CW00566145

Popular Pro

Popular Protest in Palestine

The Uncertain Future
of Unarmed Resistance

Marwan Darweish and Andrew Rigby

PlutoPress
www.plutobooks.com

First published 2015 by Pluto Press
345 Archway Road, London N6 5AA

www.plutobooks.com

British Library Cataloguing in Publication Data
A catalogue record for this book is available from the British Library

ISBN   978 0 7453 3510 0   Hardback
ISBN   978 0 7453 3509 4   Paperback
ISBN   978 1 7837 1290 8   PDF eBook
ISBN   978 1 7837 1292 2   Kindle eBook
ISBN   978 1 7837 1291 5   EPUB eBook

This book is printed on paper suitable for recycling and made from
fully managed and sustained forest sources. Logging, pulping and
manufacturing processes are expected to conform to the environmental
standards of the country of origin.

10   9   8   7   6   5   4   3   2   1

Typeset by Stanford DTP Services, Northampton, England
Text design by Melanie Patrick
Simultaneously printed by CPI Antony Rowe, Chippenham, UK
and Edwards Bros in the United States of America

To two friends who contributed so much in their different ways
and over many years to making this book possible:

Howard Clark (1950–2013)
Mahdi Abdul Hadi

CONTENTS

ACKNOWLEDGEMENTS

This book has had a long gestation period, and over the years that we have been researching and studying popular resistance in Palestine and Israel many people have given of their time and displayed amazing patience with us as we bothered them with questions and queries, emails and phone calls. The list of those who contributed in some way or another to the evolution of the book would be too long to include here.

However, it would not be right if we failed to record our deep appreciation of those people who were our direct collaborators, helping to arrange itineraries and interviews with over a hundred Palestinian and Israeli activists. To Omer Mansour and Ayman Youssef in the West Bank and to Anat Reisman-Levy in Israel go our special thanks. In our research in the south of the West Bank we received tremendous support and encouragement from Mahmoud Zawahri, whilst our dear friend Hitham Kayali was generous enough to share with us some of his research notes and findings.

Marwan's son Oscar – who Andrew used to babysit many years ago – used his considerable talent to produce the maps used in the book.

Andrew's dearest friend, Howard Clark, died during the writing of this book. Consequently, this is the first book for many years that Andrew has been involved with that did not benefit from Howard's critical comments and constructive engagement. Many people have written about Howard in his role as a writer, organiser and advocate of nonviolent action – Andrew wants to take this opportunity to acknowledge Howard as someone who was always there for him, as a friend, a critic and as a brother who was still somewhere in the background during the writing of this book.

Finally we both want to acknowledge the support and the patience of our partners – Lu and Carol … they are still hanging in there despite all!!

1

INTRODUCTION

In 1989 one of the authors (Marwan Darweish) interviewed an activist in Gaza. It was at the height of the Palestinian popular uprising against occupation, the first intifada – a time of high hopes and great expectations for Palestinians. The interviewee commented, 'You sense that the leadership is not separate from the Palestinian people, but that it is present everywhere. … You feel a unity and an amazing solidarity which differs from anything else we have felt in the twenty or so years since the PLO was formed.'[1]

At around the same time Andrew Rigby was interviewing a former political prisoner living in the refugee camp at Far'a in the West Bank. This informant echoed the sense of solidarity and hope expressed by his Gazan contemporary as he described the key feature of the popular resistance at that time: 'Everyone helps each other … all the people have the same way now, the same struggle against the occupation – from the children to the old men, all the same, they want to get rid of the occupation. One soul through many bodies, through many voices.'[2]

More than 20 years after these interviews took place both authors interviewed a senior Fatah official and member of the Palestinian Authority (PA) at his offices in Ramallah. We were trying to discover how such a person in a leadership position within the party and the administration viewed the spread of popular resistance that had started amidst the violence of the second intifada in opposition to the construction of the Separation Wall and had spread to challenge settlement expansion and land expropriation in other parts of the West Bank. Like the politician he was, he provided us with an up-beat assessment:

Popular resistance is spreading and intensifying … we are planning a more comprehensive approach to nonviolence which will include not just demonstrations but other areas such as the economic boycott of all Israeli goods, not just settlement produce. This will impact on Israel. The aim is to create a culture of popular resistance, a way of living. … We are planning a publication on how to become part of the popular resistance. … There is a degree of consensus amongst all the parties on the importance of popular resistance. Even Hamas supports this form of resistance. In the reconciliation talks between the PA and Hamas this strategy was accepted and agreed.

Nearly two years later, in November 2013, we interviewed another senior Fatah member and district governor with the PA. He was far less sanguine in his assessment of the 'state of play' with regard to popular resistance (the term used by Palestinians to refer to their civilian-based unarmed resistance to occupation):

> If there was a massive popular resistance, there is a possibility of success. ... As a Fatah person I feel that if we do not lead the movement, then it will not move – but Fatah has no programme, so how can we lead? We need a plan, not just an ad hoc reaction to events. But some of the leaders have a personal interest in the status quo. ... There is a price to be paid in resistance, and the leaders should be to the fore. It should not just be the people paying the price. So this is part of the cycle of mistrust. People want to see their leaders to the fore, as an example to people on the ground. ... At the moment popular resistance is very localised, every Friday the same few villages, the same thing. It is not popular as it does not include the mass of people. If we were serious we would make life hell for the settlers, blocking the roads, making the soldiers work. That would be popular resistance.

Through the voices captured in these four quotes we can begin to grasp the trajectory followed by many Palestinians over the past quarter of a century: from a time of hope in the late 1980s and early 1990s when there was confidence in the power of popular unarmed resistance as a means of bringing an end to the Israeli occupation, through to the waning of that hope and the acknowledgement of the weakness of leadership that has accompanied the failure of the wave of popular resistance that started in 2002 to halt the construction of the Separation Wall. The aim of this book is to delve deeper into the dynamics of this trajectory by examining the Palestinian struggle against occupation through the lens of unarmed civilian-based resistance.

THE RESEARCH PROCESS

Both authors have had a personal and professional interest in the role that unarmed civilian resistance might play in bringing an end to the occupation since the 1980s. As part of this involvement we have made repeated family and research/consultancy related visits to the West Bank, the Gaza Strip and Israel itself. Over time our friendships with Palestinian and Israeli activists have deepened and our contact lists have grown accordingly. In late 2010 we felt that Palestinian interest in unarmed modes of popular resistance had grown to such an extent that the time might be ripe for an in-depth study of the potentialities (and limitations) of such an approach, in the context of the disaster of the second intifada and the clear indications that the so-called 'peace negotiations' were leading nowhere. So it was with that intention that we made contact once again with our friends and associates. From them we gathered a basic guide to the main sites of contestation within the West Bank and contact details for key members of local popular resistance committees in each location. Essentially these consisted of those villages that had been active in the struggle to protect their land and their well-being by trying to stop the advance of the Separation Wall; those were the sites where Palestinians had been inspired by the resistance to the Wall and had taken up the struggle to resist the expansion of local settlements that threatened to expropriate more of their land, and those sites – both rural and urban – in territory designated by the Oslo Accords of 1995 as Area C where Palestinians were engaged in an ongoing struggle to protect not just their land but also their homes and their way of life from the assaults of Israeli settlers supported by the Israeli occupation forces.

Starting in 2011 we began to make contact with these local activists, and we stayed in touch with them through to late 2013 when the main body of our fieldwork was completed. During the early period of our fieldwork we shared with our respondents their sense of hope that the struggle against the occupation was taking on a new power with the spread of resistance to new sites. As one of our contacts observed, 'We came alive in the first intifada. Then we died in the second. Maybe now we are being reborn.' But over the following months we witnessed the decline in people's hopes and expectations regarding the leverage power of popular resistance as a means of dislodging the Israeli occupation. This was not something we wanted to experience – like them we had been energised and enthused and so we also shared in the disappointment felt by many who had come to acknowledge that for all their initiative, courage and struggle, they had not managed to impact on Israeli publics and decision makers who remained as committed as ever to the continuation of the occupation and the accompanying abuse of Palestinian human rights. So our focus changed – from trying to understand the factors that had led to an upsurge in popular resistance we had, by late 2013, begun to spend more time with our informants looking backwards in an attempt to understand why the movement had failed to make any appreciable progress towards achieving its basic objective of bringing the occupation to an end.

Accordingly, the analysis that is developed in the following pages is based very much on the insights and judgements of the activists themselves. Each of the face-to-face interviews and conversations – of which there were in excess of one hundred – with Palestinian and Israeli activists, politicians and opinion leaders was carried out in either their own language (Arabic and Hebrew) or in English.[3] Marwan, being proficient in all three languages, would normally take the lead in the interviews. If the medium was Arabic or Hebrew, he would also provide Andrew with a simultaneous translation in English, with Andrew busily scribbling notes and checking that the voice recorder was still operating. The notes and the recordings were then transcribed, coded and analysed using one of the standard social science software programmes for the analysis of qualitative data. We gave considerable thought to whether or not we should provide basic source references for the quotations taken from the interviews, which we have used throughout the book. In the end we decided that our paramount concern should be to avoid any actions that might undermine the security of our informants, and this required taking all reasonable measures to guard their identities.

Our approach to the study was informed not just by our long-term personal and professional involvement with different aspects of Palestinian resistance to occupation, but also by our deep value-commitment to nonviolent means of struggle for peace and justice. However, it became very clear early in our fieldwork that Palestinian activists were uncomfortable when we talked about 'nonviolent resistance'. As one of them explained, 'When we started we used the language of popular resistance. We did not want to use the term nonviolence – we practised it but did not talk about it. We try to internalise it, so that it becomes part of our culture, but the word itself sounds strange.' Accordingly we have tended to use the term 'popular resistance' to refer to the civilian-based modes of resistance pursued by Palestinians. Moreover, we ourselves felt that nonviolence was not the most appropriate term to use to refer to the methods of resistance typically pursued by Palestinians. In normal usage nonviolent resistance involves a refusal to inflict, or threaten to inflict, direct physical harm or injury upon an opponent in a conflict situation.[4] Consequently it has to be acknowledged that many of the clashes that have taken place between Palestinians and Israeli occupying forces and settlers have not been nonviolent insofar as stone-throwing by Palestinians has become a standard part of their repertoire of protest in such situations.[5]

CIVIL RESISTANCE STUDIES

Our analysis was also informed by the body of literature on civil resistance to tyranny and injustice that has grown in recent years. Most definitions of civil or civilian resistance emphasise that it is a mode of challenging opponents that are not averse to using violence by civilians, relying on the sustained use of methods that are predominantly nonviolent, unarmed or 'non-military' in nature, in pursuit of goals that are widely shared within the society.[6] It has been noted by a number of scholars and commentators that there has been something of a surge in publications on civil resistance in recent years.[7] For example, April Carter observed in 2012 that 'the increasing number of unarmed resistance struggles in recent decades has led to a growing literature discussing the theory, strategy and methods of such resistance and describing individual movements.'[8] Much of this work draws on the original contribution of Gene Sharp who began publishing on nonviolent resistance in the 1950s and whose three-volume study, *The Politics of Nonviolent Action* (1973) remains a keynote work in the field.[9] More recently the work of Erica Chenoweth and Maria Stephan has received attention with their evidence-based claims that over the past century nonviolent forms of resistance to oppressive regimes have been more likely to succeed than violent forms of insurrection and armed struggle, a fact that they have attributed primarily to the higher rates of popular participation possible in nonviolent struggles compared with violent ones.[10] However, the prime focus of such works has been on unarmed civilian-based resistance to authoritarian domestic regimes by citizens struggling for democratic change. Thus, a recent study by Sharon Nepstad focuses solely on such domestic 'uprisings', arguing that the key determinant of success in such struggles is security force defections.[11] It is a stimulating study, but the models presented in this and other works are of limited relevance as frameworks for the analysis of cases of unarmed resistance against foreign domination and occupation.

There have been a host of books written about resistance to occupation in continental Europe during the Second World War, but only a limited number have focused on unarmed resistance during that period. Those that have included such a concern within their frame of reference have proven to be particular helpful for our purposes. Jacques Semelin's work on civilian resistance in Europe during the period 1939–43 has been a source of considerable insight which has informed our study. Particularly important has been his understanding that the aim of unarmed resistance to Nazi occupation was never that of defeating the occupier by nonviolent struggle. People realised that they lacked the means to drive them out. Rather:

> The goal of this spontaneous struggle was instead to preserve the collective identity of the attacked societies; that is to say, their fundamental values. ... When a society feels less and less submissive, it becomes more and more uncontrollable. Then, even if the occupier keeps its power, it loses its authority. This expresses how much civilian resistance consisted primarily of a clash of wills, expressing above all a fight for values.[12]

Hence, the prime aim of civil resistance was to deny the occupier's claims to legitimacy, whilst waiting for eventual liberation that was expected to come from outside intervention by the armed allied forces. So, for Semelin, the first act of resistance is 'to find the strength to say *NO* without necessarily having a clear idea of what one wants'.[13] From this perspective the core of resistance is the determination not to give in to the will of the aggressor for, as Semelin has argued, 'The founding act of a resistance process against an occupation is basically an affirmation of the superiority of the de jure authority over the de facto one.'[14]

Another study of civilian resistance to occupation that has been a key source has been Werner Rings' examination of different types of collaboration and resistance in occupied Europe during the Second World War.[15] Rings' work helped us develop our categorisation of types of resistance to occupation that has informed our study throughout, and which complemented our understanding of the dynamics of unarmed resistance based on the mainstream literature within the field of civil resistance studies; these are summarised below. In addition we have drawn on Mazin Qumsiyeh's detailed and comprehensive account of nonviolent resistance in Palestine, especially during the period from the Ottoman rule to the first intifada.[16]

BASIC ASSUMPTIONS REGARDING DYNAMICS OF CIVIL RESISTANCE

1. 'Dependent power'

The basic assumption informing most studies of nonviolent civil resistance in pursuit of social and political change is that all forms of domination and oppression are dependent on various sources of support, including the cooperation (willing or forced) of significant sectors of the population.[17] Repressive regimes depend not only on fear and intimidation and the coercive power of the police and armed forces, but also on the habits of obedience of citizens and their preparedness to pay taxes and generate other forms of revenue required. To the extent that citizens can overcome their fear and their habits of obedience, then it becomes increasingly costly for regimes to impose their will.

2. The importance of identifying and undermining 'pillars of support'

Many students and activists attempting to understand the dynamics of regime change through civilian-based resistance focus on identifying the key pillars of support of a regime, and explore the ways in which these pillars might be undermined and regime support eroded.[18] In identifying the pillars of support, analysts and activists have typically focused not just on internal props such as the loyalty of key sections of the administration and security personnel, but also on those external sources of support on which a regime relies.[19] An integral part of attempts to undermine external sources of support involves searching for transnational allies that can exercise leverage directly on targeted regimes or indirectly by influencing those external actors upon whose support a regime relies.

3. Raising the costs of regime policies

Some scholars have emphasised the significance of nonviolent resisters influencing regime policies by means of activities that raise the costs of its repressive policies. Frequently such activities involve actions that are intended to provoke reactions on the part of the regime that can 'backfire' and result in a loss of legitimacy in the eyes of significant internal and external actors, including in certain cases members of the regime's own security forces whose loyalty can be stretched to such a degree that they refuse to carry out orders.[20]

4. The chain of nonviolence/influence

Johan Galtung developed the strategic concept of a 'chain of nonviolence' to refer to that process whereby civil resisters who cannot impact directly on the decision-makers against whom they are struggling can sometimes make links with groups and 'intermediaries' who can, in turn, connect with others, so that the chain of influence approaches closer to the power structures that are being challenged.[21] Galtung located the theory (and the practice) of links in the chain of nonviolence within the context of social distance – that is, when there is too great a social distance between adversaries for them to identify and communicate with each other, then there is a need for intermediaries who can more readily exercise some kind of leverage over the adversary and its supporters.

TYPES OF NONVIOLENT ACTION

Gene Sharp has identified three main categories of nonviolent action: protest and persuasion, non-cooperation, and interventions.[22] In his study of civilian-based resistance to occupation during the Second World War, Werner Rings identified four main categories. The following characterisations are derived from Rings, but developed through the prism of nonviolent resistance and will be used throughout this study as a framework for characterising different forms of nonviolent or unarmed resistance.

- *Symbolic resistance*: 'We remain what we were and communicate to others by means of gestures, actions or dress continued allegiance to our cause and its values.'
- *Polemical resistance*: 'We oppose the occupier by voicing protest and trying to encourage others of the need to maintain the struggle.'
- *Offensive resistance*: 'We are prepared to do all that we can to frustrate and overcome the oppressor by nonviolent means, including strikes, demonstrations and other forms of direct action.'

- *Defensive resistance*: 'We aid and protect those in danger or on the run, and thereby preserve human beings and human values endangered by the occupying power.'
- *Constructive resistance*: 'We challenge the existing imposed order by seeking to create alternative institutions that embody the values that we hope to see flourish more widely once we are free.'[23]

CONDITIONS NECESSARY FOR EMERGENCE OF COLLECTIVE RESISTANCE TO OCCUPATION

Research into civilian-based resistance to occupation and oppression has identified a number of conditions necessary for sustained collective resistance to oppression in general and occupation in particular.[24] The most obvious is that sufficient people share a strong commitment to a common cause, based on a shared experience of oppression and injustice. However, a number of other 'enabling conditions' would seem to be significant:

1. A strong sense of identity and social solidarity shared by members of the subject population. One of the necessary conditions for a high degree of social cohesion is the absence of deep horizontal and vertical divisions in society.
2. An effective leadership with a vision, able to articulate the concerns and needs of the population and respond constructively to changing circumstances and emerging opportunities.
3. A strong 'democratic culture' based on a tradition of active citizenship and respect for basic human rights, which thereby renders the experience of oppression and injustice all the more intolerable and about which 'something must be done'.
4. Ownership at the grassroots level with a central role being played by community-based and civil society organisations and networks.

CONDITIONS NECESSARY FOR COLLECTIVE RESISTANCE TO TAKE AN UNARMED/NONVIOLENT FORM

Certain types of conditions seem to be necessary for the resistance to take a nonviolent form:

1. The presence of experienced practitioners and advocates of unarmed modes of resistance within the leadership.

2. Extreme imbalance in the means of coercive power available so that any resort to violence in the struggle against a regime would invite massive retaliation and consequently be counter-productive.

3. The absence of strong 'counter-movements' within the society advocating and pursuing violent means of resistance.

NECESSARY CONDITIONS FOR SUSTAINABLE CIVIL RESISTANCE STRUGGLE

Based on the above, it is possible to identify a range of conditions that could strengthen and improve the likelihood of an unarmed civilian-based resistance movement sustaining itself and thereby making progress towards achieving its goals. These include the following:

1. A strong sense of solidarity throughout the subject population and within a movement that encourages the widest possible participation and within which all kinds of people can play a role.

2. Clear achievable goals that are widely supported by activists and citizens in general.

3. Organisational strength throughout all levels of the movement, enhanced by the participation of people with experience of nonviolent resistance.

4. Capacity to generate a clear strategy with a repertoire of tactics and action that can be adapted to changing contexts by activists trained in nonviolent action and sufficiently disciplined and aware to avoid responding to provocation with violence. Such repertoires can include bold, high-risk actions that dramatically challenge the legitimacy of the regime alongside lower-risk activities that perhaps erode fear or at least involve people not ready to run greater risks.[25]

5. The capacity to maintain communication within the resistance movement itself, and with wider publics, including sympathetic bystanders, third parties and external actors prepared to act as links in the chain of nonviolence. This also extends to include communication with opponents, aimed at encouraging 'loyalty shifts' amongst security personnel and armed forces by reassuring them that they can have a role to play in the anticipated future.

6. Widespread recognition of the legitimacy of the struggle with regard to aims and methods which can lead to significant third parties exercising their leverage power on behalf of the 'just cause'.

7. Reliable supply of the resources required to sustain the struggle. This includes economic, financial and material resources as well as symbolic support.

8. Sources of external support from state and non-state actors that strengthen the resilience of the population to continue its resistance and do not undermine the legitimacy or the solidarity of the movement.

Of course a resistance movement might meet all the conditions identified above, and yet fail to achieve the goal of liberation from domination and occupation. For this to happen it is vital that conditions are created such that the target regime is forced to concede that the status quo is unsustainable. This can only come about if the 'sticks' wielded by its opponents and concerned third parties carry such salience and impose or threaten such costs that the 'carrot' of an alternative future relationship between the parties becomes more attractive than the continuation of the old pattern of domination, subjugation and occupation. In this book we shall examine the ways in which Palestinians and their supporters have tried to use unarmed means of resistance in order to bring about such a situation.

2

PALESTINIAN RESISTANCE TO THE ESTABLISHMENT OF THE STATE OF ISRAEL

The aim of this chapter is to trace the thread of Palestinian unarmed resistance against the expropriation of their land and the threat to their livelihoods posed by Jewish migration prior to the establishment of the state of Israel. What becomes clear in this review of Palestinian resistance during the latter years of the nineteenth and the first half of the twentieth century is the manner in which the struggle against the Zionist project was dogged right from the start by factionalism and division that reflected in part the fractured nature of Palestinian society. This handicap was exacerbated by the failure of external sources of support.[1]

PALESTINIAN PROTEST AGAINST JEWISH IMMIGRATION UNDER THE OTTOMANS

Jewish migration to Palestine in order to establish a homeland commenced in the 1880s. On the eve of the initial wave of immigration in 1882 the Jewish community in Palestine numbered around 24,000, 5 per cent of an estimated overall population of 500,000. By the end of the second wave of Zionist-inspired immigration in 1914, their number had risen to 85,000.[2] The establishment of agricultural settlements on land purchased from Arab landowners caused friction with local farmers. They had been accustomed to their livestock grazing on what had become settlement land, and as early as 1886 there were reports of clashes between the newcomers and the peasants evicted from the newly purchased land.[3] Palestine at that time was part of the Ottoman Empire, and as early as 1891 Palestinian notables voiced their protests in Constantinople against the Jewish migration, and in June 1891 the first of a number of petitions was presented to the Grand Vizier requesting that Russian Jews be stopped from entering Palestine and acquiring land.[4] In addition to such petitions there were early forms of what might be characterised as defensive resistance. For example, in 1897 the Mufti of Jerusalem presided over a committee which scrutinised applications for the transfer of land, and so hindered Jewish land purchases for a number of years.[5]

Resentment against the incomers continued to grow during the first decade of the twentieth century, and after the relaxation of press censorship in 1908 was expressed in newspaper articles warning that there was a mounting danger of Arabs becoming strangers in their own land. It was during this early period that anger was also directed against those landowners who were selling land to the newcomers. In 1910 there was a call for more offensive resistance in the shape of an Arab boycott of Jewish goods and businesses in retaliation against a Zionist boycott of Arab labour and shops. This boycott call became a standard component in the repertoire of the early anti-Zionist organisations and was a regular feature in the manifestos of Palestinians standing for election to the Ottoman parliament.[6]

So, by the end of the Ottoman period of rule a pattern of protest had formed. The traditional landowning families saw Zionism as a threat to their position and responded by appealing to the authorities with petitions and delegations, as came naturally to those whose traditional role in the patron–client structure that permeated Palestinian society was to act as intermediary between the Ottoman authorities and their subjects. The more polemical forms of protest such as newspaper articles and pamphlets were the domain of the middle-class professionals, particularly journalists and students who were most vocal in their opposition, whilst the offensive resistance was primarily the response of those who were the direct victims of Zionist land acquisitions – the peasantry. As Kayyali has summarised the situation prior to the establishment of British military rule in Palestine in 1917: 'within the ranks of the nationalist movement in Palestine, the notables performed the role of the diplomats; the educated middle classes that of the articulators of public opinion; and the peasants that of the actual fighters in the battle against the Zionist presence.'[7] There were also some initiatives during the early twentieth century that could be characterised as constructive forms of resistance, which included the establishment of private secondary schools in Palestine that served as precursors of nationalism through the dissemination of European ideas.[8]

BRITISH MILITARY ADMINISTRATION: 1917–20

In November 1914 the Ottoman Empire entered the First World War alongside Germany and Austria. A British and allied army advanced into Palestine and by the end of the war was in occupation of the whole of Syria, whilst another British and Indian force held the whole of Iraq. The Ottoman Empire, under whose political rule Palestinians, like the majority of Arabs, had lived for centuries, was in collapse and Palestine by the end of the war was under British occupation. These changes had a significant impact on the manner in which politically conscious Arabs thought of themselves, with the emergence of the first stirrings of Arab nationalism.

In 1916 Hussein, the Sharif of Mecca, had provided a force that fought alongside the British and their allies. This allegiance came about in the context of what became known as the McMahon–Hussein Correspondence in which Hussein was led to believe that the reward for his intervention would be some kind of recognition by the British of Arab nationalism and its aspiration for an independent state.[9] However, unbeknown to the Arabs, an Anglo-French agreement (Sykes–Picot Agreement, May 1916) divided the Middle East into two zones of imperial influence. And in November 1917 the British government affirmed its support for the establishment of a homeland for the Jews in Palestine in the Balfour Declaration, provided that nothing should be done to prejudice 'the civil and religious rights of existing non-Jewish communities in Palestine.' In the words of Hourani, 'It was these documents, and the interests reflected in them, which determined the political fate of the countries.'[10]

When news of the Balfour Declaration reached the Palestinians it led to a new awareness of the need to organise. A Muslim-Christian Association (MCA) was established as a counter to Jewish organisations, with branches around the country alongside new youth clubs and other organisations. On April 12, 1918 some Palestinian literary figures put on a theatre presentation in Jerusalem before a big map of Palestine, calling on people to defend their land and not to sell it to the Zionists.[11] Newspapers were published in the main urban centres of Jaffa, Haifa and Jerusalem, and they were used to organise a national day of protest to mark the first anniversary of the Balfour Declaration. At this time the Arabs still believed they had an assurance from the British about self-government, and as such a Zionist state was unacceptable. Therefore, the formal announcement on February 27, 1920 by the head of the British military administration that Britain intended to implement the Balfour Declaration provoked a number of protest demonstrations, with businesses closing down and protest petitions being handed in to the authorities by representatives of the various MCAs.[12] Yehoshua Porath noted, 'The organisation of these demonstrations revealed the degree to which the nationalist associations in Palestine had advanced. For the first time they showed an ability to organise a coordinated action on a nation-wide scale in which all the associations took part. The almost identical language of the protest notes strengthens this impression.'[13]

There was considerable support amongst the politically literate strata of Palestinian society at this time for union with Syria under the rule of Sharif Hussein's son, Faisal. His coronation in Damascus on March 7, 1920 was the occasion for a series of demonstrations on the following day in Palestine. The protests spilled over into violence, with attacks on Jewish shops and passers-by accompanied by open threats to use force as a means of preventing the realisation of the Zionist project.[14] The clashes heightened tension in the country as April approached, an important month in the calendar of the three main faith communities. Sure enough, at the annual Muslim Nabi Musa festival on April 4, 1920 some 60,000 gathered in the Old City of Jerusalem, speeches were delivered urging the assembled to stand up for their homeland, and before long an angry crowd was ransacking the Jewish Quarter, attacking passers-by and looting from Jewish-owned properties.[15] On April 24, 1920 the San Remo Conference confirmed the British Mandate over Palestine and thereby brought an end to the Pan-Syrian vision.[16] Furthermore, the British then proceeded to appoint as High Commissioner a well-known Zionist Jew, Sir Herbert Samuel, who took up his post on July 1, 1920.

On the eve of the British Mandate a number of observations can be made regarding the resistance to the Zionist project.

1. There had been a growth in the organisational capacity of the protest movement, which manifested itself particularly in the spread of various forms of protest and resistance. But it still remained very much an urban phenomenon.
2. When people were mobilised in forms of offensive resistance such as demonstrations and other types of active protest, events could turn violent.
3. It was during this period that the weak and divided nature of the Palestinian political leadership started to become apparent. A younger and more dynamic strata of leadership was beginning to emerge, mainly middle-class professionals from the ranks of the Palestinian notable families. But their effectiveness was undermined by the rivalry between two of the Palestinian notable families, the Husaynis and the Nashashibis – a tension that was to mark Palestinian politics throughout the British Mandate period.

BRITISH MANDATE IN 1920s

Once the British received the Mandate, the focus of Palestinian pressure was to convince their new rulers to abandon their commitment to a Jewish national home as adumbrated in the Balfour Declaration. However, the efficacy of their entreaties, deputations, petitions and protest actions was weakened by a number of factors, not least the fractures within the Palestinian political elite and the society as a whole.

The Husayni–Nashashibi split permeated its way through the Palestinian social structure, insofar as each of the families could lay claim to the loyalty and fealty of families and clans in the rural hinterland, on behalf of whom the elite had acted as patrons in representing their interests to the Ottoman authorities.

This network of patron–client relationships was one of the core elements of a fractured and divided Palestinian social structure which was overwhelmingly rural, with a 1921 census revealing that 80 per cent of the indigenous population depended on agriculture for their livelihood. The Palestinian peasantry occupied a life-world vastly different from that of the urbanised political elite. Their loyalty and sense of belonging was to the family, the clan and the village. Theirs was a sense of locality, not nationality. In a society with weak central government and poor communications, it was to the local institutions that people looked for security. As Rosemary Sayigh observed, 'From time immemorial Palestinian peasants had found solutions to their problems in village-based collective action.'[17] So, not only were there vast inequalities along the vertical axis of wealth and class, there were also significant divisions along the horizontal axis between members of different families, clans (*hamulahs*) and villages. Moreover, it was a society where the institution of the feud ensured that divisive conflicts could continue over generations. This was not ripe soil in which a national resistance movement might grow.

Examining the first decade of British Mandate rule in Palestine through the prism of popular protest and unarmed resistance a number of features become apparent.

1. 'Spontaneous' clashes between peasantry and Jewish settlers

For the peasantry who experienced eviction through Jewish land purchases, the immediate response was anger and resentment that could lead to clashes with those directly responsible for their dispossession. But these clashes were localised. There were no attempts to engender a sustainable nationwide movement of active resistance based on the peasantry.

2. The absence of a national leadership

The main reasons for the failure to develop a truly active national movement were twofold. First, as has been noted above, the world-view of the peasantry was very particularistic and localised. They had no experience of coordinating collective action with those beyond their own village. Second, there was no 'national leadership' to lead and direct them along such a path. The social gulf between the urban political elite and the peasantry was immense – they occupied completely different life-worlds. Moreover, the notables had no experience of leading large-scale political movements. In the words of Rosemary Sayigh, 'Not only did the indigenous ruling class have no experience of mass leadership, but the individual notable would never attempt such a course since it would only jeopardise his access to government, and it was on this access that his influence and status depended.'[18]

3. The commitment to negotiation

Throughout the Mandate period the main impulse of the Palestinian political elite was to continue in the role they had traditionally performed under the Ottomans – representing their interests and those of their clients who owed them allegiance to the authorities. They were most at home as members of delegations to the British or the League of Nations, demanding the revocation of the Balfour Declaration, an end to Jewish migration and land expropriation, and the establishment of representative self-government in Palestine.

4. Symbolic and polemical resistance

In addition to the formal and informal representations to the British, there were numerous instances of collective forms of symbolic and polemical protest. Regular items in the press urged people to oppose the Zionist attempts to establish a homeland in Palestine. Imams spread the message at Friday prayers in the mosques. As early as December 1920 a conference was held in Haifa that rejected the Balfour Declaration.[19] Strike days were observed to mark the anniversary of the Balfour Declaration and commemorate other days of national historical significance. In March 1925 Balfour himself visited Palestine, and on the day he opened the Hebrew University in Jerusalem he was met by black flags and a complete boycott of the occasion by the Palestinians.

5. From offensive resistance to violence

From time to time the political leadership would try to mobilise people for protest marches and demonstrations, usually as part of an effort to strengthen their hand in an upcoming round of negotiations with the British. This was what happened on March 25, 1921 when Churchill visited Haifa and was met by a demonstration. On the same day there was a large demonstration in Jerusalem where the Muslim shops also closed. This had minimal impact, insofar as Churchill reaffirmed his commitment to the Zionist project before leaving the country. A few weeks later, a May Day march by Jewish socialists in Jaffa clashed with a communist demonstration of Arabs and Jews. The next day a large Arab demonstration was held. There were violent clashes and, driven by rumours that the Jews were killing Arabs, the violence spread to other parts of the country. Thousands of Jews fled Jaffa for the safety of nearby Tel Aviv, a state of emergency was declared and reinforcements were summoned from Egypt.[20] After several days order was restored, leaving 48 Arabs and 47 Jews dead, and over 200 from both communities wounded. Just as with the Nabi Musa disturbances in Jerusalem of the previous year, the Jaffa Riots showed just how little it took for people to give violent expression to their anger, resentment and frustration at the growing Jewish presence in their land.

The British were shaken by the scale of the violence, and on May 14, 1921 agreed that henceforth Jewish immigration should be regulated according to the 'economic absorption capacity' of the country. There were further disturbances in November when people assembled to mourn the anniversary of the Balfour Declaration, but by then the High Commissioner had taken steps intended to defuse some of the opposition to the Mandate by appointing Haj-Amin Husayni to be head of a newly created Supreme Muslim Council (SMC), which was to become, in the words of one contemporary observer, 'the vanguard of the Nationalist Movement'.[21]

6. The timidity of the Palestinian political elite

Not all forms of offensive resistance resulted in violence. In 1922 the British sought to introduce a legislative council for Palestine. However, its remit was such as to exclude any questioning of basic issues like the status of the Balfour Declaration, migration and bans on the sale of land. Furthermore, its proposed structure was such that the combined votes of the Jewish members and the government appointees would outnumber the Arabs. Consequently, at the 5th Palestinian Arab Congress held in Nablus in August 1922, it was resolved that elections to the proposed council be boycotted. The boycott campaign was taken up with vigour, with the mosques acting as important vehicles for spreading the message and generating commitment. Non-participation was presented as a religious duty, and in some cases those assembled for prayer would take collective vows to take no part in the process. The result was that when the elections were held in February 1923 only a small minority of the Palestinian Arab population participated, and the boycott was almost total in some areas, supported by Muslims and Christians alike. The proposed legislative body never met.

But despite this relative success, the Palestinians did not seek to extend the boycott into a fully-fledged non-cooperation movement. If people had resigned from their administrative posts at all levels of the government, they would have presented the Mandate with a major administrative challenge. But this would have been a step too far for many, as was revealed a few months later when, in June 1923, the issue of non-payment of taxes was raised at the 6th Palestinian Arab Congress. The suggestion was rejected. Too many of the participants were landowners who feared being targeted by the British with punitive fines and other sanctions.

7. Accommodation to occupation

There were no significant outbreaks of violence between 1922 and 1928. One reason for this relative calm was the decline in Jewish migration during this period.

The second reason, according to Kayyali, was 'the over-riding predominance of factionalism, the ascendancy of personal rivalries and self-interest among the Palestinian political nobility' as the Husaynis and the Nashashibis fought for control of the SMC.[22] In addition, people had been intimidated by the severity of the individual and collective punishments meted out by the British after the 1921 Jaffa Riots. In such circumstances most Palestinians, like people throughout history, tried to make the best of a bad situation and adapt and accommodate to the harsh and apparently unyielding reality that confronted them. After all the Palestinian peasantry had little experience or confidence in their capacity to change the world they inhabited. Their focus was on the development of coping mechanisms to enhance their chances of survival. The same was true for members of the political elite, as Porath noted,

> When at the end of 1923 it became clear to everyone that the political effort to effect a change in the pro-Zionist policy of the British government had failed, the reaction of many Palestinians was one of disappointment, despair, and sometimes a search for ways to get some good out of the situation by a policy of cooperation with the authorities. Under these circumstances it was difficult to resort to violence again. In this fashion Zionism gained seven years of undisturbed activity in Palestine, in the course of which it succeeded in nearly doubling the size of the Jewish *yishuv* and in enlarging the area of its map of settlement.[23]

8. Religion as a prime driver of resistance

The calm of those years 1922–28 was superficial; nothing had changed in terms of the basic dynamics and it did not take much to spark off another round of clashes. Throughout 1928 religious tensions had been rising as the Jews sought to extend their right to worship at the Western Wall, just adjacent to the *al-Haram ash-Sharif* housing the Al-Aqsa Mosque and the Dome of the Rock. Rumours abounded that the Jews had designs on the space. On August 15, 1929 Zionist extremists at the Western Wall provoked a counter-demonstration by Palestinians. The perceived threat to one of their most sacred spaces enabled the Palestinian leadership to cast the struggle in a religious light, and thereby mobilise those who had remained untouched by secular appeals to nationalism and the right of self-determination – rather alien notions to the mass of Palestinians who had virtually no exposure to such ideals, nor any experience of self-determination in their own lives. What moved them were direct perceived threats to their material and ideational (including spiritual) interests. Thus it was that on the next Friday, August 23, 1929, worshippers emerging from Al-Aqsa Mosque attacked the Jewish Quarter in the Old City. The violence spread, with the Palestinian political leadership remaining aloof. By the next day 67 Jews had been slaughtered in Hebron and a few days later 45 Jews were killed in Safed. The final death toll was 133 Jews and 116 Arabs, with over 500 wounded.[24] Most of the Jewish casualties were at the hands of Arabs, but the bulk of the Arab deaths and injuries were caused by the British as they sought to protect the Jews and restore order. The violence of 1929 marked a turning point. According to Kayyali,

> For the villagers and the masses of Palestinians two important facts were made clearer and sharper by the events of 1929. The first was that Zionism and the Jewish National Home depended, ultimately and inevitably, on British bayonets, and it was therefore necessary to fight Britain if the struggle against Zionism was to achieve its goals. The second concerned the cowardice of the Palestinian notables and their inadequacy to lead the Arabs in the struggle against Zionism and British policy in Palestine.[25]

FROM UNREST TO UPRISING: 1930–36

The harsh measures meted out by the British in the aftermath of the 1929 clashes, with collective punishments on whole villages and neighbourhoods, caused added bitterness and strengthened the hand of those calling for violence. So the tension continued to rise through the 1930s. It was a period when the economic situation deteriorated, and the suffering of the Palestinians was exacerbated by the rising tide of Jewish immigration, new land purchases and the Jewish boycott of Arab labour, all of which contributed to increased unemployment and indebtedness amongst the Palestinian people. The response was one of heightened active resistance, which can be analysed using the basic categories of resistance introduced earlier.

Symbolic and polemical resistance

The level of media activity intensified, so much so that in the summer of 1931 the British banned the Arabic newspapers for a while. Different organisations continued to meet and pass resolutions and once again the mosques were important venues for encouraging people to be steadfast in their opposition to land sales and the Zionist project. A new initiative during this period was the formation of the *Istiqlal* (Independence) political party, which called for independence from British rule. To coincide with its launch August 27, 1932 was celebrated as marking the anniversary of Saladin's victory over the Crusaders at the Battle of Hattin.

Offensive resistance

Reading the accounts of this period the sense one gets is of a rapid heightening of the tempo of events and developments running way beyond the control capacity of the established political leadership, whose influence consequently declined. Agencies such as the Arab Executive Committee (AEC) which organised the regular meetings of the different political organisations in Palestine were very good at passing resolutions, calling for boycotts of Jewish businesses, demanding an end to land sales and the like. But they continued to drag their feet in ensuring that there was some subsequent substance to such resolutions. The following saga is not untypical. In September 1932 *Istiqlal* persuaded the AEC to pass a resolution calling for resignations and non-cooperation with the government. By February 1933 *Istiqlal* was urging a more developed non-cooperation campaign involving a social, political and economic boycott – including refusal to pay taxes. Unfortunately, the wealthy landowners that constituted the bulk of the AEC were worried that they might be targeted by the government if they stopped paying tax. As a consequence, the agreed protest was confined to a weak form of symbolic resistance – the boycott of government receptions and other formal events alongside the boycott of Jewish goods.[26]

During this period, as noted, there was a rapid increase in the number of Jewish immigrants which, when combined with the policy of Jewish businesses hiring only Jewish labour, led to an intensification of clashes between Jewish and Arab labour at the picket lines set up by the Jewish workers to enforce the ban.[27] The violence spread to the countryside in 1933 when a number of peasants from a village near Haifa were killed by Zionist paramilitaries after they had resisted their expulsion from land that had been sold by the Lebanese landowners.[28] All this led to intensified pressure on the Palestinian political leadership to be more proactive. In response the AEC called for a general strike, which commenced with a demonstration on October 13, 1933. This was violently dispersed by the police and a decision was taken to hold another demonstration in Jaffa on October 27. This met with even more violence and the result was 26 dead (including one Arab policeman) and 60 wounded. This inflamed public opinion and there were further clashes in Haifa, Nablus and Jerusalem, and troops occupied Tulkarm, Nazareth and Safed. In identifying these demonstrations as significant milestones in the history of the Palestine national movement, Porath observed, 'They demonstrated the grave reaction of the Arabs to growing Jewish immigration; they uncovered the growing readiness of the Arabs to challenge the authority of the Mandatory government and to begin their struggle; they revealed that the readiness for sacrifice was far greater than it had been in the past.'[29]

Defensive resistance

As part of the increasing tempo and level of activity during this period, there was a significant growth in the number of initiatives to strengthen the resources and the resilience of the resistance movement.

- In the Spring of 1932 the Arab National Fund established an 'Arab Redemption of Lands Corporation' in order to purchase land that would otherwise have fallen into Zionist ownership.
- The Supreme Muslim Council also attempted to buy land that was for sale, and repeatedly reminded landowners of their religious duty not to sell to Jews, encouraging small landowners to register their land as part of a religious endowment and therefore inalienable.
- An Arab Agricultural Bank was started to help develop Arab agricultural land.
- Arab Labour Garrisons were formed to protect Arab workers against intimidation in cities with mixed populations such as Jerusalem and Haifa.
- In January 1932 a national youth conference was held, and the participants resolved to mobilise the youth in the villages, in part through organising a national Scout movement. One of the activities of the Scout troops was to patrol the coast and sound the alert whenever they spied vessels with illegal (Jewish) immigrants.

THE PALESTINIAN REVOLT: 1936–39

Despite the intensified nature of the protest, the situation for Palestinians seemed to worsen – by the end of 1935 about 20 per cent of Arab villagers were landless and immigration that year was at an all-time high of 60,000. The need to escalate the resistance was imperative. A new element had been injected into the mix by a paramilitary group made up of recruits from the working-class neighbourhoods of Haifa and led by a Syrian-born preacher called Izzadin al-Qassem. During the early 1930s they started attacking Jewish targets and sabotaging government property, but in November 1935 Al-Qassem was killed by the British military near Jenin. His funeral attracted thousands who saw him as a powerful symbol of self-sacrifice and as someone who pointed the way forward in the struggle.[30] This was the context for the Palestinian revolt of 1936.

There were two phases to the uprising. The first lasted for six months from April to October 1936. This was a period when the dominant forms of resistance were overwhelmingly unarmed, with a whole range of symbolic, polemical, offensive and defensive forms of resistance practised: protest marches and demonstrations, strikes and boycotts, non-cooperation and civil disobedience. These were complemented by attempts to involve wider constituencies of support such as the leaders and the citizens of neighbouring Arab states. The second phase lasted for about two years from September 1937 and took on much more of the character of a guerrilla struggle, a violent one that eventually degenerated to a level where the targets were increasingly those Arabs considered to be insufficiently loyal to 'the cause' rather than the Jewish incomers.

Phase one: April–October 1936

It was noted above that tension increased throughout 1935. There were also the stirrings of revolt in the wider region. In November 1935 there had been anti-British riots in Egypt, and in January 1936 a general strike was called in Syria which had a powerful impact not only in Syria itself but also on those in Palestine who observed the action with considerable interest. Early in 1936 there were further clashes against Jewish contractors who were refusing to hire Arab labour, and then in April two Jews were murdered whilst travelling on the Tulkarm-Nablus road. A revenge attack in Petah Tikva resulted in the killing of two Palestinians.[31] The funeral in Tel Aviv of one of the murdered Jews led to assaults on Arabs and their property; the violence spread and on April 19, 1936 nine Jews were killed in Jaffa.

The next day in Nablus an Arab National Committee was formed which declared a general strike. Strike committees were formed in all the main urban centres, and on April 25, 1936 the Arab Higher Committee (AHC) was formed with Haj Amin Husayni at its head. The strike was almost completely solid. Merchants and shopkeepers put up their shutters and there was a complete transport shut down except for some trains which continued to function. The port of Jaffa was closed, although Haifa, where there was more Jewish labour, remained open. Schools and factories closed and there were public demonstrations throughout the country. Poets and folk singers used their talents to support and encourage the struggle. On May 15, 1936 the call went out that people should stop paying taxes and observe a total boycott of Jewish firms and products, with Boy Scouts and others enforcing compliance at the neighbourhood level.[32] But once again the timidity of the Palestinian political leadership manifested itself. They resisted calls for the strike to be extended to include government officials. It would seem that a key reason for this failure was that the leadership still had faith in the power of negotiation, and Haj Amin Husayni did not want to damage his relationship with the High Commissioner.[33] If the officials had joined the strike, it could have crippled the administration and heightened the impact of the resistance.[34] As it was, the effect of the strike was limited in a number of ways:

1. The refusal to pay taxes was not a significant problem for the British, as very little revenue was obtained from direct taxation.
2. The economic impact of the strike was limited. Unlike in Syria, there was a significant Jewish sector that did not strike and continued to provide goods and services.

3. The strike actually encouraged the Jewish sector to become more self-reliant. In Jewish-owned enterprises that had hired Arab labour Jewish workers came forward to take their place.[35]
4. Although the Jewish sector suffered from shortages of fresh vegetables and fruit, alternative supplies were obtained from the vegetable merchants of Egypt and Syria.
5. The boycott of Jewish goods and services had a significant impact on Jewish-owned industries, but the effect was alleviated by the sale of the goods to Lebanese merchants, who then resold them to the Palestinians.[36]
6. The strike caused considerable suffering amongst the poorer sections of Palestinian society who depended on their earnings to survive. Nourishment and Supply Committees were formed to provide staple food items to the needy. In addition, some key workers/strikers received strike pay from the Central Relief Committee. Funds were raised from the levy on government officials. Women's Committees organised house-to-house collections, and funds were also received from sympathisers in the Arab and Muslim worlds.

The British responded to the strike with draconian emergency measures including mass arrests, house demolitions, collective fines and deportations. Such actions provoked the protesters to take to the streets in anger. In late May 1936 a large crowd tried to attack the government offices in Tulkarm. Such actions were met with force which further escalated the tension and in some cases led to an armed response. In Jaffa there was repeated sniping at the British forces, who responded by bulldozing much of the old quarter in order to create clear lines of fire. In fact, although the strike continued until mid-October 1936, after the first few weeks the resistance was never wholly nonviolent. There was plenty of violence against property, including sabotage of the Egypt–Palestine rail link near Gaza. Then, on May 16, 1936 someone fired at a crowd leaving a cinema in Jerusalem and killed three. There were also attacks by armed groups of peasants on Jewish settlements and British guard-posts during the latter half of May. By July 1936 the Samaria area was in full revolt, with Nablus at the centre, leading a British official to report: 'Armed bands which a fortnight previously consisted of 15–20 men were now encountered in large parties of 50–70. The bands were not out for loot. They were fighting what they believed to be a patriotic war in defence of their country against injustice and the threat of Jewish domination.'[37] Matters were far beyond the control of the nominal Palestinian political leadership, who were coming under increasing pressure from citrus-growers to end the strike so that the harvest could be gathered.

Their problem was how to find a way out so that it did not appear as if the leadership were submitting to the threats of the British. Eventually a face-saving formula was generated. It was agreed that if the leaders of the Arab world issued an appeal to end the strike, then their wishes would be followed. On October 10, 1936 an appeal from the Arab rulers was duly issued. The Palestinians were urged to bring an end to the disorder so as to avoid further bloodshed, and trust the good intentions of the British. The AHC called for an end to the strike that same day.

Phase two: September 1937–September 1939

Following the cessation of the strike the British appointed a Commission of Inquiry led by Lord Peel. Its report was published in July 1937 and was met with anger and indignation by the Palestinian leadership. There were petitions of protest and the AHC rejected the proposed partition of the land not only because of the loss of central and northern Galilee to the proposed Jewish state, but also because it proposed that the Palestinian sector be linked with Abdullah's new kingdom of Transjordan on the east bank of the River Jordan. The spark that set alight the second phase of the revolt occurred some weeks later. On September 26, 1937 the British district commissioner for the Galilee was assassinated in Nazareth. This was the first time a senior British government figure had been targeted, and the British responded quickly, outlawing the AHC and arresting its members.[38] A protest strike was called and by mid-October armed groups were roaming the countryside attacking Jewish settlements, destroying railway stations and cutting communication lines. Jewish paramilitary groups such as Irgun responded in kind, and the wave of violence only eased with the onset of the rainy season in November. The violence resumed in June 1938 with the end of the harvest season. By August armed groups controlled most of the roads and many of the towns, leading one British military officer to note that by September 1938 'the situation was such that civil administration and control of the country was, to all practical purposes, non-existent.'[39] According to Kayyali there were three types of resister at this time: the full-time guerrillas, the 'town commandos' who passed as civilians but who carried out particular tasks as requested, including the targeting of alleged collaborators, and the 'auxiliaries' – civilians who took up arms if there was an engagement in their vicinity.[40] It has been estimated that at the height of the armed revolt there were 3,000 full-timers, 1,000 'town commandos' and 6000 auxiliaries who could be called upon in time of need.[41]

Mao Tse-Tung is quoted as saying: 'The guerrilla must move amongst the people as a fish swims in the sea.' He was drawing attention to the principle that the guerrilla depends upon 'the people' and must be in harmony with them, like the fish is at home in the sea. He went on to assert that: 'It is only undisciplined troops who make the people their enemies and who, like the fish out of its native element, cannot live.'[42] This is what happened during the armed revolt of

1937–39, as the armed resistance forfeited the support of many of their fellow citizens. In 1937 they established their own courts to deal with all criminal, civil and personal disputes that occurred within their area of control.[43] At one level this was a classic piece of constructive resistance alongside the network of committees that had been created to provide support, sustenance and other resources to the armed groups and to the ordinary Palestinians during the period of the revolt. By 1938, however, there were allegations of corruption and excesses. The military successes of the British had restricted the flow of weapons and other supplies to the rebels, who were therefore forced to rely increasingly on the villages for support. However, the levies on villagers and others started to seem like extortion for private ends, whilst the charge of collaboration was being levelled against those moderates suspected of being in favour of partition, in addition to those accused of selling land to the Zionists and being informers. Those associated with the Nashashibis were targeted in particular, and so they formed their own defence groups for self-protection.[44] Other villages followed their example, establishing their own militias to defend themselves against the predations of the rebels. The British obviously encouraged such moves, providing them with weapons in exchange for information. Also contributing to the degeneration of the revolt was the age-old phenomenon of clan rivalries and feuds within Palestinian society. From the start, but particularly during the second phase, the rebel groups were torn by political, family and regional divisions and personal jealousies. A British teacher based in Bir Zeit observed that in early 1939,

> ... the rebellion seemed now to be turning into a struggle between the two Arab political parties: the Mufti's faction, who had organised it and who commanded the loyalty of the great majority of Arabs, and the Nashashibis, who hoped to get the power away from them by making up to the British.
>
> More and more the rebellion was tending to degenerate from a national movement into squabbles between rival rebel bands. Bir Zayt, like many other villages, was no little better than a hornets' nest of long-standing family feuds, stirred up afresh in the hope of getting some advantage through the help of this or that party of rebels.[45]

As the revolt weakened, more left the ranks and increasing numbers of villages felt sufficiently emboldened to turn their backs on the revolt and align themselves with the British. The result was the creation of more feuds that were to scar the face of Palestinian society for many years to come. Even though there were sporadic acts of violence through the summer and autumn of 1939, there was no disguising the fact that the rebels were weary, short of supplies and lacking in popular support, and so the revolt died out.

The failure of the revolt

The failure of the Palestinians to achieve their aims during the 1936–39 revolt can be attributed to a number of factors.

First, theories of nonviolent resistance advise us that all oppressive regimes rely on different sources of support, and the challenge is to develop a strategy to undermine and erode those pillars of support. One of the means by which this can be achieved is by getting key workers and personnel to withdraw their cooperation and deprive the regime of their essential services. The British Mandate was dependent on its many Arab administrative officers and officials, from the level of the local municipality up to the office of the High Commissioner himself. If these officers had withdrawn their labour and cooperation, the impact on the capacity of the British administration to function would have been significant. But the strike call was not issued, primarily because the Palestinian notables were too reluctant to risk their vested interests (property, wealth, status and influence) which, to a significant degree, depended on maintaining good relations with the government. They prioritised the protection of their personal and family interests above that of the nation.

Second, the economic impact of the general strike was limited in part because there was a whole sector of society (the Jewish sector) that continued to work and provide for the basic needs of their population. In the Palestinian case, the real suffering was borne by the strikers themselves.

Third, the Palestinian leadership revealed a single-minded persistence in their pursuit of achieving their goals through the power of persuasion and sitting around the negotiating table. Again and again representations were made to the British, delegations sent to London, and memoranda scripted. They failed to grasp the absolute commitment of the British to the Zionist project of establishing a Jewish national home in Palestine.

Fourth, the Palestinians suffered from a severe imbalance of power which they were unable to rectify. Their appeals to the Arab and Muslim worlds failed to produce significant interventions, in part because the targets of such appeals were themselves under foreign domination and had their own interests. For example, Abdullah of Transjordan had his own aspirations to absorb Palestine into his kingdom.

Fifth, the Palestinian leadership was weak and divided, reflecting in some way the fissured social structure from which they had emerged. They faced a Zionist movement that was highly organised, well-financed, with a determined leadership and constituencies of support in key centres of influence around the world. Thus, whenever it seemed that the Palestinians might have gained some concession from the British, the Zionists would arrange counter-lobbies in Jerusalem and London, mobilise supporters from the Jewish diaspora, and get the concession reversed.[46]

THE PERIOD OF PARTITION: 1939–49

The divisions in the Palestinian camp that had been such a debilitating factor undermining the resistance during the 1936–39 revolt continued to be a feature of the last decade of the Mandate leading up to partition. The British declared war on Germany on September 3, 1939. In Palestine the Arab population was relatively quiescent. The members of the Arab Higher Committee (AHC) were in exile or jail, and the local-level cadres who were not in prison were exhausted and demoralised. The Jewish population in Palestine was driven by concern about the plight of their fellows in Europe. They were encouraged by their leadership to volunteer for the British military, and the *Haganah* (Defence) force coordinated its actions with the British forces, whilst using every opportunity to build up its infrastructure and resources.

Germany surrendered on May 8, 1945 and Japan a few months later. The British were exhausted and war-weary. The Zionist movement and associated Jewish organisations were desperate to channel every possible Jewish refugee from Europe to Palestine in order to create facts on the ground and prove the necessity of a Jewish Homeland. Much to their anger the British stood by their pre-war commitment to maintain quotas on immigration, which provoked a violent reaction from Jewish groups in Palestine. A state of emergency was declared and around 100,000 British troops were stationed in Palestine to combat the threat of Jewish armed struggle. On February 25, 1947 the British announced they were handing over the responsibility of Palestine to the United Nations (UN). During June and July of that year the UN Special Committee on Palestine (UNSCOP) carried out its enquiries. It was boycotted by the Arab League, which had been established in 1945 and to whom the enfeebled AHC had handed over its negotiating rights. On August 31, 1947 UNSCOP issued its majority report recommending partition, and on November 2 the UN General Assembly passed Resolution 181 in favour of partition. The Jews were delighted; the Arabs were appalled. Fighting began almost immediately.

On December 1, 1947 the AHC issued a call for a three-day general strike. As in 1936 a network of local committees came into existence to coordinate action and organise resistance. Armed groups began to form, and in January 1948 the first Arab volunteers entered Palestine as part of an 'Arab Salvation Army'. Eventually they were to number 5,000, but they remained poorly organised and ill-equipped.[47] Zionist forces, meanwhile, had started to seize control of abandoned British military bases. The sense of insecurity and fear amongst Palestinians grew as those who lived in mixed-cities such as Haifa were driven from their homes. The confusion was heightened by the flight of significant sections of the local Palestinian elite who left in fear of becoming embroiled in the intensifying violence, anticipating that they would return once matters had quietened down. But as the spring of 1948 progressed the level of ethnic cleansing increased as the military campaigns on both sides began in earnest. For the Zionists the aim was to cleanse those zones scheduled for them by the UN partition proposals, along with gaining control of other areas where there was a significant Jewish population or particular security interests to be safeguarded.[48] Both sides committed atrocities. On April 9, 1948 over 100 people were killed in the Dir Yassin massacre, whilst a month later 130 Jews were slaughtered in Hebron after they had surrendered.

In such a situation of bloody conflict it is difficult to imagine how any unarmed initiatives other than defensive could have any impact on the unfolding events. But even such initiatives proved ineffective against the power of armed might. The villagers of Dir Yassin were raped and slaughtered despite having signed a non-aggression pact with their Jewish neighbours.[49] Further north in the mixed-town of Tiberias the community leaders of both communities had also signed a non-aggression pact in March 1948. The following month the *Haganah* took control of the city and expelled the Arab residents. So it was that by the time the British left and the State of Israel had been declared into existence on May 15, 1948 one-third of the Palestinian population had been evicted or fled from their homes.[50] This was when the armies from the Arab League entered the fray. The newcomers were poorly equipped and there was no significant coordination between the different divisions. Indeed, according to Krämer, every attempt at coordinated action failed as a result of inter-Arab rivalry.[51] This is a verdict echoed by Pappe:

> That the Arab states succeeded in fielding any soldiers at all is remarkable. Only at the end of April 1948 did the politicians in the Arab world prepare a plan to save Palestine, which in practice was a scheme to annex as much of it as possible to the Arab countries participating in the war.[52]

The most significant example of such machinations was the intrigue of Abdullah of Jordan who, with the connivance of the British, had reached an understanding with the Zionists to divide Palestine between them, with the territory apportioned to the Palestinians by the UN to come under the control of the Hashemite kingdom. As a consequence of this understanding Abdullah kept his well-trained Arab Legion in check during the war, restricting its advances to the control of the territory it was intended to annex.

By the end of October 1948 what had now become the Israeli army controlled 77 per cent of the former Palestinian territory. A final comprehensive ceasefire was agreed on January 7, 1949 and over the following months a series of armistice lines were agreed between Israel and its Arab neighbours setting borders which were to last virtually unchanged until 1967. The defeat for the Palestinians was total. Over 400 villages had been destroyed or rendered uninhabitable. Around 75–80 per cent of the Palestinian population had been displaced and dispossessed and the social, economic and political fabric of their society destroyed. The Gaza Strip was under Egyptian military rule, whilst Jordan annexed the West Bank and installed Raghib Nashashibi as governor. In the new State of Israel all immigration restrictions were lifted for Jews, who flooded in and took over the abandoned properties of their previous Palestinian owners. Israel celebrated victory whilst the Palestinians mourned the catastrophe (*Nakbha*) that had overcome them.

Reviewing this period during which Palestine was partitioned, the impression is that the fate of the Palestinians had moved out of their hands. Bigger forces were at play – the British, the United Nations, and a vigorous and driven Zionist movement whose goal, a Jewish state, was acknowledged as legitimate by the major powers of the USA and the Soviet Union. The Palestinians had emerged from the 1936–39 revolt exhausted and demoralised, divided and dispirited. They handed over their representation in the international arena to the newly formed Arab League, but their Arab neighbours faced their own challenges as newly independent states and failed dismally to live up to the trust invested in them by their Palestinian cousins. It is almost as if the Palestinian experience of these years followed the pattern of a Greek tragedy, where the tragic outcome is an inevitable result of the protagonists' weaknesses.

A SMALL VICTORY IN THE MIDST OF TRAGEDY: THE CASE OF BATTIR[53]

There were some spaces for manoeuvre available to the Palestinians, but it needed people with the insight and imagination to identify these zones of relative autonomy, the courage and determination to try to widen them, and the status and authority to mobilise and influence others in pursuit of what can only be described as 'small victories' in the context of the overall tragedy that was the Palestinian experience of partition.

Battir in 1948 was a small village of about 1,000 inhabitants some six miles south-west of Jerusalem, abutting the Jerusalem–Jaffa railway line. It had been on the front line during the fighting, experiencing shelling and skirmishing but had never been overrun. As has been noted, Abdullah's war aim was to annex what subsequently became known as the West Bank (of the River Jordan), and in pursuit of this goal had come to an understanding with the Jewish Agency that his Arab Legion would not attack Jewish troops. The only contentious issue concerned Jerusalem, and it was understood that the future of the city would be decided on the battlefield. In May 1948 the Jordanians eventually advanced and took control of the Old City and the eastern neighbourhoods. The Israelis occupied the western sector, and by September 1948 Jerusalem had become a divided city.

In March 1949 a bilateral armistice agreement was signed between Israel and Jordan, with the agreed border being based largely on the front-line positions held at the time of the UN-sponsored ceasefire of June 1948. Where there was disagreement two boundary lines were drawn on the map with the land in between designated 'no-man's-land' (NML) and the matter was referred to a special bilateral armistice committee charged with reaching agreement over such disputes. Battir was one of the villages that fell within the strip of NML south of Jerusalem, which meant that the village should have been evacuated. However, Battir avoided the trauma of neighbouring villagers who were dispossessed and displaced, largely due to the resistance campaign orchestrated by a 'son of the village', Hasan Mustafa.

Mustafa was a respected member of the village community who had been active organising the defence of the village during the war and was determined that a village that had remained unoccupied during the hostilities should not be lost as a consequence of the peace. To defend the village he followed a two-pronged strategy: 1. Active and persistent lobbying of the members of the armistice committee, arguing that Battir had never been conquered and therefore should not be evacuated; and 2. Creating the appearance of a village that was fully inhabited and ready to defend itself against attack in order to deter the Israelis from making any pre-emptive assault.

Mustafa was helped in his lobbying by the fact that there were several Jordanian military officers involved in the deliberations who were unhappy with Abdullah's conduct of the war and were sympathetic to Battir's cause. On April 18, 1949 his efforts bore fruit when the armistice line was routed such that the bulk of the village remained under Jordanian control, whilst allowing Israel to take control of the railway line running alongside the village. The decision was to come into force May 1, 1949 and to deter any unilateral action by the Israelis, Mustafa organised young men to go and light lamps in the village houses at night, put out washing lines, make as much noise as possible, and generally do all that they could to give the impression that the village was fully inhabited, when in fact most of the villagers spent their nights in a neighbouring village out of fear of an Israeli assault.

On the day when the agreement about the new armistice line came into effect Mustafa went to meet the Israeli officer (Moshe Dayan) and came to an agreement with him that the villagers would be allowed to cultivate their lands on the other side of the railway line, as long as they only used the access routes under the railway bridges and did not cross over the railway track itself. Once this agreement was reached Mustafa sent vehicles to collect those villagers who had been staying outside the village so they could get back to their homes as quickly as possible. He then had to persuade them to start farming their fields, after all it took some nerve to cross the new 'green line' in order to access their land under the watching presence of Israeli troops. So Mustafa accompanied them, knowing that if the agreements were to be recognised and respected, they needed to be implemented to the full.

Despite the various examples of offensive resistance displayed by the villagers under Hasan Mustafa's leadership, they could not escape the collective trauma of partition and the loss of the old familiar world. Mustafa was to recall, 'the days passed into months and the effect of isolation, loss of income, of health and educational services began to be reflected in bitterness and unhappiness. Something needed to be done if this village was to be saved.'[54] It was in this context that Mustafa led the village in various community development schemes that could be characterised as forms of constructive resistance. Improvements to the water supply and irrigation system was followed by the opening of a girls' school, adult literacy classes and vocational training facilities. He persuaded UNWRA to construct a road linking the village with Bethlehem and encouraged an ongoing tree-planting programme. In the words of one of Mustafa's grandsons, Jawad Botmeh:

> This community development drive managed to foster hope, provide employment and make the villagers understand that not only could they survive but they could also improve their lives markedly. This strengthened internal discipline in the face of the continued Israeli threat to the village and its land. In addition, Battir became an example of community development and its success brought the village many external admirers. Hasan Mustafa harnessed the power of external allies to make sure that outsiders had a stake in or at least witnessed Battir's prosperity and progress, bringing it protection and support. His real achievement, though, had been in harnessing the power of the indigenous concept of a'aoneh (community service/public help), infusing it with enlightened thinking and transforming it into a collective, potent, positive community force.[55]

Observations on the Battir case study

The small victory that Battir represented in the broader context of the overwhelming catastrophe experienced by the bulk of Palestinians during the partition period was only possible because there was a space, a window of opportunity to be exploited in the edifice that was being constructed by the key players in the drama. A number of factors seem significant in explaining the relative success of this resistance movement.

1. Strong leadership

The resistance would not have taken place without the leadership of Hasan Mustafa. He was involved in organising the armed defence of the village during the war that meant that it was never overrun by the Israeli troops. He was the key player in the civil resistance during the deliberations of the Armistice Committee and initiated the community development programme that enabled the village to survive during the post-partition period. The fact that he was not only a 'son of the village' but also the son of the headman gave him the status and authority to influence and mobilise people. He also had the courage to lead by example, accompanying the villagers as they risked their lives in accessing their fields across the 'green line'. He also had the self-confidence and the status to negotiate with Moshe Dayan, the officer in charge of the Israeli troops facing the village on the day the new border was to come into force, asserting the villagers' right of access to their farmland.

2. Social solidarity and shared commitment to the cause

As has been noted above, loyalty to one's clan and one's village ranked higher for most Palestinians than loyalty to an abstract concept like the nation. Moreover, nothing mobilises people more than a perceivable and immediate threat to their homes and their means of livelihood, and this is what confronted the villagers of Battir. The alternative they faced was dispossession and displacement.

3. Imbalance in the means of coercive power and absence of any significant 'counter-movement'

The challenge facing Hasan Mustafa in the immediate aftermath of the war was to display the appropriate degree of defiance to deter the Israelis from attacking whilst avoiding any action that might provoke such an attack. In such circumstances, and in the context of the ceasefire having been agreed and the overwhelming military resources of the Israeli military, violent resistance was not a serious option, except conceivably as an absolute last resort in the event of an Israeli assault.

4. Recognition of the legitimacy of the struggle and good communications with sympathetic bystanders, third parties and constituencies of support

Hasan Mustafa was able to convince disgruntled Jordanian officers that the village had never been occupied, and as a consequence their case was presented to the Armistice Committee which agreed on a re-routing of the border. Later, during the post-partition period he was able to attract the interest of external humanitarian relief agencies who supported him in his constructive activities aimed at restoring the social, economic and cultural well-being of the village community.

The experience of Battir stands in contrast to that of the 400 or more Palestinian villages that were destroyed or rendered uninhabitable during the 1947–49 period. As such it bears repeating that it was made possible by a particular conjunction of factors and conditions that created a slight 'window of opportunity' that Hasan Mustafa chose to exploit to the full. It also seems appropriate to remark that the quality of his leadership stands in stark and painful contrast to the woeful role played by so many of his contemporaries amongst the ranks of the national and local leadership strata of Palestinian society – a pattern that has been repeated over the succeeding years.[56]

Battir: A postscript

On February 20, 2005 the Israeli government approved a new route for the Separation Wall which required the expropriation of large tracts of Battir land and thereby threatened the 1949 agreement. In 2007 the village council sued the Israeli Ministry of Defense in an attempt to protect their land. They were eventually supported in this by the Israel Nature and Parks Authority which argued that the 2000-year-old terraces of the village were an important heritage site and should be safeguarded. In May 2013 the Israeli High Court required the Israeli Ministry of Defense to submit new plans for securing the border that would not destroy the terraces. Then, in June 2014, UNESCO recognised Battir as a World Heritage Site, thereby affording it a further degree of protection against the Israeli bulldozers.

3

PALESTINIANS IN ISRAEL: FROM QUIET RESISTANCE TO AUDIBLE PROTEST AND POLITICAL MOBILISATION

INTRODUCTION

Asef Bayat has pointed out how little attention has been paid by analysts of Middle East political change to the manner in which subaltern populations and communities of the disenfranchised can bring about changes in their life-world through their 'quiet and unassuming daily struggles'.[1] In this chapter we begin by exploring the ways in which the traumatised remnants of the Palestinian population, who found themselves living under alien rule in a country that was once their own, attempted to reclaim some degree of autonomy and control over their lives through the years of military rule from 1948 to 1966. We then move on to examine the different forms the political mobilisation of the Palestinian citizens of Israel took as they developed increased assertiveness and collective self-confidence in the years after military rule had come to an end.

In many ways the Arab minority within Israel in the years immediately following the *Nakbha* could be depicted as what Bayat has called a 'social nonmovement', which he characterised as: 'the collective actions of noncollective actors; they embody shared practices of large numbers of ordinary people whose fragmented but similar activities trigger much social change, even though these practices are rarely guided by an ideology or recognizable leaderships and organizations.'[2]

Bayat has attempted to use this conceptual framework of the collective nonmovement to study the ways in which the subaltern within authoritarian regimes engage in a prolonged struggle to survive by quietly impinging on the domain of the propertied and powerful by means involving the unlawful acquisition of those resources necessary to enhance their life chances. This is the strategy to which the Palestinians in Israel[3] after 1948 had to resort – modes of resistance that were not so much overt acts of defiance but extensions of the mundane practices of their everyday life whereby they were able to make claims

THIS IS NOT OUR HOUSE

Umm al-Fahim is a small peaceful town of farmers who filled their hilly land with olive, almond, and fig trees besides the seasonal crops of wheat, barley, lentils, beans and vegetables. To marry was the great anticipation of the youth at the end of each summer season when the festivity of marriage celebrations would be at its peak. My father grew up in the twinned towns of Umm al-Fahim and Lajjun that were later turned into rubble by Zionist forces and its residents expelled. He went to pursue his higher education in Birziet and later joined the growing ranks of city labourers and worked in the British Oil Refinery in Haifa. Working day and night shifts as a trained professional, he earned a good monthly salary.

My father had built a dream house, the house that made his marriage possible. A two-storey stone structure in a luxurious setting. A house in a small town of four thousand, where people mostly live in traditional mud houses, was a new novelty and beyond the dreams of even the richer villagers. Unlike the mud houses, the stone house was internally painted and decorated. Jasmine, carnation, basil – used in Palestine only for its fragrance – and other plants. The family house was in the middle of the town, very close to the centre where all four quarters of the town met. It was placed high up, and noticed by everyone who approached the town by ascending the road through the valley to reach the town on top of the mountains. Inside the house there was a wide bedroom and a balcony. The rooms were separated by a shared dining room, a practical device that also served as a privacy buffer.

My parents declined an offer to move to the Gulf States where professionals were in demand due to the intensive development. They hoped for peace and saw it on the horizon. Following the armistice agreements, Umm al-Fahim was transferred from Jordanian to Israeli rule. The United Nations approved agreement guaranteed autonomy, protection of property, culture, education, and self-policing of Umm al-Fahim until a final peace agreement would be reached.

One day without any notice my parents found themselves in a death threatening nightmare. Israeli forces entered the two-storey house, asked no questions and talked to no one. The soldiers kicked all the family out, removing and throwing away whatever their hands picked from the neatly organized items of the newly wed couple's household. Their vandalism was accompanied by an order for all women to leave the house. Another group of soldiers climbed the stairs to the bedrooms and left shortly after examination. They returned with military and office equipment and their commander settled in at my parents' bedroom. My parent's house was turned into a military headquarters. The town was ordered under curfew, and movements of its people were curtailed for sixteen more years. My father refused the abusers' offer to make him a school teacher and never felt happy again. My

▶

mother maintained her personality by telling us the stories and joining my father's militant position and with an inner anger and sadness. I inherited the injustice and the traumatic experiences of both of my parents.

We moved to live in the Haddad's house, owned by a Christian family. I grew alien to that place, internalizing my parents and grandparents alienation. 'This is not our house' was probably the first complete sentence I learned to master. And I heard it every day in various forms: through my mother and grandmother's cursing of the military 'that took our home', through the long prayers to God to bring us back to 'our home'. My parents hardly did any maintenance on the building, and never made any permanent changes. Thirteen years later in a stormy winter, the whole structure began to collapse. Big stones rolled with each stroke of lightening and thunder. I found the school hours of that winter particularly protective from the threat of big stones and falling mud, I would rush to school every morning in the hope that I would get to stay all day.

One day I was called by the principal to see my older sister who had come especially to see me. My sister insisted that I go back home with her. When we got closer to our home, I mean the Haddad's home where we were living, my sister asked, 'Do you promise not to tell anybody?' I did not know what to promise. 'I heard nothing.' I replied. She insisted and I shouted 'I promise, promise, promise ...' Sabah, my sister pushed me as if to bring me back from my shouts and she whispered: 'Today, we are going back to our home.' After that she struggled hard to keep up as I speedily ran toward the Haddad's home.

There I found my mother in control like a commander, her older sister next to her and the kids ready to move. The rain was heavy and lightning and thunder in the sky. But we moved toward our own real home where my parents got married and enjoyed their first days of love together. We had reached the 'headquarters' as our home had come to be referred to by the people of Umm al-Fahim. A group of workers were filling the stairs leading to the gate. The Israeli flag was high in the column, and an Israeli soldier watching the workers and the road below. The workers were hesitant and slow in stepping aside in front of my mother and the trailing line of kids. She was determined and paid no time to the workers apparent confusion. She moved forward, entered the gate, looked above and inside as if seeing the place for the first time. We followed her to the second floor, to her first and original bedroom, the Military Governor's office. The two moms and eight kids entered the offices and sat there refusing to move or obey the soldier's request to move. We were happy and scared, orderly and chaotic, we played, exchanged ugly faces and pushes. We were kids at their home. My mom was silent and worried in anticipation of something happening. The heavy storm continued and the Military Governor, the ruler of the town and area, with his military vehicle, could not make it through the road that day.[4]

on resources and spaces that had been expropriated from them with the creation of the State of Israel.

The types of 'quiet resistance' pursued displayed all the features of the noncollective actors studied by Bayat:

1. The activities were undertaken by individuals and their families rather than by unified groups.
2. They eschewed dramatic acts of protest, which would not have been tolerated by the military government under which they lived. Their activities were overwhelmingly 'quiet' extensions of their everyday practices, like encroaching on land for cultivation from which they were officially banned or rebuilding their homes without permits.[5]
3. Such noncollective acts of quiet resistance differed from everyday actions insofar as they involved contentious and often extra-legal practices that subverted the existing regulations and ordinances enacted by the Israeli authorities.
4. The Palestinians in their resistance engaged in a special form of nonviolent direct action, that is, they directly practised what they claimed, like encroaching on land expropriated from them, rather than attempting to put pressure on the authorities to grant their demands. As Bayat has phrased it, 'theirs is not a politics of protest, but of practice, of redress through direct and disparate actions.'[6]

The establishment of the State of Israel in 1948 had a devastating impact on the Palestinian people – it was the year of the *Nakbha*, 'the Catastrophe'. The immediate impact was that the majority of the Palestinians were either forced out of their homes or fled as result of the war to become refugees in the West Bank and Gaza Strip and the neighbouring Arab countries such as Lebanon, Syria and Jordan. It is estimated that about 700,000 became refugees and those who remained within the newly established State of Israel were reduced to a minority within their homeland, cut off from the rest of their fellow nationals.[7] Estimates of how many Palestinians remained in Israel in 1948 range between 80,000 and 160,000, somewhere in the region of 10 per cent of the original population.[8] As a result of the *Nakbha*, Palestinians faced the destruction of their political, economic and social structures. The bulk of the political and religious leadership, the intellectuals and the middle classes had left and most of the people who remained were peasants.

Israel was established as the Jewish homeland and opened its doors to Jews from all over the world. To maintain the fragmentation and control over the Palestinian minority, the Israeli state reinforced their economic dependence on the Jewish sector. The majority of the Arab land was confiscated, water sources controlled and the Islamic Waqf property expropriated.[9] Palestinians were excluded from economic development plans and from taking part in decision-making regarding any economic development. This left them detached from their land as an unskilled labour force dependant on the Israeli economy. Arab villages became the source of cheap labour and the villages became dormitories for Arab workers. Socially, the family as the main social economic unit was deeply shattered. Some family members had been killed in the war, others became refugees or internally displaced and destitute. Sami Khalil Mar'i summarised the situation of the Palestinians remaining in Israel as follows: 'Emotionally wounded, socially rural, politically lost, economically poverty stricken and nationally hurt. They suddenly became a minority ruled by powerful, sophisticated majority against whom they fought to retain their country and land.'[10]

THE MILITARY GOVERNMENT

The Palestinians in Israel lived under the heavy-handed military rule which was imposed on them immediately after 1948 until 1966. The Palestinian areas were divided into three main districts, each directly administered by a military governor. Strict restrictions were imposed on the lives of the Arab minority, drawing in particular upon the Emergency Regulation Laws inherited from the British Mandate. The movement of the Palestinians was restricted and they needed a permit from the military governor to leave the village – whether it was to work, visit family, obtain medical treatment, study or to carry out any other purpose outside the village. The heads of the extended families (*mukhtar*) became key contacts for obtaining permits from the military governor. The Israeli authorities employed a divide and rule policy, extending privileges to those *mukhtar*s who were willing to cooperate with them. This became one of the key means by which the Israeli authorities maintained the subordination of the Arab minority and reinforced patterns of social and spatial fragmentation within the Arab population.[11] Israel also attempted to exacerbate the pre-existing fractures within that society, doing what was possible to widen the divisions between the different religions, regions and clan networks (*hamulah*s).[12]

RESISTANCE THROUGH CULTIVATION

Large Palestinian areas of land were confiscated or designated as closed military areas to which entry by Arabs, including the landowners themselves, was forbidden. In addition the Israeli authorities would restrict access to certain tracts of Arab land to certain days such as the weekend or Jewish holidays as a way of undermining the local agricultural economy and weakening the

Palestinian attachment to their land. However, local people found ways to circumvent the restrictions as they were aware that Israel would confiscate any land left uncultivated. One farmer from Umm al-Fahim explained how they persisted in cultivating their land:

> Farmers and landowners in Umm al-Fahim did not accept such a closure and they used to go in secret or undercover, without the approval or knowledge of the army, to work on the land and cultivate it in order to protect and maintain the ownership of the land and to prevent the risk of confiscation. Farmers tried to work all year round to maintain their ownership of the land and strengthen their presence.

There was a particular emphasis by Israel on combatting the planting of trees such as olives and almonds because, no doubt, such trees represented a long-term claim on the land. Instead the local farmers were encouraged to cultivate vegetables and seasonal produce. In this context the planting of trees came to be seen as a form of resistance. A more obvious type of resistance, according to one shop owner, was the formation of foraging teams to go to the nearby Jewish settlements in order to reclaim (or steal) grain and other produce that was often grown on land expropriated from the families of the raiders.

Sometimes villagers reclaimed their property by a combination of quiet stealth and courage. Mua'awiya was a small hamlet near Umm al-Fahim and in 1948 the Israeli military forced the 370 residents to leave the village before proceeding to destroy their homes. The displaced arrived in Umm al-Fahim with very little because they had left all their possessions behind. However, the village leaders refused to accept their expulsion and dispossession as a fait accompli. One of the residents explained how they proceeded:

> We used the livestock as a method of returning to the land. We started immediately to take animals to graze on the land of the village, step by step we got closer to our homes and then recovered food and possessions, gradually we began to stay there. Another strategy we employed was to work on the land and harvest it. Eventually the military issued temporary permits to work the land. Finally this culminated in the military agreeing to allow the residents to return to their homes and rebuild them with one condition – that they would not ask for any compensation.[13]

DETERMINATION TO REMAIN: RESILIENCE IN THE FACE OF HARSH LIVING CONDITIONS

The destruction of hundreds of entire villages and the accompanying infrastructure resulted in the kind of humanitarian crisis that accompanies the aftermath of any war, particularly as experienced by the Palestinian minority who were subjected to extremely harsh living conditions. Umm al-Fahim, the largest village in the Wadi A'ara region, became a staging post for the thousands of dispossessed driven from their homes in neighbouring villages. The displaced lived in schools, deserted homes, mosques and anywhere they could find a semblance of shelter. As one resident depicted the situation in those days, 'Olive trees were covered with plastic sheets and became homes for the refugees, the little water springs became a magnet for refugees to stay in the area, and the whole village became like a big tent.' In fact many of the internally displaced continued to live in caves for several years – examples of what is perhaps the 'quietest' form of resistance: the determination to stay in one's homeland whatever the suffering incurred.

The displaced and dispossessed received virtually no support from the UN or any other international agency, whilst the newly established State of Israel showed little concern for the well-being of those they considered to be former enemies and as such suspect aliens in their midst. As a consequence most forms of relief were provided by relatives and local inhabitants who had managed to hold on to some of their property. Villagers would organise community-wide collections of basic supplies such as flour, oil, rice, eggs and vegetables to distribute amongst the needy families. It all helped engender a very strong sense of communal solidarity between the locals and the displaced, a feeling that has endured over the years. As one informant recalled: 'After we were expelled from our village, we lived with distant relatives for two weeks. They welcomed us and agreed that we could stay with them. They fed us and cared for us. We had nothing with us; no food and no money.'

One consequence of the harsh living conditions and shortages experienced by the Palestinian minority living under military rule was a renewed focus on developing means of self-sufficiency. Residents started to grow their own vegetables and rear chickens and rabbits secretly in their gardens and on rooftops in defiance of the military authority's regulations. Anyone discovered contravening regulations risked a significant fine or imprisonment. Refugees and local residents alike started to forage for wild plants and vegetation such as spinach, asparagus and the like. There were also figs, grapes, different types of berries and grains and pulses to be gathered, if you knew where to look. Others made the most of whatever opportunity arose to trade and survive. A displaced person living in Sakhnin explained the manner in which his family managed after they were expelled from their village: 'We used to buy eggs, barley and flour and then sell it to the Jewish communities; this was a way of supporting our family and our extended family. This was done against the laws and regulations of the military authorities. Sometimes we were arrested and imprisoned and we paid a fine.'

The Israeli authorities exerted strong pressure on social and political leaders to leave the country, even offering compensation for their land and property. Mohammed Abed Al-Qader Younis, a leading figure amongst the Arab minority, was a particular target of the military authorities. His son explained: 'My father was aware of the political implication of the attempt to get him to leave, and rejected all the pressure put on him by the government. For that he paid a high price: there were arrests, harassment and obstacles put in his way by the Israeli authorities.'

In Umm al-Fahim the head of one of the larger landowning families had been out of the country in April 1948, but decided to return to the village and follow developments on the ground. The return of the landowner, who represented social, political and economic authority in the village encouraged many people to remain steadfast and stay on in their homes and hold on to their land.

CULTURE, IDENTITY AND RESISTANCE

Of the different types of resistance to occupation identified by Werner Rings that of symbolic resistance can be viewed as the 'quietest', carrying the least risk of sanctions. Arabs in Israel found ways to express their resistance in such a manner. In 1949 the village of Umm al-Fahim was handed over to Israel by the Jordanian forces. The Israeli military commander required all the residents to gather in the centre of the village and demanded that they hand in all their weapons to mark the end of the fighting. The residents were then instructed to celebrate the arrival of the Israeli army through singing and dancing. As an expression of resistance and defiance of this order women sang songs expressing their sorrow and anger rather than joy. This was an early instance of the manner in which Palestinians in Israel expressed their opposition to the Israeli military rule through literature, song and other cultural forms of resistance. The Arab and Palestinian culture became a means to highlight their national identity. Poetry festivals and public meetings were held in Nazareth, Haifa and other villages providing people with the opportunity to express opposition to the military rule and the discrimination they experienced as Arabs citizens of the Israeli state in ways which did not provoke the military administration. Saud al-Asadi, a poet and traditional singer from the Galilee, recalled celebrating the birthday of the tenth-century Arab poet Al-Mutanabbi at the YMCA in Nazareth in 1965. He recalled: 'It was a large gathering. In this way culture brought people together and was a very powerful means of struggle. Al-Mutanabbi was proud of his Arab identity and he was used as an outlet to express our own Arab identity in Israel.'

Weddings, national and religious celebrations became a medium for political expression and singing national songs as a quiet way of challenging the military rule. Sometimes traditional songs would be sung in the local dialect denouncing the military governor and describing him in a scathing and disrespectful manner whilst he was actually present, sitting unawares as one of the important guests at the wedding. Al-Asadi described one occasion when his father used a wedding to sing the praises of an Egyptian general who was respected for his stand against Israel, British and French forces during the war of 1956. The general's name was Abed Al-Muna'im Riyad, and it so happened that the groom was also called Riyad:

> My father used this occasion to highlight the groom's steadfastness, courage and resilience but in fact he was referring to the Egyptian General. Everyone in the celebration understood this play on names and metaphor. He was accused of incitement and praising the enemy but he totally denied that and insisted that he was singing about the groom.

In 1952 an association for Arab poets was established in different villages in the Galilee and Triangle area. The centres became a focal point for political, cultural and social activities against the military rule and the discrimination against the Arab population. Pappe summarised the critical role of culture in the struggle of Palestinians in Israel for civil and national rights as follows:

> Poetry was the one area in which national identity survived the *Nakbhah* unscathed. What political activists did not dare express, poets sang out with force. Poetry was one medium through which the daily events of love and hate, birth and death, marriage and family could be intertwined with the political issues of land confiscation and state oppression and aired in public at special poetry festivals ... The Israeli secret service was powerless to decide whether this phenomenon was a subversive act or a cultural event.[14]

As part of the control system of the Palestinians in Israel the security forces created a network of informers and collaborators. The education system was entirely controlled by the Israeli security services and any appointment required their approval. Head teachers and teachers were co-opted to inform and spy about their colleagues and any activity in the village. Schools would organise celebrations of Israel's Independence Day and head teachers competed amongst each other to show loyalty to the military administration. However, some parents and students refused to take part in such events. One informant explained, 'I remember that I was asked by a teacher to bring money to cover the cost of the celebration of the Israeli Independence Day held in the school, and my Dad refused to give me the money as a sign of rejection to the Israeli authorities.' Mahmoud Darwish, then a child in school and later to become a Palestinian national poet, was summoned to the military governor after reading poetry critical of the military authority during a school commemoration of Israel's independence day.[15] It is understandable that teachers were afraid of expressing their views openly. One teacher explained how he managed in a quiet manner to express his rejection of the military government.

Once I wrote one of Al-Mutanabbi's poems on the wall of my classroom. Its theme was that those who are used to accept humiliation will continue to be humiliated and controlled. I was then called up to the military governor's office and was reprimanded and humiliated because I wrote such a piece of poetry. My argument was that this poetry was written a thousand years ago.

Part of the nonviolent resistance against the military rule was refusing to recognise the symbols and the leadership of the state. Umar Ibn Al-Khattab was one of the most powerful caliphs in Islam and renowned for his commitment to justice and speaking the truth. His image was hung on the wall of a school in Umm al-Fahim but the headmaster was asked to replace it with the photo of Chaim Weizmann, a Zionist leader and the first President of Israel. One of our informants, then a student aged 12, recalled 'secretly I went and smashed the photo of Weizmann, nobody knew who did it, but the message was clear.'

The 1950s witnessed the growing support for the pan-Arab movement led by the president of Egypt, Gamal Abdel Nasser. He challenged Israel and the colonial powers, which earned him wide support such that he became an iconic figure across the Middle East. Supporting Nasser was seen by many Palestinians in Israel as a symbol of their rejection of the military rule. One interviewee explained, 'I had the radio on the balcony and turned it on high so that others could listen to nationalist songs praising Abdel Nasser as an Arab leader and listen to his speeches. The military governor reprimanded and threatened me for doing that.'

RESISTANCE TO RESTRICTIONS ON MOVEMENT

Israel imposed curfews and other measures as a way of controlling the movement of Arab residents. In response, the targets of such measures explored ways to bypass the controls. For example, anyone wishing to leave their village or town needed to apply for a permit at the military governor's office. As noted above, the military authorities appointed *mukhtar*s as the link with the governor. One obvious way to overcome this obstacle was bribery. As one interviewee explained, 'It was possible to bribe both the military officers and the *mukhtar*; I gave them two kilograms of almonds so that they might give me a permit to work.'[16] Others who were refused permits travelled to work without one. Workers would stay away from their families for months at a time to avoid risk of arrest and save the cost of travel. The harsh conditions endured by these workers fostered solidarity and mutual support amongst them. One of those who worked in Tel Aviv recalled: 'Life in Tel Aviv was harsh; we learned how to cook and to make bread and to live with basic supplies. We used to help each other and support each other to the point that strong friendships were forged and remained for years.'

Occasionally the Israeli police would raid work places and arrest workers, impose fines and send them back to the villages. Someone who used to work in Jaffa recalled how they used to sleep in the orange groves: 'We would make hammocks up in the trees as our beds in order to hide from the police. As we were up in the trees the police would see no bedding on the ground and assume there were no workers there.'

Workers who went to the population centres such as Tel Aviv were under pressure to change their names to Jewish names, so Mahmoud became Yossi and their employers could pretend that they were employing Jewish rather than Arab workers. Here is a story from one who was a teenager during those years:

> I went to high school in Haifa. I used to take the risk travelling every two weeks without a permit to Haifa at the age of 14. I used to travel on the bus and to disguise being an Arab I would buy a Hebrew newspaper and I would sit and read it, so when the soldier or police would ask everyone to come off the bus to show their permits, I would stay on the bus and pretend not to be an Arab. So my permit was the Hebrew daily newspaper *Yediot*. The driver was Jewish and he knew I was an Arab, and he kept it quiet, because I brought him presents such as olives and olive oil and other things. In 1965 I was arrested and taken to Afula police station. I was fined and then released late at night.

Israel imposed the restriction on the movement of the Arabs to prevent the displaced returning to reclaim their land and their homes. Lustick quoted a former Adviser to the Israeli Prime Minister on Arab Affairs who explained the rationale for such restrictions:

> The Arabs who used to live in the empty villages, egged on and organized by the Communists, would go back and squat on their ruins, demanding their land back ... and then, when they have made as much trouble as possible about their own lands, they will start clamouring for the return of refugees.[17]

FROM QUIET RESISTANCE TO AUDIBLE PROTEST

The overt purpose of the military rule was to maintain political and social segregation and control of the Arab community in Israel. The only political party that sought to involve both Jewish and Arab members as equals was the Israeli Communist Party (ICP), which was established in 1948. The ICP was a key vehicle for early campaigns against the restrictions and discriminatory practices imposed on the Arab population within Israel. As such the ICP played an important role not only in the struggle for full equality for the Arab minority but also in the maintenance of an Arab national identity and consequently became the political home of leading Arab intellectuals, writers and poets.[18]

Residents were threatened if they indicated a preparedness to vote for the ICP or any other party that opposed the military rule. *Al-Ittihad*, the official newspaper of the ICP, was sold and distributed clandestinely because of the risk of arrest and punishment. As one interviewee recalled: 'The communist party used to deliver their own newspaper secretly in the village. There were three or four members of the party who would do this. But if you met or visited openly with known members of the communist party or openly read their newspaper you would be punished.'

The ICP was one of the groups who organised the first open political protest against the military authority which took place in Nazareth on May 1, 1958. Thousands of demonstrators came from the surrounding villages to Nazareth, with the police attempting to block entrances to the town to deter people from participating. By the end of the day more than 350 people had been arrested and scores injured. These May Day demonstrations became the occasion for the Palestinians in Israel to demand their civil rights and express their national identity through proclaiming their solidarity with nationalist and anti-colonial movements throughout the Arab world. As someone who worked in the military government office in Nazareth recalled, 'The communists and nationalists would use the celebration of May Day as an occasion to confront with the military. Activists would spend hours preparing themselves to confront the army and the police.'

As the Arab minority within Israel grew in political confidence and assertiveness, the authorities responded with expulsions of political activists to remote villages far away from their families. Others were placed under house arrest and were required to report – sometimes twice a day – to the local police station. Activists were also punished by denying them and their families travel permits. Pressure was also exerted on the heads of families to prevent their relatives from taking part in political activity. One interviewee told of how the military governor 'threatened my father that they would expel my brother to the Galilee if he took part in a national meeting opposing military rule.' As a consequence his father did not go to the meeting and his brother avoided expulsion. The military government had a wide network of informers to enable them to identify anyone who spoke out of line. As White noted, 'By reporting on the day-to-day speech of Arabs and by summoning and interrogating those Arabs who spoke against the state, the security authorities "taught" the minority what was fit to be said and what was unacceptable, thus shaping the contours of Arab political discourse in Israel.'[19]

Despite such measures to suppress dissent there was, by the late 1950s, a growing number of attempts to give public expression to the emerging aspirations of the Palestinians in Israel. In 1958 one of the first public meetings against military rule was held in Umm al-Fahim. The organisers had invited Tawfeek Tubi, a Knesset member from the ICP, to address them. But the military governor was intent on frustrating these plans and attempted to block all the entrances to the village. One of the organisers recalled how they side-stepped such measures.

> We went and met him at Lajoun junction (Megido) and disguised him as a woman on a donkey and sneaked him through one of the back entrances. The number of the police and army present was equal to the number of demonstrators. The meeting was held and a confrontation broke out with the military and more than 40 people were arrested and many were injured. They attacked us with batons but we responded with stone throwing. We physically attacked the governor and he hid underneath the military jeep.

Alongside the struggle for civil and political rights the Arab population also focused on social and economic justice issues. The high unemployment caused by restriction on travel and the confiscation of the land caused deprivation and poverty amongst many. The scarcity of commodities and food rationing further worsened the situation and many families suffered severe hardship. Mahmoud Younis, then a member of Mapam, the Zionist Socialist Party, recalled that 'The first demonstration organised in Aa'ra was in 1952 and we raised slogans like "We refuse to die hungry" and demanded "Our right for work and bread". The army shot at us but there were no injuries.'

A few years later in 1957 nationalists and communists established the Arab Front which ideologically was part of the pan-Arab nationalist movement. Israel refused to register the organisation under this name and so it became the 'Popular Democratic Front'. Its main aims were equality between Arab and Jews in Israel, an end to land confiscation and the end of military rule. In 1965 the Front was banned from participating in the Knesset election. Also banned from the Knesset elections that same year was the Arab Socialist List created by another political movement to emerge during this period – *Al-Ard* (The Land). Established in 1958 it also located itself within the context of the pan-Arab nationalist movement, seeing the Palestinian question as an integral part of the wider Arab nationalist cause. Although it was banned from participating in Knesset elections, *Al-Ard* was influential through the different cultural and sports centres it established (under different names) in those areas of Israel where the Arab population was concentrated, and became a significant driver of the struggle against military rule.

FROM PROTEST TO POLITICAL MOBILISATION FOR CIVIL AND NATIONAL RIGHTS

In 1966 the period of military rule came to an end, but the Arab minority within Israel continued to face discrimination in most walks of life with the status of 'semi-citizens'.[20] Then came the war of 1967 and the occupation of the West Bank and Gaza Strip, which paradoxically 'united' the Palestinians from both sides of the Green Line after years of separation. It enabled the Palestinians in Israel to renew family relations and commercial links with the newly occupied Palestinian territories (OPT). This new situation exposed Palestinians in Israel to the struggle of the Palestinian national movement in the OPT and the PLO and led to political cooperation. The reunification led to a growing recognition of their shared history with the Palestinians in the OPT and consciousness of their Palestinian national identity. This process was also accompanied by economic and social changes in the status of the Palestinian minority within Israel. In the early 1970s the expansion of the Israeli economy provided jobs for Arab workers and facilitated their integration into the Israeli economy. Palestinian workers from the occupied territories also became part of the labour market in Israel, a development that changed the status of the Palestinian citizens of Israel who found themselves no longer at the foot of the status ladder. As part of these changes, they began to obtain higher positions as a consequence of their expertise, familiarity with the majority culture and associated knowledge of the Hebrew language. During the 1970s, then, there was an economic improvement in the situation of the Arabs in Israel and an increase in their standard of living, which also saw an expansion of Arab-owned enterprises.

The economic changes which affected the structure of the Arab community in Israel was accompanied by the erosion of the influence of the traditional clan-based leadership as a new generation of educated and articulate Arabs emerged to challenge the old regime. The assertiveness of this new younger generation was emboldened by their perception of the vulnerabilities of Israel as exposed during the 1973 War. All this fed into a significant increase in the self-confidence of the Arab community within Israel during the 1970s, which in turn fed into the emergence of new movements and organisations seeking to articulate and represent the interests of the Palestinian minority within Israel. One of these was the National Committee for the Defence of Arab Lands (NCDAL) which was formed in 1975 as a coalition of various political groupings and community-based organisations to oppose land confiscations and expropriation by Jewish municipalities and the state. The NCDAL called for the first national strike for the Arabs in Israel on 'Land Day' March 30, 1976 during which six protesters were killed by the Israeli police. After years of military rule and relatively quiet resistance, Land Day 1976 was the first act of mass resistance by the Palestinians inside Israel against the ongoing expropriation of their land. Furthermore, after years of virtual ostracism by the PLO leadership and the Arab states, Land Day of 1976 led to the acknowledgement of the Palestinian minority within Israel as inseparable members of the Palestinian nation.[21] Since that date Palestinians from both sides of the Green Line and throughout the diaspora have continued to commemorate Land Day with demonstrations and strikes to protest against the continuing confiscations of Palestinian land and settlement building in Israel and the OPT.[22]

It was in the same year as the formation of the NCDAL that the Democratic Front for Peace and Equality (DFPE) was established as a political party in Nazareth. It consisted of communists, nationalists and academics and in 1975 it gained control of the municipal council of Nazareth, the largest Arab town in Israel. Three years later the DFPE had taken control of 19 Arab municipal councils in Israel, all of which had been under the control of the older generation of traditional leaders. It was also during this period that efforts were intensified to establish community-based organisations in response to the various demands of different sectors of the population. The most important organisation was the National Committee of Heads of Arab Local Authorities (NCHALA) which was founded in 1975 as a lobby to pressure government departments for a greater allocation of national resources. Other organisations formed during this period were the Union of Arab High School Students, established in 1974, and the Union of Arab Students in Israeli Universities, established a year later.

The Israeli government was concerned about the growing politicisation of the Palestinian minority. A report submitted in 1976 by Yisrael Koenig, a member of the ruling party, put forward a number of strategic goals and tactical steps aimed at reducing the number and influence of Arab citizens of Israel in the Galilee region. Outlining what he viewed as 'objective thought that ensures the long-term Jewish national interests,' Koenig stressed the need to 'examine the possibility of diluting existing Arab population concentrations' and recommended various measures including restricting their employment opportunities, restricting their access to universities, reducing their family benefits, and giving preferential treatment to Jews. Koenig was especially concerned with the Arab majority in the Galilee and urged the expansion of Jewish settlements to break up the contiguity of Arab communities in that area, stressing the importance of using law enforcement agencies to control and crack down on the actions and movement of Arabs, and to generally facilitate Arab immigration out of the country.[23]

What we see in the late 1970s and the years leading up to the first intifada is the emergence of new Arab political movements and parties within Israel. Their platforms generally included the demand that the Arabs should be recognised as a national minority within Israel, mutual recognition between Israel and the PLO, the withdrawal of Israel from the territories occupied in 1967 and the establishment of a Palestinian state alongside Israel.[24] It was during this period also that Islamist political parties began to emerge and play a role in the political life of the Arab communities in Israel, reflecting to some degree the resurgence of Islam in the Middle East in the late 1970s. For a number of years the movement focused on social welfare, health and education projects, but by 1989 they enjoyed sweeping victories in the local elections for the Arab councils.

In addition the mid-1980s saw another expression of politicisation with the emergence of professional associations seeking to represent the interests of different occupational groups and professions. All these different organisations, parties and movements came together in the mid-1980s under the umbrella of the High Follow-Up Committee for Arab Citizens of Israel (HFCACI).[25] The broad representation of this coalition meant that it enjoyed a significant degree of legitimacy amongst the Palestinian minority within Israel, as indicated by the broad support for the four national strikes it called during 1987–88. During the 1980s the growing political assertiveness of the Palestinian minority began to make itself felt nationally. They were the first to organise protests against Israel's invasion of Lebanon in June 1982. A few months later, on September 22, a general strike was called in response to the massacres of Palestinian refugees at Sabra and Shatila. Thousands heeded the call and clashes broke out with the Israeli police in many localities including small villages and mixed cities such as Haifa, Acre and Jaffa.[26]

THE FIRST INTIFADA

Palestinians within Israel were quick to show their solidarity with their cousins in the West Bank and Gaza Strip after the outbreak of the first intifada. A general strike was called on December 21, 1987 – designated as 'peace day'. The HFCACI issued a statement affirming their engagement, 'The events in the occupied territories directly concern the Arabs in Israel as an inseparable part of the Palestinian people and as citizens of the state of Israel. We proclaim our full solidarity with the struggle of this people, our people, against Israeli occupation.'[27] The strike call met with a solid response in the Arab towns and villages, accompanied by protest marches and demonstrations that led to clashes with the police and the arrest of over a hundred protesters. The strike actions and demonstrations in support of their compatriots continued throughout the early years of the intifada, with the largest taking place in Nazareth with a reported 50,000 participants. Support also took on a more substantive form, with a number of the communiqués of the intifada leadership being printed in Arab-owned print-shops within Israel. In addition people organised relief committees for the provision of humanitarian aid and supplies for delivery across the Green Line.[28]

The intifada had a significant impact on the Palestinians within Israel. There was a deep sense of pride and admiration for their fellow nationals resisting the Israeli occupation. It strengthened the sense of shared identity with those living in the occupied territories. It also served as an example and a stimulus for their own struggle, feeding into a new sense of empowerment and solidarity, with the HFCACI as a recognised representative of this new mood. Be that as it may, in the aftermath of the intifada the Palestinians within Israel were reminded of how marginal they were in the eyes of the Israeli state, the PLO and the wider world. They played no part in the run-up to the Oslo Peace Accord that was signed in Washington on September 13, 1993, and were not mentioned in any section of the agreement.[29] It was in this context that the politically active amongst the Palestinian minority began campaigning for 'a state for all its citizens', recognising that whatever the bonds of solidarity that existed between different sections of the Palestinian nation, they were citizens of Israel with their own concerns and priorities, centred primarily on their continuing status as second-class citizens in the eyes of the state.

THE SECOND INTIFADA

On September 30, 2000 the HFCACI called for a general strike to protest the killing of several Palestinians in the Al-Aqsa compound in Jerusalem on the previous day. Demonstrations spread across the Arab towns and villages in northern Israel over the following days, with protesters enraged by the shooting of a 12-year-old boy in Gaza whilst sheltering with his father from gunfire. Molotov cocktails were thrown in some actions, and the Israeli security forces used live ammunition, resulting in the death of 13 protesters. It was as if the Green Line had disappeared. As Graham Usher reported at the time:

> ... what pulled Palestinians out onto the streets of their villages was televised murder – relayed again and again on Arab TV – of 12-year-old Mohamed Al-Dorra at the Netzarim junction in Gaza after 45 minutes of continuous Israeli army fire. And what put rocks into their hands was the lethal response of the Israeli police, for whom there has never been a Green Line as far 'their' Palestinians are concerned.[30]

The strength of the response reflected not only the level of support for those Palestinians resisting the occupation in the West Bank and Gaza Strip, it also grew from the deep sense of frustration felt by the Palestinian minority at the discriminatory treatment they experienced as marginalised second-class citizens of Israel. Indeed, the lethal force used by the Israeli police only served to highlight the manner in which the whole community was discriminated against.[31] As Ilan Pappe noted,

> If one can summarize the Palestinian take on what lay behind October 2000, it would be to say that this was an institutional use of state power to deliver a message to a fifth of its population: be docile and accept your status as second-class citizens, or encounter the wrath of the army and security forces.[32]

A relatively new development of this period was the emergence of Israeli solidarity groups composed of Arab and Jewish citizens of Israel. Amongst the groups with both communities represented were Anarchists against the Wall, Tarabut and Ta'ayush. One of our informants outlined the significance of such joint-action: 'Our message was genuine and clear; end the occupation, build Jewish–Palestinian partnerships, build trust in time of suspicion and give political, moral and humanitarian aid to the OPT.'

CONCLUSION

The 1948 war, the *Nakbha* and the establishment of the State of Israel had a traumatic impact on Palestinians generally. But whilst the majority became refugees a minority found themselves living as an alien group within the land that was once their own. They witnessed the destruction of their socio-economic institutions and way of life and were subjected to military rule for almost two decades. In many ways they were a 'forgotten people' separated from their fellow Arabs elsewhere in the Middle East. But it would be wrong to view them as mere passive victims of fate during those first decades of life in the new state of Israel. As we have attempted to illustrate in this chapter they engaged initially in quiet forms of struggle to preserve what autonomy they could find as they strove to survive in the face of the harsh living conditions that accompanied their displacement and dispossession. What we have also shown is that during the second decade of military rule they started to move on from quiet and to a large extent hidden forms of resistance to more audible and open forms of protest and resistance – primarily through the formation of political movements and parties that sought to represent the interests of a minority that was to become increasingly assertive over succeeding decades. A development that received a mighty impetus after the 1967 war when Palestinians within Israel were able to re-establish direct face-to-face contact with their fellow nationals in the newly occupied West Bank and Gaza Strip. Over the years since then the political assertiveness of the Palestinian minority within Israel has continued to grow as their struggle to achieve full civil and national rights within the Israeli state has continued.

4

FROM THE *NAKBHA* TO THE SEPARATION WALL: 1948–2002

In this chapter we trace the different modes of resistance pursued by the Palestinians outside the State of Israel as they sought to come to terms with the catastrophe of 1948 and their new status as refugees and dispossessed. We then look at the period, leading up to the establishment of the Palestine Liberation Organization (PLO) in the mid-1960s and the subsequent glorification of 'armed struggle' as the path to an independent Palestinian state. It was the abject failure of this mode of resistance that fed into the outbreak of the first intifada – a period of sustained unarmed popular resistance to which contemporary Palestinians can only look back upon with wonder and regret that the hopes it engendered came to naught during the subsequent years of the so-called 'Oslo peace process'. It was the anger and the despair brought on by the failure of the peace process that sowed the seeds of the second intifada, a period of violence and horror that in turn created the environment within which the Israeli state could justify its construction of the Separation Wall/Barrier by which it was able to encroach even further onto the diminishing territory of the Palestinians.

THE LOST YEARS OF THE 1950s

Between the disaster of 1948 and the establishment of the Palestine Liberation Organization (PLO) in 1964 there was virtually no significant public manifestation of Palestinian resistance of any sort. The reasons for this are not hard to find.

1. Dispersal, dispossession and division

Palestinian society had been devastated and fragmented by the defeats of 1947–48, which were in fact the culmination of a long chronology of failure. The immediate result was the dispersal of the majority of the Palestinian population to refugee camps in Lebanon, Syria, the Gaza Strip and the West Bank. Not only were they divided geographically, but they also confronted different host regimes. In the West Bank, which was annexed by Jordan in 1949, they received Jordanian nationality. The Gaza Strip was under Egyptian military administration, whilst – as noted in Chapter 3 – the Palestinians left in Israel lived under military rule until 1966. Conditions for the refugees in Lebanon and Syria varied over time and according to the political climate.

2. The trauma of loss

Whilst they were scattered and separated from each other, Palestinians were also disempowered by the deep trauma and shock suffered by those with a deep attachment to place who found themselves uprooted, no longer a majority in their own homeland but relegated to minority and subordinate status in states that were not their own.

3. Faith in pan-Arabism

Another reason the Palestinians were so quiescent through the 1950s was their identification with the ideology of pan-Arabism, as embodied above all in Nasser's rise to power in Egypt in 1952. The claim was that the Arabs constituted a single people, sharing language, history and culture, who had been divided by the machinations of imperialist powers. It is easy to understand the appeal of this movement for a people who had been dispossessed – they could regain their strength and their agency through the resurgent power of the Arab nation. It offered the hope of support from their fellow Arabs in their struggle against the Israeli enemy. Palestine would be 'liberated' in the context of the renewal of the Arab nation and associated political unification. The role for Palestinians in the meantime was to be patient and await deliverance.

4. The priority of economic survival

For most Palestinians reduced to poverty and subordinate status in their new anomic conditions, the priority was survival – particularly economic survival. This was particularly challenging in the face of discriminatory regulations and practices that limited employment opportunities in Jordan, Lebanon and Israel. For many, education became the main avenue for personal advancement.

THE EMERGENCE OF THE PALESTINE LIBERATION ORGANIZATION AND THE ISRAELI OCCUPATION OF THE WEST BANK AND GAZA STRIP: 1964–87

Historical experience shows us that a major spur for radicalism in whatever political context is the experience of discrimination and unemployment by educated young people – and this is what also happened with the Palestinians. In 1950 Yasser Arafat who was a young engineering student at Cairo University set up a 'Union of Palestinian Students' with some friends. A short while later in Beirut, George Habash, a medical student at the American University, set up another student group with the rather grand title of the 'Arab National Movement'. Grass-roots organisations were also being established in the Gaza Strip, and by the mid-1950s there was the beginning of a network of nationalist organisations, all of them very small and very weak. Incursions into Israel from Gaza and the West Bank started in ad hoc fashion, monitored closely by the Egyptian and Jordanian authorities who had no desire to provoke Israel. It was out of this network that the main resistance organisation, Fatah, emerged. In 1964 the Palestine Liberation Organization (PLO) was formed. In 1967 the debacle of the Six Day War rang the death knell of popular faith in pan-Arabism and boosted the fortunes of Fatah which became the prime agency of the Palestinian national movement.[1]

Looking back on the period prior to the first intifada through the lens of unarmed popular resistance, a number of observations come to mind.

1. The glorification of armed struggle

It was with the rise of Fatah and the PLO that we witness the growth of the iconic figure of the Palestinian fighter with a Kalashnikov rifle that became the symbol of Palestinian resistance in subsequent decades. A Palestinian state was to be achieved through armed struggle. Indeed, resistance was synonymous with armed struggle. The gun became the symbol of power. In this the PLO was sharing the iconography and the rhetoric of other contemporary liberation movements that voiced the language of third world nationalism and anti-imperialist struggle. An element in this was a belief in the transformative power of revolutionary violence. Violence was the only language that the oppressor understood. Violence would set the oppressed free![2]

Following the 1967 war the initial strategy of the PLO was the fanciful one of using the occupied territories as a base for a popular guerrilla struggle. After a few months this was abandoned and Jordan was identified as the most appropriate launch pad for guerrilla raids. This was complemented by a violent campaign of plane hijackings and other actions intended to force a change in Western policies towards the Palestinian–Israeli conflict.

2. Palestinians as victims

In an insightful discussion of the sources of Palestinian identity Rashid Khalidi has pointed to the fact that according to Palestinian perceptions they have experienced a series of crushing defeats throughout their recent history at the hands of an array of enemies so powerful as to have been virtually unassailable. Again and again Palestinian history is presented as one of heroic struggle against impossible odds by a people betrayed by traditional leaders and perfidious Arab states.[3] One consequence of this world-view is that in the context of such asymmetric power relationships, the Palestinians can be absolved from responsibility for their failures. As Khalidi remarks, 'From this perspective, if their enemies were so numerous and powerful, it is hardly surprising that they were defeated.'[4]

3. The portrayal of defeat as triumph

Developing his analysis Khalidi has pointed to a related peculiarity of the Palestinian experience: the manner in which failures have been portrayed as victories, or at least as heroic perseverance against impossible odds. According to his analysis, 'This narrative of failure as triumph began during the Mandate, but reached its apogee in the years after 1948, when it was picked up and elaborated by the grassroots underground Palestinian nationalist organisations that would emerge and take over the PLO in the mid-1960s.'[5]

Amongst the examples he cites are the martyrdom of Izzadin al-Qassem, the 1936–39 revolt, the 1947–49 *Nakbha*, the battle of Karama on March 21, 1968, Black September of 1970 when the PLO was expelled from Jordan by force of arms, and the subsequent expulsion from Beirut in 1982. A few months after the exodus from Lebanon, there was a meeting of the Palestine National Council (PNC) in Algiers, when attempts were made to present the evacuation as a victory. Khalidi quotes the caustic comment of Issam Sartawi who observed, 'One more *victory* like this one, and we will have the next meeting of the PNC in the Seychelles Islands!'[6]

4. Shifts in the Palestinian political centre of gravity

During the years when the PLO, and Fatah in particular, was a burgeoning force, the Palestinian political centre of gravity shifted. After 1967 the move was from the territories that were once part of the Palestinian Mandate to the refugee communities and camps in Jordan, and after 1970 to Lebanon. It was the refugees who were seen by the PLO as potential recruits for the armed liberation struggle, and it was amongst the refugee communities, especially in Lebanon, that the PLO pursued a form of constructive resistance with the establishment of its own broad welfare infrastructure, which in turn enhanced its standing among the refugees. It also established a number of cultural and research institutions in Lebanon and supported various cultural activities aimed at expressing and strengthening the Palestinian sense of their own identity as a people dispossessed of their patrimony. This focus on the refugees distanced the

PLO from the Palestinians in the occupied territories, a separation heightened by the problems of communication after the 1967 war and the ensuing Israeli occupation.

THE SITUATION OF PALESTINIANS IN THE OCCUPIED TERRITORIES PRIOR TO FIRST INTIFADA

The message for the Palestinians in the occupied territories embodied in all these developments became clear: stay steadfast and eventually you will be liberated as a consequence of the pressure generated by the PLO and its allies outside. In essence their allotted role was a passive one. In truth, the space available for organising any form of collective resistance to the occupation was severely circumscribed. Any signs of opposition to the occupation met with severe repression. Four East Jerusalemites were expelled as early as July 1967 after calling for an unarmed resistance campaign of non-cooperation and civil disobedience.[7] That same month the Israelis destroyed half the homes in Qalqilya after reports of armed resistance in the town – the first of many acts of collective punishment directed at those regarded as resisters. In the Gaza Strip there were numerous protests and demonstrations against the occupation, some of them involving Molotov cocktails and other weaponry, but all were quashed. The assault on the basic human rights of the Palestinian population continued, accompanied by the confiscation of land and the establishment of settlements.[8]

The emergence of any coordinated leadership that could organise resistance to the occupation within the Palestinian territories was hampered by the Israeli tactic of deporting any suspected resistance leader, but it was also exacerbated by the suspicions of the external PLO leadership regarding potential rivals to its own leadership position. The grouping they were most wary of was the communists who constituted the most advanced underground political organisation. As early as 1968 the communists had established National Guidance Committees, but in 1973 it was the PLO that was instrumental in establishing the Palestinian National Front (PNF) as an attempt to coordinate nationalist activities in the occupied territories within a PLO framework. The Front was led by an eight-member committee representing the communists and various PLO organisations. Although most of its activities were carried out clandestinely, its work was severely curtailed by the Israelis, and it was eventually outlawed in October 1979.

Denied the opportunity to express themselves openly in any overtly political organisation, activists within the occupied territories established other vehicles for education and mobilisation. Student and professional associations, trade unions, women's societies, social and cultural associations, and other grass-roots organisations were formed. These institutions and organisations engaged in various forms of constructive resistance providing services such as education, health, agricultural support and other social and cultural initiatives, whilst they also became the main agencies for promoting the struggle against the occupation. The activists received encouragement in this constructive resistance work from the outside leadership after the PLO participated in the Arab League Summit held at Rabat in 1974 and agreed upon an intermediate goal of establishing a 'national authority' on any part of Palestine from which the Israelis might withdraw.

In anticipating the establishment of a Palestinian state alongside Israel, the leadership of the PLO was concerned to create the institutional infrastructure for such a state as early as possible. In fact, the grass-roots organisations that were established during the 1970s were seen as having a dual role. As noted above they served as agencies for both offensive and constructive resistance – organising and mobilising the people whilst also providing the basic services that were not provided by the Israeli occupiers. As a consequence, such grass-roots organisations gained the allegiance of the majority of the Palestinian population, and as such constituted the nucleus of an alternative structure of authority and power to rival that of Israeli military government. Indeed, according to Salim Tamari: 'This strategy of informal resistance or institutional resistance was actually far more successful than even its own designers envisioned. By the late 1970s, it had established the complete political hegemony of Palestinian nationalism and the PLO as the single articulator of Palestinian aspirations.'[9]

The occupation of the West Bank and Gaza Strip by Israel in 1967 had opened the door for re-establishing political, cultural and social linkages between Palestinians on either side of the new border or Green Line after years of separation. This fed into the growth in nationalist sentiment on both sides of the divide. Within the West Bank and Gaza Strip, however, the main factor feeding the impulse to resist was the growth in anti-Israeli sentiment aroused by the burgeoning settlements and the harsh treatment of protesters meted out by Israeli troops. The spread of nationalist feeling was illustrated most graphically in the 1976 municipal elections, which the Israelis allowed to be held. Most of the councillors and mayors elected were openly identified with the PLO. Although the bulk of the new mayors were young members of old established families, the 1976 elections nonetheless marked the political ascendancy of a newer, more radical, nationalist constituency. Whilst the PLO outside was heartened by the 1976 results, there was continuing concern that the newly elected representatives would be cultivated by the Israelis as an alternative Palestinian leadership.

Following the election of the right-wing Likud government in 1977 and the subsequent Camp David Accords, the new mayors were instrumental in establishing the National Guidance Committee.[10] Formed in October 1978, the Committee reflected a very wide spectrum of Palestinian nationalist political orientations, including the nationalist mayors and representatives of trade unions, societies and associations. The aim was to organise and coordinate an open political struggle against the occupation in general and the autonomy proposals of Camp David in particular. However, its non-clandestine form and the fact that many of its members were public figures made the Committee particularly vulnerable to Israeli counter-measures. Its effectiveness was greatly reduced by the imposition of restriction orders, arrests and the deportation of its leading figures, whilst in June 1980 the mayors of Nablus and Ramallah were severely maimed by car bombs. In March 1982 the remaining mayors were dismissed and the Committee outlawed by the Israeli Defence Minister, Ariel Sharon.

In fact the effectiveness of the National Guidance Committee had been debilitated before its banning due to the divisions between the different political factions. Unable to organise openly they had used the trade unions, professional associations, student union groups and the different grass-roots organisations as arenas for political competition. Even in the 1970s there had always been considerable rivalry between the different political organisations, with a consequent duplication of service-provision agencies in some areas, each affiliated with a different political faction. In the first half of the 1980s relationships between the different nationalist groupings deteriorated to such a degree as to create fertile ground for mutual suspicion and rumour, with rampant allegations of corruption relating to the receipt and use of funds from outside. The divisions also facilitated the task of the Israelis in trying to prevent the emergence of an all-Palestine political authority that could command allegiance and coordinate the collective resistance of the inhabitants throughout the occupied territories. The Israelis also attempted to encourage the fragmentation process by trying to promote Islamic groups as rivals to the secular nationalists.

The level of disunity and factional rivalry within the nationalist camp in the occupied territories was a reflection of the condition of the PLO itself during the years after 1982. Arafat's seeming preparedness to consider some kind of Jordanian–Israeli condominium over the occupied territories, helped to provoke a rebellion from within the ranks of Fatah that was undoubtedly fomented by Syria, who also sponsored the formation of a National Salvation Front in opposition to Arafat.[11] However, in February 1986, negotiations between Hussein and Arafat finally broke down, whilst the pressure for the reunification of the PLO grew as Palestinian refugee camps in Lebanon were besieged by Syria's clients, the militia forces of Amal. Increasingly urgent demands were also coming from the inhabitants of the occupied territories, who were calling for some political initiative before it was too late and all their land was expropriated for the use of Israeli settlers. The USSR also played a key role as mediator helping to bring about a reconciliation between the different groupings. All this came to fruition at the 18th Palestine National Council (PNC) meeting of April 1987 in Algiers. It was at this meeting also that the communist party was welcomed as a full member of the PLO for the first time. This unprecedented display of unity provided a necessary basis for coordination and cooperation between the different nationalist factions within the occupied territories which became manifest with the outbreak of the first intifada – a mass civilian-based unarmed resistance movement initiated by youths who knew no other existence beyond that of living under occupation.

THE FIRST INTIFADA: DECEMBER 1987–OCTOBER 1991

In looking at the first intifada through the lens of popular unarmed resistance it is useful to distinguish two phases – from late 1987 through to early 1990, and the subsequent period through to the Madrid Peace Conference of October 1991.

Phase one: Horizontal escalation of the struggle, December 1987–1990

Emergence of Unified National Command

In early December 1987 riots broke out in the Gaza Strip and there were violent clashes between Palestinians and Israeli forces. The confrontations spread from the refugee camps to the cities, from the Gaza Strip to the West Bank, and developed into a sustained attempt to throw off the burden of Israeli occupation by means of mass protest, non-cooperation and various forms of unarmed resistance. The outbreak of the uprising came as a surprise to the leadership of the PLO in their headquarters in Tunis. They were even more surprised by its scale and its coordinated nature. This was achieved through the creation of a 'Unified National Command' (UNC) representing the different political factions. This clandestine body attempted to coordinate the resistance through regular communiqués and leaflets, the content of which was usually agreed beforehand with the PLO leadership in Tunis. The UNC was supported by an organisational infrastructure of popular committees, and together they took on the character of an embryonic state – coordinating activities, administering the provision of basic services and seeking to control the use of force within its territorial boundaries. The goal was to create a counter-authority to that of the Israeli occupiers, thereby undermining the Israeli capacity to command obedience. With such an organisational framework, organically linked to the different sections of Palestinian society, the months following the outbreak of the intifada saw a mass social mobilisation – a horizontal escalation of the struggle which embraced all sectors of society.

Symbolic resistance

Whilst stone-throwing and other direct offensive confrontations with the occupiers was primarily the preserve of young males, the majority of Palestinians bore witness to their resistance by less drastic yet symbolically powerful means. They boycotted Israeli products as much as possible. They wore clothes in their national colours, women wore pendants and jewellery incorporating the outline of historic Palestine. People followed 'Palestinian time' by switching between summertime and wintertime a week earlier than the Israelis.

Polemical resistance

The authority of the UNC and the popular committees was revealed during the first phase of the intifada by the solidarity of the response to strike calls and the instructions to merchants to restrict their opening hours to the mornings on non-strike days. Moreover, as part of its attempt to undermine the authority of the Israeli occupiers, the UNC called on all those Palestinians who worked for the Israeli administration to resign. Those who ignored such instructions faced sanctions – Palestinians referred to this process as 'cleaning out our national home'.

Offensive resistance

Whilst the closure of shops and workplaces at midday represented a powerful display of the authority of the UNC and the solidarity of the population, it also meant that by mid-afternoon the streets and public spaces were clear of 'civilians' and could become the domain of the strike forces in their direct confrontations with the Israeli occupiers. This was the dimension of the intifada that lent itself most to the world's media – stone-throwing youths with keffiyahs wrapped round their faces clashing with Israeli soldiers armed with tear-gas grenades, rubber bullets and other weaponry. This was the visual representation of the 'David versus Goliath' conflict that the Palestinians sought to communicate to the rest of the world.

Defensive resistance

Each neighbourhood and community had its own 'strike force' of young men engaged in direct confrontations with the occupier. Rarely would they spend more than one night a week with their families. They moved from house to house (and cave to cave) in order to avoid arrest and imprisonment, depending on a network that also included medical relief and other support services.

Constructive resistance

Less visual than the confrontations was the constructive work that was integral to the first phase of the intifada. As people began to suffer economic hardship as a consequence of the calls to disengage from the Israeli economy, the loss of income through strikes, and the boycott of Israeli produce, so families began to develop their household economy in their efforts to become more self-reliant, cultivating vegetable plots and rearing poultry. Women's committees were particularly active in promoting new forms of home-based economic activity. Homes were also the base for the clandestine education classes that were held as a means of countering the Israeli closure of schools and colleges.

Dimensions of the Intifada strategy

Underpinning the different types of unarmed resistance were a number of strategic goals.

Regeneration of a spirit of resistance

One of the main targets of the different forms of resistance was the Palestinians themselves. The verb from which the term intifada is derived refers to the action of 'shaking off' or 'shaking out'. It can also refer to recovery or recuperation. This expressed the fundamental aim of generating a national spirit of solidarity necessary for the liberation struggle to be sustained. The strikes, the boycott of Israeli goods, the efforts to disengage from the Israeli economy and state, the confrontations, the different forms of symbolic resistance, the constructive programme – they were all symbolic of the 'shaking off' of subservience and dependency and the restoration of communal and national pride.

Increasing the costs of occupation

Through the various forms of resistance the Palestinians sought to inflict pain upon the Israelis, causing them to question whether the costs of occupation outweighed the benefits. These costs were not so much the loss of lives and physical injuries suffered as the impact on the economy, the erosion of morale within Israel and within the Israeli occupation forces, and the damage to Israel's standing in the world and in the eyes of significant sections of world Jewry.

Shame power and links in the chain of nonviolence

Gandhi laid considerable emphasis on the transformative power of self-suffering in the struggle for justice. He believed that through a preparedness to suffer in the 'firm holding on to truth', resisters might touch the emotions of the oppressor, revealing to them the shameful consequences of their actions and offering up the possibility of mutual liberation in the creative struggle for a better future. Such was the belief, but in practice we know that oppressors can remain immune to the suffering of their victims as long as they see a significant social distance between themselves and the 'other'. Aware of this, Palestinians adopted a step-by-step model for influencing the Israeli public and decision makers. They developed a dialogue first of all with Israeli peace groups opposed to the occupation. These Israeli sympathisers were then able to exercise a greater impact on their fellow citizens closer to the mainstream of Israeli politics, and so on link by link along what Johan Galtung depicted as the 'great chain of nonviolence' towards decision-making centres and significant opinion leaders.[12]

The intervention of third parties

It was hoped that the combined impact of these different forces and pressures would bring about a situation in which significant third parties – the United States in particular – would intervene to exercise pressure on Israel to agree to begin peace discussions leading to its eventual withdrawal from the occupied territories.

Phase two of the intifada: post-1990 deterioration

Over the Christmas/New Year of 1989–90 thousands of international peace activists joined Israelis and Palestinians in a series of demonstrations in Jerusalem under the banner of 'Time For Peace'. In retrospect this was the high point of the intifada as an unarmed mass-based popular resistance movement. The months following were to see a deterioration in the 'health' of the movement. There were a number of reasons for this weakening of the struggle.

1. *The relative failure of disengagement and non-cooperation*

As was noted in the introductory chapter, it is one of the axioms of unarmed civilian resistance that if sufficient people, especially those in strategic institutional positions, withdraw their cooperation then they will thereby undermine the pillars that support the oppressor's power. One of the goals of the intifada was that by means of the Palestinian active unarmed resistance and the withdrawal of cooperation they would raise the costs of the occupation to such a level that the Israelis would consider withdrawing. The weakness was that whilst Israel desired the territory of the West Bank and Gaza Strip, it has never wanted the people – the Palestinians. Therefore it was prepared to carry the costs of the intifada whilst increasing the screws of repression. In a nutshell, the Israelis did not require Palestinian cooperation to maintain the occupation, and this seriously weakened the impact of the unarmed resistance.

2. *The escalating costs of resistance*

Furthermore, it turned out that in many ways the Palestinians were more dependent on the Israelis than the other way round. The Israelis could find replacements for the Palestinians who withdrew their labour, the Palestinians could not find alternative sources of employment and income. Moreover, for the majority of Palestinians Israel remained the only source of many of the basic necessities of life within the occupied territories. Therefore, as the months passed the costs of resistance borne by everyday Palestinians rose, whilst Israel showed no weakening of its resolve. People began to question the commitment to unarmed resistance: Was it causing the Israelis sufficient suffering to force them to consider withdrawing?

3. The weakness of 'shame power' and the appeal of 'vertical escalation'

There were two dimensions to the Palestinian attempt to influence the Israeli public and decision makers – the attempt to convert and persuade by means of the Palestinians' preparedness to suffer for their just cause and the attempt to force the Israelis to consider withdrawal by increasing the costs of continued occupation. Unfortunately these two dimensions – conversion and coercion – have never rested easily together. Thus, the vulnerability to shame power of the many liberal Israelis uneasy about the morality of occupation could be (and was) negated by any act of Palestinian violence resulting in injury and death for Israelis. The dominant emotion within Israel, then as now, was fear and any act of violence triggered the escalation of that fear. Therefore, as the months passed and Palestinians became frustrated with the lack of tangible achievements realised through unarmed resistance, so the appeal of a 'vertical' escalation of the struggle towards armed resistance grew. As the incidence of violent attacks on Israeli targets increased, so the gains achieved through 'shame power' were eroded, sympathy for the Palestinian cause being replaced by a fear of Palestinian 'terrorists'.

4. The fragmentation of resistance and the weakening of political control

One of the strengths of the intifada lay in the coordination between the different political factions achieved through the UNC and the popular committee structure. However, by 1990 not only were the tensions between the different factions increasing in the light of the perceived weaknesses of the unarmed struggle and the temptations of vertical escalation, but the majority of the experienced cadres who had been able to maintain cohesion in the struggle had been apprehended and imprisoned (or deported) by the Israelis. Their places were taken by relatively inexperienced young men from the ranks of the strike forces who lacked the political skills and organisational experience of the older generation.

5. Third parties and the impact of external events

Palestinians lacked the resources to affect the self-interest of the United States, and thereby prompt it to intervene constructively in the conflict. This was highlighted by the American response to Iraq's invasion and occupation of Kuwait in August 1990. Within days the build-up of American troops in Saudi Arabia was under way. Inexcusable as the invasion was, Saddam Hussein's actions were popular in many parts of the Arab world, including Palestine – here was a man who refused to be intimidated by American power and hence restored some sense of pride to the Arab nation. The result was that financial support for the Palestinian cause from the Gulf States dried up. During Operation Desert Storm Iraq launched missiles at Israel, which meant that Palestinians were subjected to lengthy curfews, the hardship and the suffering intensified and so did the bitterness. By mid-1991 more Palestinians were being killed by their fellow Palestinians than by the Israelis as anger and resentment turned against those suspected of collaboration and betrayal of the uprising.

The Oslo Process: September 1993–September 2000

In October 1991 peace talks commenced in Madrid sponsored by the USA and the USSR. Seeking to use the political capital generated by Operation Desert Storm (and meet the commitments made to their Egyptian and Syrian allies who had lent their support to the war against Iraq) in order to kick-start an Arab–Israeli peace process, the US administration under the presidency of George H. W. Bush had exerted significant financial leverage on Israel to force the Likud-led government to the table.[13] The multilateral talks continued intermittently for a number of years, with no apparent progress. However, changes were taking place. In June 1992 a Labour-led coalition came to power in Israel that was publicly committed to 'land for peace', whilst the PLO was feeling diplomatically isolated on the world stage and feared the growing influence of Hamas within the occupied territories. This was the context for the 'track two' negotiations facilitated by Norway that came to be known as the Oslo Process, and which resulted in the joint Israeli–Palestinian Declaration of Principles (on Interim Self-government Arrangements) that was signed at the White House in Washington on September 3, 1993. In the preamble to the Declaration both sides agreed: 'it is time to put an end to decades of confrontation and conflict, recognize their mutual legitimate and political rights, and strive to live in peaceful coexistence and mutual dignity and security and achieve a just, lasting and comprehensive peace settlement and historic reconciliation through the agreed political process.'

There was widespread euphoria at the announcement, which we now know to have been tragically misplaced. Israel continued to negotiate from its position of strength, imposing its demands on its weaker partner.

'OSLO II' AND THE FRAGMENTATION OF THE PALESTINIAN TERRITORIES

By July 1, 1994 Arafat had established himself in the Gaza Strip, but despite the Palestinian flag flying, it was a very limited form of autonomy circumscribed by

Israel's continuing control of the borders. What followed was a cycle of violence fuelled on the Palestinian side by a growing sense of frustration at the lack of any substantive progress towards the realization of any significant 'peace dividend'. It was also driven by those Islamist political groups who considered the Oslo Accords to be a sell-out and betrayal of the Palestinian patrimony and who recruited suicide bombers to target civilians within Israel. The Israelis responded with targeted assassinations, collective sanctions (particularly the closure policy that prevented movement of Palestinians within the occupied territories), new expropriations of land for settlements, the suspension of negotiations, and renewed pressure on the Palestinian Authority (PA) to deal with the 'terrorists'.

The impact of the closures was particularly harsh, resulting in escalating unemployment and levels of poverty, whilst enforcing the separation of the West Bank from the Gaza Strip, with Israel controlling all movement between the two territories. In the meantime Israel continued to construct and expand the settlements along with a large network of connecting roads to serve them. In effect the territories were being divided into separate segments by these new 'facts on the ground', a situation that was formalised by the second 'Interim Agreement' signed on September 28, 1995. 'Oslo II', as it came to be known, divided the West Bank into three administrative divisions categorised as Areas A, B and C, each to enjoy a different degree of Palestinian self-government until a final peace agreement was established.[14] Area A covered 3 per cent of the West Bank, encompassing the main Palestinian population centres but excluding East Jerusalem. This was to be under the full civil and security control of the PA. Area B covered 23–25 per cent of the West Bank and included those rural areas where there were no Israeli settlements. Within this area the PA would exercise civil control but security would be the joint responsibility of the Israeli and Palestinian authorities. Area C covered the remainder of the West Bank, approximately 73 per cent of the territory and here Israel was to continue to exercise complete civil and security control (see Map 4.1). It was widely presumed that once the interim agreement was in place and progress towards a final settlement underway then Israel would gradually transfer increasing tracts of territory over to Palestinian control. The presumption was that over a period the Palestinians would move towards self-government over expanding stretches of contiguous territory rather than in the separate pockets separated from the others by territory over which Israel retained control as established under the interim agreement.[15]

The combined impact of these developments was to bring about a set of conditions that undermined any possibility of launching any new mass-based unarmed civilian resistance movement against the occupation.

First of all, any initiative had to deal with the PA that had been tasked by Israel and its international backers with controlling dissent within the Palestinian community. From the start the PA had shown a marked suspicion and antipathy

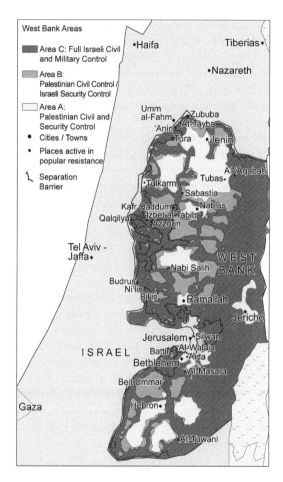

Map 4.1   West Bank: Area C map

towards any civil society organisation that evidenced signs of independence of thought, action and funding.[16] Moreover, the PA had rapidly developed a track record for corruption and nepotism rather than respect for human rights and democratic processes.

Second, for the majority of the Palestinians within the population centres designated as Area A the occupation was experienced 'at a distance'. The Israeli soldiers were no longer entering the streets of the towns and villages on a daily basis, they were manning the checkpoints that controlled the movement of Palestinians between their zones of relative autonomy. Moreover, the settlers now travelled along highways specially designated for them from which Palestinians were banned. As a consequence there were no immediate sites of contention at which Palestinian protestors might confront the agents of the occupation, except at the growing number of checkpoints and roadblocks.

Third, the leverage power over the Israelis that could be exerted by Palestinian non-cooperation was virtually nil. Drawing the lessons from the intifada, Israel had attracted guest workers from around the globe to take the place of the Palestinian labour upon which significant sectors of the Israeli economy had once depended.[17]

Fourth, there was a lack of potential leaders of any coordinated unarmed popular resistance movement. The cadres from the intifada followed different trajectories, but two career paths were common. Some joined the new PA, whilst others founded or joined non-governmental organisations concerned with themes like democratisation and peace-building, a trend encouraged by foreign donors who directed funds towards the promotion of warmer relationships between Palestinians and Israelis through 'people-to-people' dialogue projects. Such programmes often included conflict resolution training and capacity-building components, but they did not include training for unarmed civil resistance.[18]

As a consequence of these factors, by the summer of 2000 the occupation seemed more firmly entrenched than ever. Since the signing of the Declaration of Principles the confiscation of land and the expansion of settlements had continued at an accelerated pace. The West Bank and Gaza Strip had been divided into cantons separated from each other by Israeli-controlled territory. Innumerable checkpoints and barriers had been set up throughout the territories controlling the movement of Palestinians and enabling the Israelis to lock them into their particular enclaves, with disastrous consequences for economic activity and general living standards. Moreover, as Sarah Roy observed, 'In these policies Israel relied on the Palestinian Authority and its vast security apparatus to maintain control of the population, suppress any visible forms of opposition, and provide protection for Israeli actions.'[19]

THE SECOND (AL-AQSA) INTIFADA

The Al-Aqsa Intifada began in September 2000 following Ariel Sharon's provocative entry into the Temple Mount/al-Haram al-Sharif area. But the deeper cause was the build-up of frustration, resentment and anger resulting from seven years of a peace process that only served to deepen Palestinian dispossession and deprivation whilst strengthening the Israeli occupation, a situation made worse by the malfunctioning of the Palestinian administration and its leadership. The rapid militarisation of the uprising effectively sidelined any significant role for civil society groups in the struggle, as a younger and more militant generation of cadres came to the fore, superseding to some extent the discredited older generation of leaders. They were influenced to a significant degree by the example of Hezbollah in Southern Lebanon whose guerrilla tactics had succeeded in forcing Israel to withdraw in May 2000. Thus it was that within a short while every Palestinian faction, secular and Islamic, had spawned its own armed militia, each seeking to contribute to the collapse of the occupation through violent confrontation and armed struggle. Amongst these the armed wing of Hamas re-emerged and took the fight beyond the borders into Israel itself. The suicide bombings inevitably brought about massive Israeli retaliation. Following the murder of 30 Israeli Jews in a suicide bombing at a restaurant in Netanya on March 27, 2002 the Israelis launched Operation Defensive Shield and re-occupied the Palestinian enclaves from which they had withdrawn under the terms of the 'Interim Agreement' of September 1995. They then intensified their domination of every aspect of Palestinian life – enforcing curfews and closures, demolishing dwellings and forcing people out of their homes, effecting mass arrests, assassinating alleged militants and other 'terrorists'. Amidst the violence and the associated destruction of the socio-economic fabric of Palestinian society, there was little space for any large-scale unarmed resistance. Indeed, sometimes it seemed as if the prime role of Palestinian civilians was to act, like their Israeli counterparts, as vehicles for propaganda in their capacity as 'innocent victims' of the barbaric outrages of the 'other'.

The second intifada thus stood in stark contrast to the first, its violent character limiting both internal participation and external third party involvement and support.[20] The main points of contrast are summarised in Table 4.1.

Table 4.1 The main points of contrast between the first and second intifada.

First intifada	Second intifada
Predominantly unarmed resistance	Predominantly armed/violent resistance
Mass civilian involvement	Civilians confined to 'support' functions
Cohesion and unity via popular committees	Fragmentation with power to local militias
Predominantly secular	Enhanced confessional character
Attempts to influence Israeli publics through dialogue of words and actions, shame power etc.	Attempts to influence Israeli publics through intimidation and fear.
Active support from Israeli peace groups	Limited role for Israeli peace groups in context of suicide bombings/terror attacks
Significant international support and third-party pressure for peace settlement	Particularly after September 11, 2001 resistance viewed through the lens of 'war on terror'

CONSTRUCTION OF THE SEPARATION BARRIER AND THE RE-EMERGENCE OF UNARMED POPULAR RESISTANCE

The suicide bombings and associated targeting of Israeli civilians provided the Israeli government with the rationale to justify their decision to embark on the building of a physical barrier between the West Bank and Israel – 'to keep the bombers out'. Construction commenced in the spring of 2002, and by September 2003 it had become the focus of international attention. It seemed clear to many observers that whilst the Israeli government justified the barrier in terms of the security needs of Israeli civilians, its route was also determined by the desire to expropriate even more Palestinian territory and impose an additional layer of suffering on the Palestinians. Within a very short while it had impacted deleteriously on the lives of tens of thousands of Palestinians who were denied access to their fields, prevented from reaching their places of work, and forced to travel circuitous routes and negotiate armed checkpoints to get to school, university or a medical centre. It was the imposition of such a new, direct and visible challenge to their well-being that provoked a wave of popular unarmed resistance amongst those most directly affected – the analysis of which is the focus of Chapter 5.

5

THE RESURGENCE OF
POPULAR RESISTANCE: 2002–13

As noted in Chapter 4, the second intifada rapidly became militarised, leaving very little space for any large-scale unarmed civil resistance. Indeed, one estimate is that only 5 per cent of the Palestinian population in the OPT played any active role in resistance activities during the confrontations of this period.[1] Some people did issue repeated calls for a turn towards civilian-based popular resistance along the lines of the first intifada, but the necessary conditions for this were no longer present.[2] Since Oslo there had been an increase in social, economic, geographical and political divisions within Palestinian society which had undermined the level of social solidarity and trust necessary for large-scale civilian mobilisation. Moreover, in place of the dense network of civil society organisations that had been one of the seedbeds of the first intifada, Palestinian society was now dominated by foreign-funded NGOs with relatively tenuous links with the grassroots. Furthermore, the weakness of the PA and the debilitating impact of the Fatah–Hamas political rivalry meant that there was not the political coordination necessary for mass mobilisation. As one veteran of the first intifada observed: 'There is no unified command, no programme, no real coordination between the different political forces. … The 1987 Intifada was a complete system, which ruled our lives. And the objective of the movement was clear. Today nobody knows what we want.'[3]

The result was that throughout the second intifada unarmed civilian resistance remained localised and overshadowed by the violence of the militias. However, by 2003 the instances of popular unarmed resistance had begun to multiply, sparked by the Israeli decision to construct a Wall to act as a physical barrier between the West Bank and Israel. They commenced construction in the spring of 2002 and within a very short while it had impacted deleteriously on the lives of thousands of Palestinians who were denied access to their fields, saw their trees destroyed and their land expropriated.[4] As the construction of the barrier progressed, Palestinians found they were prevented from reaching their places of work, and forced to travel circuitous routes and negotiate armed checkpoints to get to school, university or a medical centre. It was the construction of this

Wall that led directly to the emergence of forms of unarmed popular resistance on the part of those villagers directly affected.[5]

THE EMERGENCE OF POPULAR RESISTANCE

The construction of the Wall commenced early in 2002 in the north of the West Bank in Jenin District. (See Map 5.1). Once local villagers realised the threat to their land and their livelihoods, they reacted as best they could. In villages such as Aneen, Tourah and Al-Tayba, public meetings were held and informal popular resistance committees created. These had little or no formal structure as such and were composed of those most directly affected by the barrier, local activists from different political persuasions, local council members and other community leaders. The repertoire of protest and resistance available to them included doing what they could to obstruct the construction process, using ropes to pull down the half-constructed fence during the night, cutting holes in the fence, holding protest marches and also making special efforts to cultivate the land and plant crops adjacent to the barrier.[6] Some of the confrontations attracted the support and participation of Israeli and international solidarity activists but in the main the protesters were drawn from the local communities.[7] There was virtually no involvement or support from the PA and limited coordination with popular resistance networks or activists elsewhere in the West Bank. Apart from temporarily obstructing the construction of the barrier, it has to be said that there was very little of substance achieved at this early stage.

As the construction of the Wall progressed southwards, so it sparked the emergence of new sites of contestation and confrontation. By 2003 clashes were occurring in villages affected by the construction in Tulkarm District and Qalqilya. By November 2003 the struggle in Budrus had commenced. Early in 2005 Bil'in was the focus of resistance, to be followed in 2006 by communities in the Bethlehem District such as Al-Masara. In 2007 Ni'lin joined the list of villages waging unarmed struggle against the expropriation of their land by the wall, to be followed by Beit Jala (2008) and Walajah (2010) – both were neighbourhoods of Bethlehem threatened by the Wall. The spread of popular unarmed resistance along the route of the Wall also spawned a revival of civilian resistance in other locations in the West Bank where Palestinians were threatened by the expansion of Israeli settlements. A popular resistance committee was established in Beit Ummar, south of Bethlehem in 2004 in response to settlement expansion. In 2005 a number of popular resistance committees were established in different neighbourhoods of Silwan in order to thwart Israeli plans to demolish local properties. In 2008 the Youth Against Settlements movement in Hebron was created as part of a sustained struggle to ensure a Palestinian presence in those parts of the city claimed by Israeli settlers as their domain. A year later,

Map 5.1   Showing the dates of the emergence of unarmed
popular resistance

in 2009, the first protests were launched in Nabi Saleh in Ramallah District
targeted against the expansion of the neighbouring settlement of Halamish.
In 2011 regular protests began in Kafr Qaddum, 13 kilometres west of Nablus,
challenging the expansion of the neighbouring Israeli settlement of Kedumin.

Looking back over the decade of popular resistance between 2003 and 2013
we can see the emergence of a series of localised centres of active popular
resistance against the construction of the Wall or the threat of land expropriation
from local settlements. At no stage was there anything comparable to a mass
movement of protest – at the height of the popular resistance during 2010–11
there was a maximum of 40–50 villages and neighbourhoods where there was

some form of organised unarmed resistance against the ongoing occupation. Some of these pockets of resistance, such as Budrus and Bil'in, gained an international profile during the peak of their resistance but this declined with the passage of time. As noted above, the centres of resistance changed over time – as the construction of the Wall progressed so new 'hot spots' emerged whilst other locations not directly affected by the construction resorted to unarmed forms of resistance to local challenges to their well-being. For example, in the spring of 2013 the inhabitants of Sabastia in the centre of the West Bank began a protest movement against the discharge of sewage on their lands from the local Israeli settlement of Shavi Shamron.

THE AIMS AND OBJECTIVE OF POPULAR RESISTANCE

Insofar as most instances of popular resistance emerged in response to particular threats to the well-being of local communities, most activists when asked about the aim and objectives of their activities would invariably refer to the need to defend their land and protect the livelihood and human rights of the local people in the face of the immediate threats. Thus, from the south to the north of the West Bank respondents tended to emphasise the particular localised target and purpose of their activities. Here are some typical responses:

A member of the Popular Committee of the South Hebron Hills:

> Our role as a committee in the village is to support the resilience of the residents so that they can be part of the popular struggle. ... Our aim is reopen roads, encourage work in agriculture, and accompany children to schools and shepherds to the field.

A member of the Hebron-based 'Youth Against Settlements':

> Our role is to defend our land and homes ... to support people to stay in their homes and to campaign to reopen Shuhada Street and reclaim homes occupied by the settlers.[8]

An activist in Silwan:

> We are concerned with defending the living conditions, housing, services, against attacks by settlers.

An activist with the Jordan Valley Solidarity Campaign:

> Our main focus is the human rights/needs of Palestinians in the Jordan Valley ... We are trying to highlight issues.

A villager from Azzoun, Qalqilya District:

> The aim of the popular resistance is to stay on our land.

An activist in Jenin District:

> Our overall aim has been to stop the Wall, but more specifically people want to regain access to their land. And now the main concern is how to keep the issue alive in the consciousness of people.

If pushed to expand on their broader aim activists would contextualise their particularistic objectives within the wider framework of resisting and bringing an end to the occupation. Hence, an activist in Nabi Saleh explained:

> Our overall aim? We are struggling against every manifestation of occupation – its face here is the settlement. If we removed the settlement we would still have the occupation which we resist as a whole.

An activist from Nablus area explained:

> Our aim is to create popular awareness, a campaign to carry on with the popular resistance, to create a culture of popular resistance and secondly … to shed light on the occupation and its inhuman doings in the Occupied Territories.

An interviewee from Al Aqaba village in Tubas District placed particular emphasis on establishing links with international networks, explaining:

> Our aim is to change the attitudes of the West towards the Palestinians, particularly the USA.

It is noteworthy in this regard that very few activists articulated any kind of peace framework they envisioned beyond 'ending the occupation'. Typical of this stance was an activist in Silwan who expressed himself very clearly, 'We defend Palestinian rights in the neighbourhood. We do not have a political platform about Palestine as a whole – one-state/ two-state etc.'

POPULAR RESISTANCE: TYPES OF ACTIVITIES

As noted the wave of popular resistance was sparked off by the construction of the Wall and spread to areas directly affected by settlement expansion. In challenging the route of the Wall and the associated threat to Palestinian land

and property, local groups pursued a range of activities that can be categorised as follows:

- Offensive resistance: Protest demonstrations and confrontations
- Defensive resistance: Accompaniment
- Polemical resistance: Documentation, advocacy and using the Israeli legal system
- Constructive resistance

OFFENSIVE RESISTANCE: PROTEST DEMONSTRATIONS AND CONFRONTATIONS

It is significant to point out that in very few cases did Palestinian activists proactively prepare any plan of action or strategy for their popular resistance. There was very little forward planning.[9] In most cases the call for action came when people realised that their land and their livelihoods were threatened by the construction of the Wall, and typically this was when they saw the bulldozers! Then there would be an urgent call to mobilise people. Here is an account of how protest started in Budrus:

It was a Friday, November 7, 2003. Suddenly, at around 10.00 am we saw the bulldozers arriving at our land. I started speaking with the coordinators of the different political factions ... I went to the mosque, and started shouting to the people of the village that we wanted to make a demonstration and that the target was the bulldozers; we didn't want to engage the soldiers or anyone else, but simply to stop the bulldozers from uprooting our olive trees. ...

After the prayers had finished, I stood up on some rocks next to the mosque, and I started to shout that it would be shameful for us not to demonstrate against this illegal confiscation of our land. The people knew that I, personally, didn't own any land along the route of the wall, so they knew I wasn't acting for personal ambitions. It was our first ever demonstration, so there was no media, no one coming in solidarity from outside the village.[10]

As activists around the world appreciate, without media coverage and the resultant wider public concern that can result from such coverage, the impact of unarmed resistance activities can be limited. As Arundhati Roy has posed it, 'Non-violence is a piece of theatre. You need an audience. What can you do when you have no audience?'[11] One of the reasons sites such as Budrus, Bil'in and Ni'lin came to prominence was that they were easily accessible to journalists based in Jerusalem, Ramallah or Tel Aviv, and the organisers in such locations were very 'media-savvy', knowing what was necessary to attract media coverage.

Moreover, such sites were all within one hour's drive from Tel Aviv and as such were easily accessible to Israeli solidarity activists. As one of the coordinators of resistance in Bil'in advised us, 'What made Bil'in visible was the creativity. The media is not interested in covering the same Friday protest with 20 people. They want something new ... so you have to be ready.' Here is an example of the kind of creativity to which he was referring.

> One time they announced they were going to uproot trees. We tried to think how to act. We had the idea of tying ourselves to the trees, but we did not have enough chains in the village. A store-keeper in Ramallah agreed to open up and provide us with the 100 metres of chains and twenty lengths of rope required. Then we called the media and asked that they be here for 5.00 am. We know them. They arrived and we moved to the olive trees and chained ourselves to them. This was April 5, 2005. The bulldozers arrived, and they started to film live. After 30 minutes the soldiers came – we were not throwing stones and there were more than 50 internationals and Israelis. It was a difficult situation for them. Finally around midday they started to cut the chains and beat us. There was a big contrast between our nonviolence and their violence!

One way to attract media attention and achieve a degree of resonance amongst interested constituencies and targeted audiences is by organising protests and 'theatrical events' on particular symbolic dates. Here is an example from Bethlehem.

> On Palm Sunday we sent out a message to all Christians around the world – Jesus entered Jerusalem on a donkey, so we had a pilgrimage of about 300 people led by three donkeys to enter Jerusalem. We started at the Church of Nativity and managed to get through the checkpoint and were about 200 metres along the road before we were stopped by the soldiers.

A few days after this interview in November 2013 we encountered the owner of one of the donkeys. Once introduced we laughed about his experience and the fine that had to be paid to obtain the donkey's release from custody! Activists in Ni'lin chose another powerfully symbolic date for one of their actions. On November 6, 2009 they marked the twentieth anniversary of the fall of the Berlin Wall by dismantling an eight metre concrete slab from the Wall running through the village land using a hydraulic car jack as a lever. One of the participants explained,

> Twenty years ago, no one imagined that the monstrosity that divided Berlin would ever be taken down, but it took only two days to do it. ... Today we proved that we too can pull it off, right here and right now. That is our land

beyond the barrier, and we have no intention of ceding it. We will triumph because justice is on our side.[12]

The routinization of protest and confrontations

Over time there developed a routinized, and hence predictable, quality to the protests against the Wall and settlement encroachments. By 2013 at the main sites of confrontation such as Nabi Saleh, Bil'in, Al-Masara and Kafr Qaddum, the template of protest was similar. Each Friday after prayers in the mosque people would gather and march to the site of contestation. Once the target area had been reached banners and flags would be waved, chants and songs repeated. Sometimes tyres would be burned and stones thrown at the soldiers. The soldiers would respond with tear-gas grenades, sound bombs, rubber bullets and 'skunk water' (a chemical fluid with a foul stench that clings to the body and clothing) – and live ammunition in some cases. There would then follow a kind of cat and mouse game with Palestinian youths using slingshots to harass the soldiers whilst snatch squads of soldiers tried to apprehend them. Often the chase would continue into the local village with soldiers forcing entry into homes to make arrests. This in turn could result in confrontations with family members which could easily escalate.[13]

Generally the more routinized an action becomes, the less public (and media) interest it arouses. As a consequence some activists in the West Bank tried to come up with innovative examples of the 'theatre of protest'. Some of which are reviewed below.

STONE-THROWING

Popular resistance for activists in the OPT included stone-throwing. As an activist from Walajah explained, 'Stone-throwing is violent but it is part of popular resistance. We call it popular resistance, not peaceful resistance, so it includes stone-throwing.' In our discussions with activists we queried the inclusion of stone-throwing in their repertoire of protest activities. We received three types of responses: 1. Stone-throwing is a necessary method of defence for protesters; 2. Stone-throwing is part of Palestinian culture and it is impossible to stop the youth from engaging in this form of activity, even if you might want to; and 3. Stone-throwing is counter-productive and as such measures should be taken to prevent its occurrence.

1. Stone-throwing as necessary means of self-defence
An activist from Jenin District explained, 'Stone-throwing? It is not really to hurt them, it is not shooting. They use gas, rubber and sometimes real bullets.

▶

It is our only way of repelling them, pushing them back.' A similar response came from an activist in Silwan:

> It is silly to think that resistance to the settlers will be peaceful. In the West people might see stone-throwing as violent. But we see the main responsibility for the violence lying with the occupation. We also know that there are people in our communities who advocate violence. ... And stone-throwing and Molotovs have stopped 'settlement tourists' – potential settlers who tour the area, paying money to a settler organisation that uses the funds to buy properties. ... Stone-throwing in Silwan has not killed anyone. Sometimes people are injured but it does not endanger life.

2. It is impossible to prevent stone-throwing
A number of local leaders of popular resistance explained to us that whatever their own views might be on the practice of stone-throwing, it was impossible to stop the youth from engaging in this activity. As an informant from Bil'in explained to us, 'The young have to express their feelings. We have stopped them bringing Molotovs. ... Stones are not violent resistance. It is also part of Palestinian culture. And our model is the first intifada and that involved stone-throwing. However, this person went on to explain how, on certain occasions and for tactical reasons, they would make particular efforts to prevent stone-throwing, 'Sometimes we stop them throwing stones – like if there is an important international visitor – then the Israelis do not shoot and we ask for no stones.'

3. We make every effort to prevent stone-throwing
A number of respondents made it very clear that they were totally opposed to stone-throwing and would use whatever influence they had to prevent it. Stone-throwing, from their perspective, provided the Israeli soldiers with the excuse they needed to retaliate with their weapons. As a respondent from the Qalqilya District explained, 'We make sure that there is no stone-throwing to prevent any excuse from the army to use violence.'

Israeli perspectives

There is evidence that the Israeli Army has planted undercover special forces disguised as Palestinians (*mistaravim* in Hebrew) amongst protesters to act as agents provocateurs, throwing stones and thereby presenting the uniformed soldiers with a pretext to respond.[14] As one well-informed Israeli politician confirmed, 'The Israeli Defense Force is more comfortable with armed struggle, where Israel is seen as the victim.' Clearly, to the extent that the Israeli authorities can present the image of Palestinian protest as violent, so they can legitimise their own violent response to the protest. This was a view endorsed by an Israeli media observer interviewed in 2013 who described the media presentation of Palestinian anti-Wall protesters as violent stone-throwers 'who attack our children, the soldiers.'[15]

Women-only picnic at Nabi Saleh spring

One innovative action, especially in the context of Palestinian patriarchal conservative culture, was a women-only picnic at a village spring on Nabi Saleh land that local Israeli settlers had started to expropriate and deny access to local villagers by various modes of intimidation. This had been one of the immediate factors leading to the outbreak of popular resistance in the village in 2009. One of the organisers of the action described the picnic as a way of moving beyond the ritual of confrontations, stone-throwing and the associated risks of injury and arrest.

> We organised some picnics at the spring – women only. The soldiers did not know what to do. We told them to go away – it was a women's picnic. The officer laughed and withdrew. There were no men, not even journalists. It was amazing – twice we have occupied the spring and the soldiers can do nothing. ... We need to surprise the Israelis and to teach the Palestinian men that we can achieve a lot without any violence. ... For me stone-throwing is violence – when it happens all is finished. There is no surprise, no strategy. We can't win.
>
> On these picnics – and we have had one in the local 'forest' that has been taken over by the settlement – we try to stop the women feeling intimidated. Beforehand we had a meeting and decided that if provoked, we would ignore them. At the picnic we read Palestinian stories to each other. We have to strip the Israelis of every excuse. We left the spring site very clean. It is also about having fun and enjoying ourselves.[16]

Al-Masara: 'We try to be creative'

At the village of Al-Masara, just south-east of Bethlehem, they commemorated the sixth year of their struggle on October 19, 2012 by carrying a large birthday cake with them as they marched towards the land due to be separated from the village by the Wall. They offered to share the cake with the soldiers who were unsure how to react. As one of those involved recounted.

> A Palestinian woman carried the cake on her head as if it was a wedding party. ... We broke it into pieces on the jeep ... There were a lot of Italians there so we had cooked pasta. The soldiers did not know what to do, they were surprised ... the people eating while they watched. Their commanders want the soldiers to be disciplined, but they are human. A few weeks ago (November 2013) we organised a game of football, you could see the soldiers getting involved watching the game, following the ball with their eyes. ... We

try to be creative. We aim to make the soldiers confused, so that they don't know what to do.

Another aim of such offensive resistance activities is to encourage villagers to overcome their fear of settlers and the soldiers by exercising their collective strength. Here is another example from Al-Masara as recounted by one of the organisers:

On Friday November 15, 2013 instead of marching our usual route to the entrance to the village we went to a cross-roads where a settler had erected a tent as a way to put pressure on the Israeli government to build more settlements. We tore down the tent. The army came but we got away. This is important because it helps bring about a change in people's mind about confronting the settlers. The activists in the village no longer believe in Israel as a super-power. We have the experience and the courage to challenge them … It is so important to overcome this fear, this sense that we cannot do anything.

On another occasion they gathered around 200 Palestinians and blocked the road to Herodium, the fortress constructed by Herod the Great on the highest peak in the Judean desert, just a few miles south of Bethlehem. Our informant smiled as he recalled an action in which they succeeded (however temporarily) in reversing the normal power-relations between soldiers and Palestinians: 'Some Israeli buses came up – one with soldiers and one with settlers and their children returning from school. So we allowed the children to pass but refused to allow the soldiers' bus to move. … They did not want to use tear-gas or sound-bombs as the road is used by settlers.'

Blocking Route 443

One of the main problems for organisers of popular protest was that clashes with soldiers at the Wall failed to impact in any clear manner upon members of the Israeli public. Indeed, according to one of our informants, an Israeli journalist, when Israeli civilians saw confrontations on the television news they were likely to frame it as illegitimate violence by Palestinian trouble-makers throwing stones at 'our boys' (the soldiers). With the increasing separation of the Israeli public from Palestinian life in the occupied territories, the depressing fact is that only a minority of the Israeli Jewish public have shown any significant concern about the situation in the West Bank. For the Israeli public in general what happens just a few miles away in the OPT fails to impact on their lives in any direct and clear manner.[17]

One way to address this challenge has been to organise actions that do 'interfere' with the everyday lives of the Israeli public.[18] On October 16, 2012 a group of Palestinians blocked Route 443, one of the main arterial roads linking Jerusalem with Tel Aviv. The group drove their cars on the road and at a pre-arranged spot stopped, and thereby succeeded in blocking the road for about 30 minutes. The aim of the action was to highlight the increase in settler violence against Palestinians and their property during the olive harvest. But, as one of the organisers explained, 'We organised this action today to stress that as long as Palestinians suffer under the daily practices of the occupation and settler terror, Israeli daily life cannot continue as normal.'[19]

Occupation of Israeli supermarket

A similar motive lay behind an action that took place a week after the blocking of Route 443 when around one hundred Palestinians 'occupied' an Israeli-owned supermarket located just outside the West Bank settlement of Sha'ar Binyamin, south of Bethlehem. One of those involved described how they all drove to the supermarket car park in private vehicles,

> Then we all emerged with our flags and banners and entered the store. For 20 minutes we were there. They had no idea what to do, how to get the Palestinians to leave. After a while we asked people to withdraw as there was no obvious escape route – so most of us got out before the police came.

The targeting of the supermarket was to highlight the negative impact such supermarkets have on the local Palestinian businesses and raise awareness of the importance of boycotting Israeli products by Palestinians in the context of the international BDS movement. But once again, underpinning the action was the message that 'as long as there is no justice for Palestinians, Israeli and settler daily life can't continue on as normal.'[20]

Actions like blocking Route 443 and occupying the supermarket can be depicted as 'offensive' actions insofar as one of their aims was to disrupt the daily life of Israelis for whom the occupation remained distant and separate from their own lives. A similar rationale can be used to justify labelling the regular confrontations that took place on Fridays in various locations in the West Bank as offensive, even though they originated as a form of defence against threats to Palestinian land and livelihoods. In 2013 one activist outlined to us his vision of scores of confrontations taking place every Friday throughout the West Bank. If only that could happen, he reasoned, it would radically raise the cost of the occupation, maybe to a level where some Israelis began to question whether or not it was worth continuing with the occupation. Sadly for him, his vision remained just that – a dream without significant substance.

Boycotting Israeli goods – the campaign in the OPT

As part of the renewed interest in popular resistance within the OPT a number of organisations and activists began to devote energy to trying to persuade people to boycott Israeli goods where Palestinian alternatives existed, an initiative driven in part by a felt responsibility to take action in the context of the burgeoning international BDS movement against Israel and a way to engage wider sectors of society in the popular resistance movement.

As will be explored in greater depth in Chapter 9 the spread of the international campaign can be attributed in part to the increased involvement of 'internationals' in solidarity with Palestinian popular resistance as accompaniers, co-participants in actions, and as 'activist-tourists' expressing their solidarity through their presence. One of the consequences of this involvement has been the expansion of the international grass-roots movement of solidarity with the Palestinian struggle which in turn has been one of the prime vehicles for implementing the initiative that emerged out of a meeting of Palestinian civil society organisations in July 2005 – the call for a worldwide boycott, divestment and sanctions (BDS) campaign against Israel. The campaign went from strength to strength at the international level, but prior to 2014 had made relatively little progress amongst Palestinians living under occupation. In January 2010 however an initiative was launched to encourage Palestinians to boycott settlement products. The National Dignity and Empowerment Fund (Al Karama Fund) was established as a joint initiative by representatives from the Palestinian business community and the PA early in 2010. The aim was to encourage Palestinians to boycott all settlement products, and lead an international campaign to raise public awareness about the political implications associated with accepting Israeli settlement products in international markets. Over 500 products were identified, ranging from foodstuffs to construction materials. Three thousand volunteers were then recruited to visit Palestinian households in the West Bank to explain the project and to get them to sign the 'Karama (Dignity) Pledge'. Yellow flyers were distributed so people could display the fact that their premises were free from settler products. In April 2010 a law was passed by the PA outlawing trade with the settlements. Plans were also laid to move the campaign on to the international level with three strands: 1. Approach governments at the diplomatic level, to point out that as settlements are considered illegal under international law, their products should not be allowed into the market place; 2. Identify financial institutions with investments in companies based in settlements, to persuade them to disinvest; and 3. Nurture grass-roots movements in different countries that will help maintain pressure on their governments whilst continuing to raise public awareness about the issue.[21] However, by 2012 the initiative had come to an end, in part due to the retaliatory measures threatened by Israel.[22]

The Karama initiative remained a strange hybrid – initiated and funded by a coalition between business and political elites in the West Bank, but at the same time trying to engage and empower people at the grass-roots level. An initiative along similar lines was launched by the political party, the Palestinian National Initiative (*Mubadara*) led by Mustafa Barghouti. The first step of what was called the 'Bader campaign' focused on the boycott of Israeli soft drinks, which was then expanded to include Israeli dairy products. The campaigners urged Palestinians to buy Palestinian soft drinks and dairy products. One of the activists from Ni'lin explained: 'The Bader campaign to boycott Israeli goods is the same as the Gandhian experience of boycotting British goods in India. We wanted to reduce our dependence on Israeli goods by 15 per cent and increase the national products by 15 per cent which meant creating employment for Palestinians.'

Although in general women's participation in Palestinian popular resistance has been uniformly low due to the conservative and patriarchal culture, women have played a role in campaigning for the boycott of Israeli products. As one activist from Qalqilya informed us: 'We started an awareness-raising campaign by knocking on doors. We talked to the housewives about the importance of boycotting the Israeli goods. They are responsible for the shopping. The campaign reached thousands of women and was very successful.'

It is tempting for any activist to portray their campaigns as successful, if only to bolster their belief that all the costs incurred by their activities are worthwhile. But for large segments of the Palestinian population living under occupation, especially those living in territory designated as Area C, their prime focus is on survival. In this endeavour an important part has been played by popular resistance activists fulfilling the defensive function of accompaniment.

DEFENSIVE RESISTANCE: ACCOMPANIMENT

This refers to the practice of activists accompanying Palestinians as they go about their daily lives so that, by their presence and witness, they can deter assaults by settlers and the Israeli occupation forces. This protective role has been played by different groups – Israeli solidarity activists, internationals and Palestinian activists. For example, in the South Hebron Hills activists from the Israeli solidarity group Ta'ayush and from Rabbis for Human Rights have acted as a protective presence in the area since 2000. They were then joined by international volunteers with the Italian project Operation Dove who have been accompanying local children on their route to school that passes close to an Israeli settlement since 2004.[23]

Within the city of Hebron members of Youth Against Settlements (YAS) have attempted to act as a protective presence for those Palestinians living adjacent to

Israeli settlements in the city. As one of their members explained, 'We observe the settlers ... We have 50 people ready to mobilise if any house is threatened ... We are not afraid to confront the settlers. Our aim is to empower the local people – they are not alone – so that they can hold on to their property.'

As part of their activities the YAS runs training programmes in all the different dimensions of film-making for young people. Then, we were told, 'whenever violations happen we film as much as possible and then upload it to YouTube.' Using electronic media in this manner has opened up a significant international dimension to accompaniment on the ground – international audiences can now bear witness to the violations perpetrated by settlers and others.

In other areas of the West Bank where Palestinian communities have felt threatened by settler assaults local activists have established 'Guard Committees' as a protective measure and to accompany farmers to their land. An official within the Governor's office in Nablus explained:

We set up guard committees in the villages and whenever the settlers are coming, the news is broadcast from the mosque. As a consequence there have been less mosques burnt. ... We can see there is a clear impact of the guard committees. It is working. We need to develop it. In some places we have set animal traps in order to deter the settlers from night-time attacks.

SILWAN: THE FLASHPOINT FOR A NEW UPRISING?

Silwan is located adjacent to the Old City of Jerusalem, just a short walk from the Dung Gate. Like other neighbourhoods of Palestinian East Jerusalem along with the city of Hebron, the Jordan Valley and the South Hebron Hills, Silwan has undergone an accelerated process of ethnic cleansing and influx of Israeli settlers over recent years. Two neighbourhoods in particular within Silwan have been targeted – Wadi Hilweh, called City of David by Israelis, and al-Bustan. In both neighbourhoods the process has been headed by a settler organisation, Elad, working in association with the Israel Nature and National Parks Authority and the Jerusalem municipality. Using various legal pretexts including an Israeli law that allows for the demolition of any building thought to be covering up archaeological evidence of Jewish history, significant tracts of land have been acquired and properties demolished in order to proceed with the construction of an archaeological park/tourist attraction designated the 'Garden of the King'.[24] The result of such a process has been predictable – a sustained conflict characterised by repeated clashes between locals and settlers and Israeli security forces. It is perhaps the most unstable flash-point of the whole Israeli–Palestinian conflict given the dire situation of Silwan's residents and its proximity to the Holy sites within the Old City itself.

▶

In 1996 it was the construction of the Western Wall tunnel that led to the clashes resulting in dozens of Israeli and Palestinian fatalities. In September 2000 the second intifada broke out following Ariel Sharon's incursion on the Temple Mount (al-Haram al-Sharif). Then, in 2014 there were indications that Israel is seeking to challenge the status of the Temple Mount in order to allow Jews to pray there. When this is set alongside the declared intention at the same time to construct over a thousand new settler homes in East Jerusalem localities it is difficult to foresee anything but a new explosion of violence. One indication of the mounting tension was the increased number of clashes between Palestinians and Israeli security forces after the murder of the Palestinian teenager Mohammad Khdeir in July 2014. By late October of that year it was reported that more than 900 Palestinians had been detained by Israeli security personnel and that Palestinian youth were increasingly hurling Molotov cocktails at their targets rather than stones and rocks.[25]

VOICES FROM SILWAN[26]

Community organiser, Wadi-Hilwe

The PA is doing nothing in Jerusalem – so we are doing it. Primarily it is sumud. In a way we are trying to shame the PA to take responsibility. … There are daily clashes with settlers, with confrontations and provocations from armed settlers in addition to all the social deprivation – poor schools, unemployment. The young are suffering. It makes them angry, and it is easy to provoke them.

We try to make our actions as nonviolent as possible without stones and molotovs. Organised nonviolent resistance hurts the Israelis more than violent. I am not worrying about the safety of Israelis but the safety of my people. The second intifada caused a lot of death and violence amongst Palestinians. I am not advocating nonviolence to satisfy the West!

We have experienced the effectiveness of nonviolence on the ground. One action we did in front of the City of David settlement – we covered our eyes and tied our hands behind our backs and stood there in front of the settlement. This had a bigger impact than stone-throwing – we had people asking what was going on. We saw how angry and frustrated were the settlers. … We have no other way to fight the occupation. But we are close to our limit – we cannot take it anymore.

Fatah activist, Silwan

Israel does not give a shit about international law or anything. What Israel is doing is barbaric, they have no respect for people. … It is our basic human,

▶

moral and religious right to struggle against this. Many countries in the world break international laws, and they suffer sanctions, but Israel acts with impunity. We can expect nothing from the international community.

For the last 60 years Israel has tried guns and tanks, but one thing they cannot destroy is the will to resist and our belief in our just cause. Unfortunately we went on the peace path and it has not led us anywhere. … As Fatah activists we have the right to use all means. There is no point in being narrow-minded and be fixed on military confrontation. … This is the darkest page in Palestinian history and leadership. What we are suffering in Jerusalem – this ethnic cleansing. It has been made easier because of the split between Fatah and Hamas.

We will use all means – we will live in tents, fight with all our limited means. We shall scream and shout so that the international community hears us. If people have the awareness, they will not give up. … Unfortunately there is no strategic plan for popular resistance, we are not organised. There should be a clear strategy behind the mobilisation. … If we do not make every day costly to the occupier, they will not leave.

The clearest and most honest form of resistance was in the first intifada. I doubt whether we can regain that level of purity of the first intifada, because now we have the PA. In the first intifada everybody suffered, everybody sacrificed. Now we see the salaries from the PA and the international NGOs – the people in the security forces with salaries, they are tied within the framework of the Oslo Agreements.

Community activist, al-Bustan

The major concern we have is the lack of any significant national or international protection for our neighbourhood against the Israeli plans. We have a clear strategy to prevent the threatened demolitions, but we know that if Israel decides to destroy the buildings, they can do it. We need support … The EU and the international community do not take the responsibility of holding Israel to account for its illegal activities in Jerusalem. They do not challenge the ethnic cleansing that is going on. The EU should have actions and not just position papers.

We devote a lot of energy to mounting legal challenges to the Israeli plans. We also try to lobby internationals – taking them on tours of the neighbourhood and using the media and documenting what is happening which we target specifically at the internationals. We have special commemorative events on *Nakbha* Day – that kind of thing. We have also developed alternative plans for the neighbourhood, and we also provide counselling services for the young who have been arrested and imprisoned by Israelis and suffered trauma.

POLEMICAL RESISTANCE: DOCUMENTATION, ADVOCACY AND
MEDIA WORK

As noted with regard to the accompaniment activities of the YAS in Hebron,
it became increasingly common for accompaniers to be equipped with
camcorders and cameras in order to record and subsequently document any
assaults perpetrated against local people by Israeli settlers and occupation
forces. Footage of human rights violations would be uploaded to websites such
as YouTube within an hour of them taking place. As an activist based in the
Jordan Valley explained to us, 'Our role is to expose Israeli violations, document
and bring to the attention of decision makers. We are trying to highlight issues'.
An activist from Bethlehem District smiled as he commented, 'The Israeli
soldiers have changed. They are more scared of us, or actually they are scared of
our cameras. When they shoot at us we can record all of that now.' International
accompaniers with such organisations as the Ecumenical Accompaniment
Programme in Palestine and Israel (EAPPI) also carried cameras with them
to record incidents. The images could then be used as part of advocacy and
lobbying campaigns in their countries of origin. Protest 'hot spots' such as
Nabi Saleh had very active websites where video recordings of clashes and
confrontations were uploaded. In such locations some of the local people were
employed by human rights organisations such as B'tselem to act as their local
'eyes and ears' monitoring and recording human rights abuses in their locality.
The footage shot by such people became an important means of reaching out to
international networks with the aim of influencing public opinion and thereby
the position of significant decision makers.

Wherever we went in the West Bank during our fieldwork activists would
tell us that one of their significant responsibilities was the hosting of visits by
internationals, including representatives of the international diplomatic corps.
An activist from Al-Masara told us of his meeting with Catherine Ashton when
she was the equivalent of the European Union's foreign minister and with the
then British Foreign Secretary, William Hague. Sometimes the links between
local activists and international networks and groups took on a more institu-
tionalised form. One example was the link established between YAS in Hebron
and South African human rights groups. In 2009 they escorted a group of South
Africans around the city centre, including Shuhada Street. The visitors were
shocked at the situation which seemed to them to be worse than apartheid, and
they agreed to form a partnership in order to launch an international campaign
of support and solidarity.

One of the activists from Nablus, who had been part of the popular resistance
in Palestine for many years advised us that, 'In the first intifada we won the
media battle. We lost it in the second. Now we are trying to regain it.' As part
of this strategy, films have also played a role. In the village of Tourah in Jenin

district, a film was made about the impact of the Separation Barrier on the education system and life of the community. It portrayed the story of the families cut off and left on the western (Israeli) side of the barrier and the challenges the school kids faced every day crossing the checkpoint to go to school on the Palestinian side. The film was shown on Palestinian television and a delegation from the village visited Italy and Greece for a tour showing the film organised by solidarity groups. More widely distributed films such as *Budrus* and *Five Broken Cameras* documenting aspects of the struggle against the Wall have been shown internationally with a significant impact on audiences worldwide.

POLEMICAL RESISTANCE: APPEALS TO ISRAELI LEGAL SYSTEM

Whilst demonstrations and confrontations can create an issue by drawing attention to particular threats to Palestinian interests, Palestinians have had most success reclaiming land threatened with confiscation by resorting to the Israeli legal system. Here is an example from the South Hebron Hills. In November 1999 the Israeli military issued expulsion orders against the local population occupying land adjacent to the Israeli settlements of Ma'on and Karmel. In 2000 the dispossessed, with the support of Israeli solidarity and human rights groups such as Rabbis for Human Rights, petitioned against their expulsion to the Israeli High Court of Justice and a temporary injunction was issued permitting the residents to return to the area until a final decision was reached. A case that generated more publicity worldwide was that initiated by activists from Bil'in. The Wall was constructed initially such that a significant area of village land was left on the Israeli side of the barrier. Alongside the regular protest actions local activists with the assistance of Israeli solidarity groups such as Yesh Din *(There is law)* took the matter to the Israeli courts. The court recognised the villagers' claim to the land, ruled against the construction of residential accommodation by Israeli developers on the land, and finally on September 4, 2007 the Israeli Supreme Court ordered the Wall to be rerouted.

In Qalqilya District activists also linked the legal path to that of protest. As one activist recalled:

> We raised the issue before the court. We won one case in the Israeli High Court where we had restored around 2000 acres of confiscated land. We also secured a verdict from the Israeli court to keep the villages Ras Tierah, Wadi al-Rasha and Al-Dabeha outside the Wall after they had been totally isolated.

Activists in Budrus also had some success through following the legal path, once again assisted by Israeli solidarity groups:

We used to meet the Israeli anti-Wall activists in the field. We know their names and they know our names too. They helped us to take some cases to the Israeli courts and they followed up legally. We succeeded with the help of the Israeli activists to save around 1200 acres of land and more than 3000 olive trees. In the Buffer Zone between the Green Line and the Wall – a length of approximately 2–3 kilometres – we recovered more than 200 acres of land by filing cases in the Israeli courts.

CONSTRUCTIVE DIRECT ACTION

Under Israeli law, land left uncultivated for three years reverts to the state. The fear of Palestinians denied access to their land is that after three years the Israelis will expropriate it as 'state land'. Sometimes settlers will expropriate land owned by Palestinians and prevent them from using it. Hence activists have pursued a number of initiatives aimed at 'land reclamation' in order to forestall its expropriation by Israel on behalf of settlement expansion. In 2002 an activist from Beit Ummar south of Bethlehem discovered that a neighbouring settlement had expropriated some of his land, which the Israelis subsequently designated to be a 'closed military area'. Volunteers from the village joined the farmer in working the land in defiance of the Israeli order. According to his account, 'The settlers fenced the land for three days, but then I brought a tractor to open a gap in the fence and began spraying the crops.' More than a decade later similar kinds of activity were taking place in the same district as part of the ongoing attempt to forestall settler expropriation of land. In October 2013 there had been a court order allowing villagers near Herodium to cultivate their land adjacent to a settlement. However, when the villagers approached the land they were intimidated by some of the settlers. Our informant, an experienced activist from a neighbouring village, decided to intervene as he feared that the local people were too afraid of the settlers to challenge them.

> So I went and acted as if I was preparing the land for irrigation with a tractor. The settlers came. People were afraid. One of the settlers had a knife. I called over the photographer and we went towards the settlers. They were shocked. They expect the Palestinians to run away, not face up to them. It is so important to overcome this fear, this sense that we cannot do anything. The settlers see Palestinians as hopeless; they do not expect a reaction.

In the same district activists had heard rumours that a particular tract of land adjacent to the main road linking Jerusalem with the Israeli settlements south of Bethlehem was being considered for expropriation by the Israeli authorities. The activists contacted the landowners and began working with them to renovate the dwellings, repair the terracing and recommence agricultural activities – all as part of an attempt to deter any attempt by Israel to take control of the land and properties.

In a similar attempt to underline the claims of Palestinians to particular tracts of agricultural land the governor's office in Nablus provided tractors in 2012 to enable local people to plough land adjacent to local settlements in order to forestall its expropriation by the settlers. In the words of the governor:

> We try to support people in their efforts to regain access to their land. The Israelis destroy schools, we rebuild them. They cut the electricity, we bring a generator. … One idea, taken from the settlers, is to have portable housing units, or else provide people with the materials to construct houses, in order to create a new reality, facts on the ground. … I supported farmers by providing the cost of tractors to plough the land next to the settlements which was threatened with confiscation, in total 17,300 dunums were ploughed.[27]

As with most forms of popular resistance in Palestine, international and Israeli solidarity activists have also played an important supporting role in relation to different forms of constructive direct action relating to land use, particularly through volunteering to assist in planting olive trees and helping with the olive harvest.

The Palestinians most exposed to direct violence from Israeli settlers and occupation forces have been those living in zones designated as Area C where Israel retained control over all aspects of life as if the territory was part of the Israeli state. In areas such as the South Hebron Hills and the Jordan Valley the pressure on the Palestinian inhabitants is relentless, driven as it is by the Israeli desire to cleanse the areas of Palestinians. In such circumstances the prime goal of activists has been to work with local communities in order to strengthen their steadfastness and resilience (*sumud*) in the face of unceasing assaults on their way of life and attempts to undermine their resolve. Sometimes this support was expressed through accompaniment and associated documentation and dissemination of reports of the human rights abuses perpetrated against them. But support could also be more direct and constructive: rebuilding dwelling places that had been destroyed, building schools and kindergartens, constructing play areas for children, trying to ensure the supply of basic amenities such as clean water. This commitment was most clearly expressed by someone working with the Bedouin communities in the Jordan valley: 'Our strategy is *sumud* – to stay here on the land. … Our slogan is "To exist is to resist" and we are trying to promote the right to live here in the Jordan Valley.' This has been the driving impulse behind the work of Haj Sami Sadiq, the leader of the village council in Al Aqaba village in Tubas District on the western edge of the Jordan Valley. Al Aqaba was targeted for demolition by the Israeli occupation authorities due to its location in the midst of land expropriated as military training grounds. In his efforts to create the conditions such that the village might remain 'alive' Haj Sami has networked with a range of international humanitarian agencies and involved them in different forms of community development.[28] Through such efforts the village was able to develop a kindergarten, a school and community centre – all part of the struggle Haj Sami has led to encourage villagers to return to their properties and to challenge the Israeli expropriation of the land.

Al Aqaba is a small hamlet in a relatively remote location but activists in the urban centre of Hebron in the south of the West Bank have been as innovative as Haj Sami in the forms of constructive action they have taken to help sustain those Palestinians living under the direct shadow of Israeli settlers. Interviewed in November 2013, one of the activists with YAS outlined some of their initiatives.

> We have the Steadfastness Campaign in Shuhada Street. It is about finding ways to support the resilience of people in their daily life. With all its checkpoints, you cannot drive in. People, including tradespeople, are too scared to come to this area. So, for example, you have a real problem getting plumbers and the like. So we bought materials and established a programme to improve people's housing. Also we constructed a fence to protect some residents from the stone-throwing of the settlers. When you feel part of a community you feel more confidence and it is more difficult to force you and your family out. It is about restoring the vibrant life there used to be here before.
>
> We have also created a kindergarten in the home of a Palestinian family who left it and agreed to rent it to us. They left it empty because of settler attacks. For 10 years it was lying empty. So since March 2013 we have been rehabilitating it, and during that time we have suffered physical attacks and arrests. But now it is running with 30 kids. It is free with the teachers volunteering.
>
> As with our centre here – here we are protecting the house itself, and protecting the families adjacent to the house and it is no longer available for the settlers to use as a base for intimidating the other houses.
>
> We have also created a greenhouse which we call the Freedom Machine. This is on the top of a dwelling and uses the aquaponics system. This is aimed at those who live adjacent to settlements and do not have enough safe space to grow vegetables. The partner for this is a Palestinian living in Jordan.[29]
>
> Another project is near Khiryat Arba – we constructed a house with a well for water – the house is built over the well, which is fed by a rainwater collection system.

In 2013 activists in Bil'in began planning an unusual constructive initiative for occupied Palestine – the creation of a park on the land 'liberated' by the decision of 2007 to reroute the Separation Wall. One of the prime movers behind this project outlined its genesis:

> We started the struggle against the Wall. The Wall is connected to the settlement expansion – so we sought to stop the settlement expanding. ... One day we were looking at the settlement plan – and we noted that they had identified some land as a 'green area' for a settlement park. This was in 2005.
>
> One day in 2007 Emad Burnat (the man who made the film *Five Broken Cameras*) and Bassem Abu Rahmi (who was killed by a tear-gas canister fired into his chest in 2009) – we were talking and we said we should have a park, and Bassem said 'and with a swimming pool'.
>
> We got the land back in 2011 and we thought we must do something with this land that we struggled for, to show to everyone that it was worth it. So we began to plan the park – we contacted UNDP for funding. We decided we should make a memorial for Bassem from tear-gas canisters. ...
>
> When it is completed the park will generate income from those visiting the park. Also it will create employment – more than 60 per cent of the youth are unemployed since they are no longer permitted to work in Israel. This is a real challenge – they lack education and they cannot work in Israel. Also the park will attract more people to the area, and so make it more difficult for the Israelis to control it. And it will be an example of how we can help ourselves, an example from which others can learn, using the resources from the land to create jobs. ... It is important to start, to create new things.

On a somewhat smaller and more surreptitious scale, we were told of some residents in the neighbourhood of Tourah village who had been cut off from utilities supplied on the Palestinian side of the Wall. The families now on the Western (Israeli) side of the Wall were refused services by the Israeli authorities. However, we were informed, 'One night the family dug a shallow trench and ran cables from the village (about 500 metres), so we provided water and electricity to the house despite the refusal of the Israelis.'

BAB AL-SHAMS

A protest action can be evaluated according to any number of criteria. Sometimes an activity can be deemed a success not because it achieved substantive change on the ground but because it generated media attention and boosted the morale of activists. One such Palestinian action was the establishment of a temporary encampment on a stretch of hillside in East Jerusalem over a bitterly cold January weekend in 2013.

▶

On Friday January 11, 2013 popular resistance activists from around the West Bank set off for what onlookers believed to be a winter youth camp in Jericho, a fiction circulated to maintain the element of surprise. On arrival in East Jerusalem they set to work establishing their encampment on Palestinian-owned land scheduled by Israel to be the site of a new settlement in the area known as E1 between East Jerusalem and the established Israeli settlement of Ma'ale Adumim. Mirroring the actions of Israeli settlers the activists announced that they were 'establishing facts on the ground' in order to stop the planned construction of 3,500 housing units for Israeli settlers. They gave their new village the name of Bab al-Shams, the Gate of the Sun.

They had planned for an encampment of some 250 activists and had brought with them sufficient tents, blankets and provisions for that number. But their first challenge was the speedy arrival of hundreds of Palestinian and multi-national solidarity activists who joined the encampment – such that numbers exceed one thousand with a consequent 'domestic crisis' of providing sufficient shelter and sustenance for such a number!

The main challenge, of course, was the reaction of the Israeli authorities. Lawyers acting on behalf of the Palestinian owners of the land had obtained an injunction from Israel's High Court allowing the campers to remain on site for up to six days in order to prevent the Israeli forces from immediately evicting the participants. Despite this, the Israeli special police forces arrived in the middle of the night, Saturday January 12, 2013, and forcibly evicted the campers, making up to a hundred arrests in the process. Despite the short-lived nature of the action, it generated a considerable degree of international media attention and was one of the few occasions when the PA, which funded the initiative, and grass-roots activists worked together in coordination and collaboration. Moreover, for those that participated and those solidarity activists who supported the action, it provided a very welcome fillip to their morale. As one of their number recalled:

> Throughout our time in Bab Al-Shams, local and international media covered our story intensively, recognizing it for the act of creative, strategic nonviolence that it was, while numerous messages of support poured in through social media, phone calls and text messages. Seeing how Bab Al-Shams brought a new sense of optimism and hope to people around the world helped us endure the bitterly cold nights and violent evacuation by the Israeli forces.[30]

CONCLUSION

Palestinians in particular should be thankful for small victories, because that is about all they have had alongside their history of dispossession, displacement and occupation. It is true that on occasions some of our informants amongst the popular resistance activists sketched out their dream of another large-scale unarmed popular uprising like the first intifada. Their vision was replete with 'If onlys ...': 'If only there were hundreds of protest actions every Friday ...'; 'If only Fatah would mobilise its cadres to be catalysts for popular resistance ....'; 'If only the USA and the European Union would exercise some leverage over Israel ...'. But the unfortunate truth is that in the decade leading up to 2014 unarmed resistance on the part of Palestinians has fallen far short of being a mass-based popular movement of resistance. Overall what we have reviewed in this chapter can be characterised as instances of localised pockets of resistance with a clear 'shelf-life'. That is, the protests have tended to emerge in response to immediate threats to the well-being and way of life of local people as posed by the construction of the Wall and the ongoing encroachment of settlements on Palestinian land. Our findings show that once the Wall had been constructed or the settlement fence erected, activists found it increasingly difficult to mobilise people in protest and resistance. Indeed, in one location in the north of the West Bank we discovered that local villagers were increasingly irritated by the local youths who persisted in sabotaging the separation barrier and thereby giving the Israeli occupation forces the pretext to make repeated raids on the village to apprehend those responsible, and thereby disturbing the lives of the villagers. In such locations the challenge for activists became one of combatting the growing 'acceptance' of the Wall as a fact of life. In Chapter 6 we explore in depth the full extent of the challenges facing those who prioritise popular resistance as a means of bringing an end to the occupation.

6

CHALLENGES FACING PALESTINIAN POPULAR RESISTANCE

POPULAR RESISTANCE AS SYMBOL OF DEFIANCE

As noted in the introductory chapter those Europeans who engaged in different forms of unarmed resistance against German occupation during the Second World War never thought that their activities would somehow drive out the Nazi occupiers. Liberation, they knew, would have to come through outside intervention in the guise of the military might of the allied forces. However, this is not to say that their acts of resistance were pointless and irrelevant. Their significance lay in the way the different acts of dissidence and defiance evidenced the fact that significant sections of the subject population refused to accept the legitimacy of the occupiers' regime. As Jacques Semelin noted, the goal of such activities was 'to preserve the collective identity of the attacked societies; that is to say, their fundamental values. ... civilian resistance consisted primarily of a clash of wills, expressing above all a fight for values.'[1]

It seems clear that the different forms of popular resistance examined in Chapter 5 should be viewed in the same light. The Israeli occupation of the West Bank will not be brought to an end by means of such acts of protest, confrontation and resilience. But this does not mean that the different instances of popular resistance are pointless and futile. As with those living under Nazi occupation in continental Europe during the Second World War, the popular resistance of the Palestinians in the years since the second intifada can be seen as a significant symbol of defiance, a way of enacting the determination of the activists not to acquiesce to the status quo, not to submit to the will of the occupier and to continue to reject the occupation. This was recognised quite clearly by one activist from the north of the West Bank when he explained that the regular Friday confrontations taking place at locations like Bil'in was 'symbolic, not popular resistance ... It is to say *We are still alive, still resisting!*'

Quite simply there have been too few pockets of resistance and sites of confrontation to impose sufficient cost on Israel to cause any significant section of the Israeli public to conclude that the occupation was unsustainable and not worth the price. Of course, as noted already, some of the leading activists in the popular resistance argued that if only there were regular confrontations with Israeli forces in hundreds of locations throughout the occupied territory, then the cost imposed on the occupier would be such as to erode some of the central pillars of support on which the occupation depended. But realistically the prospect of such a mass movement of popular resistance emerging within the foreseeable future remains very slight. Indeed, one of the most dedicated activists acknowledged that what had been happening since the second intifada had been 'village resistance' rather than popular resistance. As we have seen the pattern has been a patchwork of sporadic protests taking place in different locations initiated by local people affected by the Separation Wall or by settlement activity. At no time has there been a territory-wide movement of protest and active resistance such as occurred during the first intifada. In the remainder of this chapter we shall analyse some of the reasons for this.

THE WEAKNESSES OF THE CONTEMPORARY POPULAR RESISTANCE MOVEMENT

The leading figures amongst the Palestinian activist networks who we interviewed on various occasions during our fieldwork were aware of the fundamental weaknesses of the movement and its impact. When asked about the challenges they faced in terms of strengthening the popular resistance they would list a whole range of factors that needed to be overcome, including the political fracture between Fatah and Hamas, the lack of a coherent strategy and the lack of coordination between competing networks of activists. As one member of a popular committee in Silwan observed, 'A major challenge is the coordination of nonviolent activities. Some focus on the Wall, others on checkpoints and others on settlements. There is no coordination like there was in the first intifada.'

Underpinning the different challenges organisers identified as obstacles was what many observed to be a pervasive lack of trust in leadership at any level, including village-level leaders of popular resistance. As one activist observed,

> People believe that in this struggle against settlements and the Wall there are certain people who are benefitting. They are running a shop rather than a movement … They make connections, get trips abroad, funds for projects … People are saying, 'I will not be a stepping-stone for people to climb upwards where I pay the price of participation and the leadership benefit and gather the fruits.'

This cynicism about the motives of activists taking local leadership roles helped explain a core weakness of the popular resistance – the low rates of participation. As observers at more than one protest action it seemed to us that internationals, Israeli solidarity activists, photojournalists and leading popular resistance figures outnumbered local people on some of the actions. As an activist from Tubas District commented in November 2013, 'Now it is more political tourists, journalists and leaders participating rather than actual villagers.' This problem of low participation was particularly pronounced in locations where the construction of the Wall had been completed. As one village leader from Jenin District acknowledged, 'There were places that were active during the construction of the Wall, but now the Wall is there and there is no longer any protest activity.' The lack of activity in such locations can be explained by the fact that once the Barrier had been constructed it became a reality, a constituent element in everyday life, and no longer an issue around which people could be mobilised. As one activist from one of the villages directly affected by the Wall dividing the villagers from their fields explained: 'Our big concern is that the Wall has become a reality and is becoming an accepted part of reality. The Wall is becoming the de facto border. There are feelings of defeat – all this struggle and nothing achieved … What more can we do?'

This experience of having participated in the resistance against the Wall – and having suffered as a consequence of their involvement through arrests, fines and other sanctions – was one of the contributory factors to the emergence of undoubtedly the biggest challenge faced by those seeking to mobilise Palestinians in a large-scale and sustainable movement of popular resistance: the widespread sense of resignation and weakening of hope amongst so many Palestinians in all sectors of society. As one activist expressed it in November 2013:

> There has been a decline in participation. There is a sense that whatever we do, the Israelis will ignore … People do not see results … Since the first and then the second intifada people have lost trust in the political leadership and the political parties. There are so many people in Israeli prisons, but they show no real concern for them. We get empty promises. There are no results from negotiations. So there is a sense of resignation.

How to explain this disempowering lack of hope, this erosion of any belief in the efficacy of collective unarmed struggle and the pervasive lack of trust in anyone who presumes to take up any kind of leadership role? The answer lies not so much in strategic errors made by leaders of the popular resistance movement nor in the lack of substantive achievements gained as a result of such unarmed struggle. To understand the origins of this malaise we need to delve deeper and examine the changes that have taken place within Palestinian society, polity and culture since the first intifada came to an end in 1991 and the subsequent Oslo Peace Process that commenced in 1993. Our thesis is that whilst certain conditions and factors were operative in the late 1980s that constituted the backdrop to the first intifada, these conditions were undermined and eroded over the two decades of the Oslo Peace Process such that there was no longer the necessary socio-political base for a mass movement of popular resistance in the occupied Palestinian territories.

PREREQUISITES FOR SUSTAINABLE UNARMED RESISTANCE MOVEMENTS AGAINST OCCUPATION

In the introductory chapter we reviewed some of the conditions necessary for the emergence of collective resistance against occupation and identified some of the factors that heightened the possibility of such resistance developing into a sustainable and strong movement of unarmed popular resistance. Reviewing these conditions and factors, three broad areas appear to be of particular significance.

1. A strong sense of solidarity throughout the subject population

i.   The most important manifestation of this solidarity would be a shared sense of being involved in a common struggle.
ii. One of the necessary conditions for such a degree of solidarity would be the absence of deep vertical and horizontal divisions within the society.
iii. Community-based organisations and networks of civil society organisations can play a key role in generating and reproducing the bonds of solidarity between members of the subject population.

2. Organisational resilience

i.   A key factor influencing the effectiveness of any resistance movement is the existence of a coherent and unified leadership.
ii. Leadership exists at all levels within a society and a resistance movement. The most important manifestation of this quality would be the organisational strength of the movement at all levels – from the grassroots to the top.
iii. One of the key sources of resilience is the capacity to devise appropriate strategies adapted to the context within which the resistance movement operates and the absence of strong 'counter-movements' within the society advocating violent means of resistance.

3. External support from state and non-state actors

i.   Any resistance movement requires a reliable supply of material, symbolic and other resources to help sustain and strengthen the resistance. External actors can be a key source of such resources.

ii. A key role for external supporters of a resistance movement as links in the chain of influence is to exercise leverage over the occupying power's supporters, publics and decision makers.

iii. It is important that external supporters of resistance movements do not seek to pursue their own agendas and interests in the process of lending support to the movement. To the extent that such conflicts of interest can be avoided, the salience of the resistance movement will be enhanced.

In the next section we shall use this summary of the conditions necessary for a sustained civilian-based unarmed resistance movement as a template with which to analyse the foundations of the first intifada, to which so many of the contemporary generation of popular resistance activists look as a model for their own movement. We shall then compare the features of the contemporary popular resistance movement with those of the first intifada, as a means of highlighting the base factors that need to be addressed if the goal of contemporary activists – the ending of the occupation – is to be approached through unarmed popular resistance.

PREREQUISITES FOR A SUSTAINABLE UNARMED RESISTANCE MOVEMENT: THE CASE OF THE FIRST INTIFADA

Solidarity

Shared identity as participants in a common struggle

The outbreak of the first intifada in December 1987 was as great a surprise to the leadership of the PLO as it was to everyone else, although in the first few days there was little to set it apart from previous confrontations with the occupying power. However, as the weeks went by the insurrection took on a distinctive character. One aspect of this was its scale. Whereas previous outbursts had been dispersed in nature, which made them relatively containable, this time whole sectors of society became involved as the revolt spread from the Gaza Strip to the West Bank, from the refugee camps to the towns and villages. There was for a time significant evidence of mass involvement in the struggle. The resistance was coordinated through a network of popular committees. In August 1988 the Israeli authorities declared such committees to be illegal, with membership punishable by up to ten years' imprisonment. Being aware of how widespread participation in the uprising had become, one Israeli commentator wryly observed that this move was tantamount to declaring all Palestinian inhabitants of the West Bank and Gaza Strip to be illegal.

> All political organisations in the territories have long been illegal. Last week, the popular committees were outlawed, and alongside them their supporters, those who follow their instructions and those who do their work and aid them verbally, materially, actively or by default. There is a popular committee in every village and municipal district, and all residents accept its authority. We cannot, therefore, escape the pleasant conclusion that we have finally managed to outlaw all the inhabitants of the territories.[2]

Absence of deep divisions

No analyst of the first intifada would claim that the historic social divisions that had fractured Palestinian society for so long had disappeared. But there can be little doubt that for a while, during the first two years of the uprising, the traditional divisions were to some degree subordinated to a strong sense of shared identity as Palestinians living under occupation and suffering at the hands of the Israeli state. The shared experience of oppression and suffering resulted in a narrowing of social divisions, with a corresponding increase in the level of reciprocity and mutual aid amongst all sectors of society. Underpinning this there emerged – at least for a while – a common commitment to a body of values and beliefs, centred on the need to maintain the struggle in order to end the occupation.

Network of community-based and civil society organisations

This phenomenon of social solidarity in struggle did not just happen. To a significant degree it was created in the context of a sustained organising effort within the OPT from the mid-1970s onwards. In his study *Behind the Intifada* Joost Hiltermann noted that in 1974 the PLO made the decision to start mobilising Palestinians within the OPT, setting up new popular organisations and infusing existing ones with nationalist ideology. This initiative fed directly into the eventual mobilisation of the population during the first intifada. As he records:

> During the following years an intensive recruitment drive took place among students, workers, professionals, and others around issues of common concern. Organizations proliferated, not only in the urban centres but in the rural areas as well. Their membership increased dramatically and their activities expanded. By the mid-1980s one can speak of the existence of a

network or infrastructure of organisations that had a popular base and were able to provide the basic services lacking in the community, and also lead the masses in times of direct confrontation with the occupier.[3]

Organisational resilience

Coherent and unified leadership

It was not just the scale of the uprising in 1987–88 that surprised observers. Another distinguishing feature was the emergence of an instrument of political unification for all the various political factions in the guise of the Unified National Command of the Uprising (UNC). Following the first announcement of its existence in a leaflet distributed in the first week of January 1988, the UNC succeeded in establishing itself as the undisputed guiding force behind the uprising, commanding the allegiance of the vast majority of the population in the struggle to end the occupation. Along with the organisational infrastructure of popular committees that grew up, the UNC took on the character of an embryonic state: coordinating activities in civil society and seeking to control the use of force within the boundaries of its own territory. In the West Bank the membership was made up of representatives from each of the four main nationalist organisations – Fatah, the Popular Front for the Liberation of Palestine, the Democratic Front for the Liberation of Palestine and the Palestine Communist Party. In the Gaza Strip, Islamic Jihad was also represented.[4]

During this period, of course, the headquarters of the PLO was in Tunis and the leadership of the uprising within the OPT was always careful to acknowledge the sovereignty of the leadership outside and clear any new initiative with them. The result, for the first two years of the intifada at least, was an unprecedented sense of unity throughout the Palestinian body politic. As one informant at the time observed: 'It (the intifada) is not organised by the PLO, as they say. The PLO and the Palestinian people are the same. The PLO represents the aspirations, the ambitions for the future, of the Palestinian people ... The PLO is an output of the Palestinian people. The PLO without the Palestinian people means nothing.'[5]

Organisational strength at all levels

As noted above the base organisational strata of the first intifada was constituted by the popular committees that were established throughout the OPT. In essence they were neighbourhood committees, and the members were friends, relatives, and neighbours – in addition to being local political leaders.[6] A close observer of the intifada commented on the special relationship existing between the UNC and the popular committees during the period 1987–89:

The policy of the leadership to give authority and power to local committees, its willingness to listen and many times change or even reverse its own decisions, shows how close to the average person the leadership is. … This quality meant that the command was seen as a communicator of ideas and suggestions of the population, rather than a leadership trying to impose its predetermined ideas.[7]

The symbiotic nature of this relationship meant that the unity of the leadership acted as an example to the rest of society, whilst the sense of solidarity amongst all sections of the population augmented the political alliance at the heart of the UNC and the embryonic state structures that grew up around it.

Coherent and appropriate strategy

To be sustainable any unarmed resistance movement needs to be able to reassure activists that their continued participation (and the associated costs) is worthwhile. Amongst other things, this means that the leadership must be able to convince activists that significant changes have been achieved as a consequence of the resistance. Failure in this regard is likely to lead to a loss of support for unarmed resistance as a path to liberation.

The first intifada notched up many striking achievements in terms of mobilising large sections of the Palestinian population and in eliciting international support for their struggle. But it failed to end the occupation. There were a number of reasons for this failure, but crucially the resistance failed to impose sufficient costs on the Israeli state and publics to cause them to seek an end to the occupation. In part, this was due to the depth of the Israeli commitment to maintain control of the Palestinian territories and also to the relative weakness of the type of sanctions the Palestinians could impose through unarmed resistance. By the early 1990s Israel was no longer dependent on Palestinian labour to the extent that a withdrawal of that labour would threaten the economic foundations of the state and society. Furthermore, an economic boycott of Israeli goods and services by Palestinians sufficient to cause significant pain to Israel was never realistic insofar as Palestinians had no other means of obtaining the goods and services they required to meet their basic needs except from Israeli suppliers. As Rigby noted in 1991:

Palestinian efforts to impose intolerable costs on Israel through rendering the occupied territories ungovernable have been seriously hampered by the weakness of the indigenous support systems necessary to sustain such a struggle, and the relative immunity achieved by Israel in relation to the sanctions that the Palestinians have sought to impose in the process of their unarmed insurrection.[8]

Imposing a cost on Israel and Israelis for continuing the occupation was only one plank in the intifada's strategy – another was to exercise an influence over significant sections of the Israeli public such that they would come to oppose the continuance of the occupation and thereby help undermine some of the pillars on which the Israeli state relied in order to continue the occupation (such as the willingness of Israeli citizens to continue to perform their military service in the OPT). Once again this strategy failed – at least in part because the intifada was never completely nonviolent. As Palestinians began to lose confidence in the efficacy of unarmed resistance, so the appeal of violence grew. But one consequence of the violence was that many Israelis who were touched and moved by the sufferings endured by Palestinians in pursuit of a just cause – ending the occupation – were moved to fear and distrust when their physical safety was threatened by Palestinian violence.[9]

External support from third parties

A third and particularly crucial reason why the intifada failed in its ultimate goal of ending the occupation was the failure of third parties to exercise sufficient leverage on Israel to help bring about an end to the occupation.

During the intifada it became increasingly clear to most observers that the Israelis, public and politicians alike, would only be persuaded to sit down and talk peace with the Palestinians if they could be convinced that this was the least hurtful and threatening of the available options. Given the relative weakness of Palestinian sanctions to bring about such a situation the only other alternative would have been the exercise of leverage by third parties. As has been noted elsewhere, the history of unarmed resistance against occupation has shown that liberation requires the active intervention of third parties, either in the guise of a liberation army or in the form of non-military sanctions, including a sustained diplomatic offensive. To put it bluntly, during the period of the first intifada Israel was never faced with the threat of such sanctions by any third party with the capacity to implement them. Whilst the Palestinians received humanitarian assistance and expressions of support and solidarity from many sources, at no stage during the first intifada did this third party involvement extend to the exercise of effective leverage on the occupying power itself.

PREREQUISITES FOR A SUSTAINABLE UNARMED RESISTANCE MOVEMENT: THE POST-SECOND INTIFADA PERIOD

Solidarity vs social disintegration

As noted already, many observers (and activists) of the unarmed resistance movement in the OPT would dispute the appropriateness of the epithet 'popular'.

As one activist bemoaned in November 2013: 'In the first intifada people were prepared to sacrifice. But now the struggle only involves a few people ... Every movement has its ups and downs. Popular committees? We are not popular anymore. In fact there is no movement now.' A major causal factor in bringing about such a state of affairs was the erosion of any significant sense of solidarity amongst Palestinians during the twenty-first century. There have been many reasons for this fracturing of the society.

- The geographical fracturing that took place as part of the Oslo process with the division of the OPT into Areas A, B and C;
- The blockages to easy communication and movement between areas – particularly between the West Bank and the Gaza Strip;
- The political fractures – particularly the division between Hamas and Fatah;
- The economic impoverishment of large numbers of Palestinians who can no longer find employment in Israel, resulting in them prioritising the satisfaction of basic needs above participation in a common struggle for some distant goal like the end of the occupation;
- The widespread disillusionment with the cronyism and corruption that permeated the PA, which fed a country-wide lack of trust in those seeking to act as leaders.

One manifestation of this erosion of social solidarity and identification with a common struggle was the deepening of vertical and horizontal divisions within Palestinian society.

The deepening of vertical and horizontal divisions

It is noticeable to anyone who has spent any time in Ramallah since the mid-1990s that there has emerged a political class aligned with a business/entrepreneurial class that became conspicuous by its consumption patterns and the mansions that they built for themselves. There is something obscene about the ostentatiousness of the lifestyle and trappings that go with positions of political and/or economic power enjoyed by the Palestinian elite ensconced in Ramallah. Particularly when one contrasts their wealth and consumerism with the ongoing plight of Palestinian peasants trying to eke out a living on land designated by Israel as Area C in the Jordan Valley and South Hebron Hills or facing the daily assaults from settlers and occupation forces in urban locations such as Silwan and Hebron. One of the consequences of this deepening divide between the 'haves' and the 'have-nots' has been increasing levels of inward migration to centres such as Ramallah in search of employment.[10]

All this has militated against any sense of social solidarity beyond the family and clan. Indeed, there has been a resurgence in tribalism as the processes of social disintegration have intensified. According to Salah Abdel Shafi the erosion of the authority of the PA after the split between the Fatah-controlled administration in the West Bank and the Hamas administration in the Gaza Strip accelerated the processes of social fragmentation: 'The lack of central authority paved also the way for the revival of tribalism and the emergence of warlords who took the law into their own hands. A process of social disintegration was gradually taking place.'[11] When one factors into this erosion of common bonds transcending family, clan and tribe the physical obstacles to travel between different parts of the West Bank and the virtual impossibility of Palestinians moving between the West Bank and the Gaza Strip, then one begins to grasp just what has been lost compared to the period leading up to the first intifada. As one informant in Jenin told us, 'In 1982 as a young activist – I went to Gaza and again in 1983 to Khan Younis in solidarity with political activists there and to support their struggle. Nowadays I might go for a photo opportunity! No one is ready to go even a few miles to participate in an action.'

The NGO-isation of community-based and civil society organisations

In the years prior to the first intifada there had been a proliferation of community-based organisations (CBOs) and civil society organisations (CSOs) delivering services to Palestinians whilst reinforcing the nationalist message. As noted, they subsequently played a key role in mobilising people during the intifada and supplying cadres of activists. These conditions no longer prevail in the OPT. In the post-Oslo years there was a steady process of what can be termed the 'NGO-isation' of such organisations. This came about as a result of the mushrooming of NGOs following the Oslo Agreement, funded largely by foreign donors eager to channel development aid through civil society organisations. As a consequence, what were once popular grass-roots organisations and committees were transformed into professional deliverers of foreign development aid, with a number of significant consequences.

Challand has noted that the most active NGOs were the ones that had the capacity to adapt to the jargon and reporting requirements of the donors. As a consequence,

> These more successful NGOs – in terms of fund-raising – ran ... the risk of gradually losing touch with their own people, because they tend to adjust more to the agendas of their donors, to whom they are accountable for funding, rather than to focus on the population's real needs, despite claims by NGOs to be grass-roots organizations.[12]

He also noted the consequent erosion of the spirit of 'voluntarism' in Palestinian society:

> Many donors ride the fashion waves, like empowerment, awareness-raising, children's rights, mobile clinics, or mental health, etc. This translates into the emergence of a large number of new civil society organizations ... the creation of many new professional NGOs, as a result of the large amounts of money made available by donors, has contributed to the loss of the voluntary spirit that was so characteristic of the mass-movement organizations that arose around the late 1970s. Many NGOs are now guided much more by market principles than by voluntary participation in their activities.[13]

So many of the activists interviewed during 2013–14 referred to this erosion of the spirit of voluntarism, of helping one's neighbours, of going that extra kilometre for the sake of the common good. As one activist from Jenin commented,

> Everyone is looking out for their own benefit, what will they get? There is no longer the sense of contributing your efforts. Even the spirit of self-help has weakened. Now you go to the external funding agencies. During the first intifada we grew watermelons and sold them, and used the profit to support the local struggle. That would not happen now. Money and revolution is like a mouse and wheat. The mouse will eat its way through all the wheat!

The perception that popular resistance activists were driven more by their own selfish interests rather than concern for the well-being of the wider community was widespread. People explained to us how – in their view – local activist leaders were treating the movement as their own NGO, their own 'shop'. Such views reflected the lack of trust already alluded to and in turn nurtured its growth. As one activist from Tubas district observed:

> When you look around – the different popular resistance coordinating networks ... you will conclude that some people are benefitting from this. They have a car, a salary, projects – as part of popular resistance! This is the view on the street. Some of them have connections with internationals – they exchange personal email addresses. So then support and donations go to them rather than to their institutions or organisation. Then the funds for various villages that comes – these people spend some of it on popular resistance and the rest on themselves.

Fractured leadership

One of the notable features of the first intifada was the emergence of a unified leadership within the OPT that enjoyed a mutually supportive relationship with the top PLO hierarchy then based in Tunis. Even after the emergence of Hamas the political factions worked out a modus vivendi so that no side could be accused of undermining the uprising. This stands in marked contrast to the post-second intifada period where the PA has seen its popularity drastically eroded due to the widespread corruption and cronyism, the failure (prior to June 2014) to mend the disastrous split between the Fatah-dominated PA in the West Bank and the Hamas administration in the Gaza Strip, and the abject failure on the part of the PA to obtain any dividend from negotiations with Israel. All this has had a powerful impact on the popular resistance movement. As one political activist from Jenin explained to us in 2013:

> There is no unified leadership representing the majority of the people. ... The split (between Fatah and Hamas) is a reason, the parties are after their own interests and not the national agenda. .... The leaders want to keep control of some of the territories which to them has been more important than the national agenda – eight years since the split and still no resolution. This is reflected on the ground.
>
> Maybe there is some support for popular resistance from some of the leadership, but there is no actual leadership. In fact the Palestinian political leadership does not have a long-term strategy. ... It is also constrained by its security arrangements with the Israelis. They have to retreat, so they do not have a long-term commitment to popular resistance. The leadership is constrained by the Oslo agreements on all levels and this prevents them from playing a proactive role. They are chained by the agreements they signed, and they are not struggling against them. They thought it would be easy to end occupation without a struggle. This is not possible.
>
> It is 20 years since Oslo and there have been no political achievements. Nothing. No justice. More settlements. An erosion of freedom, the Wall – nothing! So why trust the political leadership?

This person was not the only one to express his disillusionment with the formal political leadership. One activist from Ramallah District was particularly scathing:

> After Oslo the Palestinians from outside came back here, they had nowhere else to go and Oslo was the answer to their dilemma of having nowhere to go. They came back here never having had experience of occupation, and they created a bubble for themselves in Ramallah where they still don't feel the occupation. Our sense is that they are nurturing different priorities of consumerism, cars etc. – not liberation. We also know about the corruption and the internal conflicts. They are frightened of popular resistance – they want to co-opt us and our methods, turn us into projects of NGOs.

It was very clear to most of the people with whom we talked during our years of fieldwork between 2011 and 2014 that the PA was ambivalent around the issue of popular resistance. A common analysis was that the PA could not be seen to condemn popular resistance, but played no significant role in mobilising people for resistance as a way of weakening what was considered to be a fundamental threat to established interests. There are, of course, other reasons why the PA failed to take a leading role in the popular resistance movement apart from the self-interest of the political elite and those who depend on them for their livelihoods. The political leadership within the main secular political organisation of Fatah who also fill the key posts within the PA have felt constrained by the terms of the Oslo Agreements and the conditions attached to the peace negotiations. In addition, by the terms of those agreements, the PA has not been in a position to intervene openly in many locations where popular resistance has taken place because they are in parts of the West Bank designated as Area C and thereby outside the formal domain of the PA. On top of this, a number of senior figures within the administration emphasised their commitment to maintaining public order and defusing situations that might incur physical injury and even death to participants. This was how they justified the occasions when Palestinian security personnel had intervened to prevent particular protest actions. Moreover, these people were well aware that if the PA did intervene in a more direct and open manner in support of popular resistance, then Israel would retaliate by imposing sanctions which in turn would impose an additional burden of suffering on the population. Most typically this would involve Israel withholding the customs duties collected on goods headed to the OPT through the border crossings which Israel controls. According to some observers 'the money accounts for approximately two-thirds of the Palestinian budget and is key to keeping its public sector functioning and maintaining stability in the Israeli-occupied West Bank.'[14]

Organisational frailty

The first intifada was coordinated through a network of popular committees, each one operating within the parameters articulated in the communiqués issued by the UNC. The movement that has emerged in the OPT since the second intifada has no such organisational infrastructure. The divisions within the Palestinian political house have been mirrored in the creation of four different popular resistance coordinating committees. The first to be established in 2002 was the Stop the Wall Campaign (STWC) aligned with the Palestinians political left. By 2012 its main activity had become international outreach. In 2008 the Popular Struggle Coordinating Committee (PSCC) was established with seed-funding provided from the office of the then prime minister Salam Fayyad. By 2012 the PSCC had become the most visible of the coordinating committees, aided in part by the funding provided from Spanish and Italian sources. In August 2009 Fatah, at its sixth annual conference held in Bethlehem, decided that popular resistance should be an integral part of its programme. Two years later, in October 2011, this decision resulted in the formation of the National Committee for Popular Resistance (NCPR). Around the same time another network of Fatah activists set up their own coordinating committee with the resounding title of Popular Resistance High Follow-up Commission (PRHFC).

For the outsider it was difficult to detect significant differences between the different coordinating committees other than the STWC is 'leftist' with board members drawn from the PFLP, *Al Mubadara* (Palestine National Initiative) and the Palestinian People's Party, whilst the other three seemed to represent different tendencies within Fatah.[15] Indeed, it would appear that at the grass-roots level the representatives of the different networks all work together on common actions. The problem seems to be one of organisational rivalry amongst the top echelons, with representatives of the different networks competing to get their names in print and their banners on photo shoots at different protest actions. There have also been instances when rival networks have organised competing demonstrations and protest marches such as happened in Hebron on one occasion.[16] Each has held its annual conferences and passed similar resolutions – from the point of view of organising unarmed popular resistance such divisions would appear to have undermined any potential for coordinated mass actions. As one activist from a village south of Bethlehem commented, 'Diversity is not a problem, but there is no shared strategy, no coordination, no pressure from the grass roots or from above for people to move beyond this division.'

Another factor that contributed to the relative frailty of the popular resistance movement has been the socio-economic changes that have taken place in the West Bank during the post-Oslo period. At one level the impoverishment endured by large swathes of the population has meant that their focus is on survival and the meeting of basic needs. In a context where few substantial gains have been achieved by popular resistance, despite the costs of detention and fines borne by activists, it is perhaps not surprising that those living on the breadline became reluctant to add to their burdens by participating in protest actions where they risked significant sanctions and for no apparent purpose.[17] Moreover, a significant proportion of the employed in the West Bank work for the PA, including the security wings, and consequently were less likely to participate in popular resistance activities.

Another relevant factor has been what one might call the 'embourgeoise-ment' of significant numbers of people who acted as local leaders during the first intifada. Whilst many of this generation have been at the heart of the more recent unarmed resistance, others of their peers have opted out. As one activist from Ramallah District explained,

> Fatah was once the main force. But there is the effect of normalisation, NGOs, fund-raising – they are trying to make us consumers. People who used to be leaders in the first intifada are now concerned about getting new cars, jobs and houses. So even they are now against popular resistance as it threatens their interests. 'I don't want to go back to being without a car or pay the price for resistance.' So they are not very active. It is not just Fatah – some of the leftists with the PFLP … they play no role.

So, to summarise, the popular resistance movement in the OPT that emerged after the second intifada has lacked coherent leadership and organisational resilience. As one activist lamented,

> It is not popular resistance. … We do not have a leader for popular resistance – there is no Martin Luther King with wisdom, who is loved and able to inspire … We have tried to coordinate actions in the main centres – Al-Masara, Bil'in and Nabi Saleh – but we do not have mass support. It is the same faces. There are probably about 150 activists.

Lack of an effective popular resistance strategy

The third factor identified as necessary for a sustainable unarmed resistance movement is the pursuance of a coherent strategy – and once again we find that the changes that took place since the Oslo Accords of the mid-1990s have resulted in a different environment from that pertaining in the years leading up the first intifada.

As noted above, there were two main planks to the Palestinian strategy during the first intifada:

1. Impose sufficient costs (moral and material, symbolic and substantive) on the Israeli state and publics so as to cause them to reconsider their commitment to continuing the occupation; and
2. Win over significant sections of the Israeli public to the realisation that the continuation of the occupation was not only morally wrong but politically disastrous for Israel.

These pathways were pursued by means of protest actions and other initiatives that were targeted not only at Israelis but also at international constituencies and stakeholders. Particular emphasis was placed on the importance of facilitating encounters between Palestinians and Israelis as a means of persuading the

Israeli participants to use their influence with their fellow citizens and decision makers to bring about a change in Israeli policy with regard to the occupation. Such encounters had been taking place for a number of years prior to the intifada – primarily with activists from the Israeli peace camp. During the intifada however, the focus changed as attention was directed more towards creating encounters with Israelis who were closer to the mainstream of Israeli public opinion than the 'peace-niks' as part of a strategic decision to exercise influence, however indirectly, over the mainstream political parties within the Israeli state.[18]

Little has changed in the strategic thinking of popular resistance activists except that the concern with facilitating encounters with Israelis had been dropped, reflecting the disillusionment and cynicism felt by Palestinians after all the many foreign-funded 'people-to-people' initiatives that accompanied the Oslo peace process, and which have come to be dismissed as part of an overall 'normalization' project. However, changes in the political geography of the Israeli–Palestinian conflict have seriously undermined the capacity of Palestinians to exercise leverage over Israelis by means of unarmed resistance. Crucially, the erection of the Separation Wall alongside the construction of separate highways for the use of Israeli citizens has achieved its goal – the separation of Israelis from Palestinians. Palestinian protest actions targeting the Wall or settlements do not impact in any direct manner on Israelis living within the boundaries of pre-1967 Israel. What they experience of such actions is mediated through the mass media, if it is reported at all. And if it is reported what is likely to remain in their mind is the image of keffiya-clad Palestinian youths using sling-shots to hurl stones at 'our boys' in the military – which in turn provides even more reason for maintaining the separation so that Israelis can continue to go about their everyday lives untroubled.

Moreover, whereas the first intifada witnessed an explosion of Israeli peace groups and organisations, their number and their influence has been radically reduced over the past decade or more. The fear that was planted in most Israeli Jews by the terror of the suicide bombings of the second intifada fuelled the rise in the popularity of right-wing political parties, which in turn has meant that those Israeli groups that campaign for an end to the occupation have become increasingly isolated and marginalised (and demonised) in Israel. Hence, there has been a corresponding erosion in their capacity to act effectively as interlocutors between Palestinian nationalists and the Israeli mainstream. All this can be very disheartening for Palestinians (and others) committed to unarmed modes of struggle for human rights and the end to the Israeli occupation. But there remains one significant ray of hope as grounds for optimism – the burgeoning influence being exercised by external actors which holds out some kind of promise for a more peaceful future in Israel and Palestine.

The burgeoning role of third party solidarity: grounds for hope?

Perhaps the most significant feature of the post-second intifada period of popular resistance has been the increased involvement of 'internationals' as accompaniers, co-participants in actions, and as 'activist-tourists' expressing their solidarity through their presence. The significance of these overseas activists has been threefold:

1. By their presence they created a kind of protective shield for Palestinian protesters;
2. They established linkages between Palestinians and wider activist networks around the world; and
3. On their return home they act as powerful advocates of the Palestinian cause amongst networks and groupings in their own countries.

One outcome of this trend has been an expansion of the international grass-roots movement of solidarity with the Palestinian struggle. This loose 'movement of movements' has been one of the prime vehicles for implementing a Palestinian initiative that emerged out of a meeting of Palestinian civil society organisations in July 2005 – the call for a worldwide boycott, divestment and sanctions (BDS) campaign against Israel.[19]

What we are witnessing with the emergence of a worldwide movement of solidarity with Palestinians in their unarmed struggle against occupation is a new phase of Palestinian resistance, where the struggle is taking place at the ideological, economic and diplomatic level. It is one in which Israeli military might, its capacity to wield the weapons of violence with apparent impunity, only serves to weaken its claim to legitimacy. Increasing numbers of people around the world seem to have come to the realisation that the continued Israeli occupation of Palestinian lands, the blockade of the citizens of the Gaza Strip and the repeated 'slaughter of the innocents' that takes place in the regular wars waged against the Gaza Strip constitute gross and unacceptable violations of basic human rights about which 'something must be done'. During the 2014 war on Gaza (Operation Protective Edge) local and national demonstrations were organised around the world to protest against the war and the civilian death toll. In the UK there were national and local demonstrations, and on October 13, 2014 the House of Commons debated the recognition of Palestine as a state alongside Israel. A majority of those members present voted for the motion, which was carried. This was a significant indicator of the manner in which Israel has started to lose its standing and status internationally as a direct result of its ongoing abuse of international and humanitarian law and its refusal to engage in serious and substantive negotiations for a sustainable peace.

As our analysis has shown, Palestinians on their own lack the leverage power to cause the Israelis to change their stance. But we have now moved into an age where transnational social movements do exercise an influence on publics around the world and hence upon political leaders and decision makers. Within this scenario the popular resistance within the OPT takes on a particular significance. As protesters continue to play the part of a brave people struggling for their basic human rights by unarmed means against an illegitimate and violent occupation, so they can widen their support base internationally. However weak the actions of Palestinian activists might appear in terms of direct leverage on Israeli publics and decision makers, it is through their persistent and unarmed resistance that they can continue to shame the Israeli regime in the eyes of sympathetic constituencies around the world – links in the great chain of nonviolence – who can in turn exercise pressure on their own governments and institutions to take action. In Chapter 9 we shall return to examine the growing significance of the international movements of solidarity and support in relation to Palestinian popular resistance against occupation. But in Chapter 7 attention is turned to the situation of the minority of Israeli citizens who continue to display the courage necessary to express their solidarity with the Palestinian struggle for justice and freedom.

7

THE ROLE OF ISRAELI PEACE
AND SOLIDARITY ACTIVISTS

HISTORICAL BACKGROUND

During the period of Zionist migration to Palestine, prior to the establishment of the State of Israel, there had been a small minority that had been concerned about the consequences of alienating the Arab population. Amongst their number was a small organisation called *Brit Shalom* (Covenant of Peace), founded in 1925, which was Palestine's first recognised peace group. Its founders, who included Martin Buber, Arthur Ruppin and Henrietta Szold, sought peaceful co-existence between Arabs and Jews through the creation of a bi-national state within which both peoples would enjoy equal rights. The group never had more than a hundred members and failed to convince any significant section of either population group of the relevance of its proposals. It eventually went out of existence in the early 1930s, but in 1942 some of its original members, along with Judah Magnes, founded the group *Ihud* (Union) with the aim of garnering international support for the bi-national vision.[1]

In 1948 the mainstream Zionists achieved their aim of Jewish statehood. A year later Buber predicted with amazing prescience the fragility of the post-war 'peace' – 'a stunted peace, no more than non-belligerence, which at any moment, when any new constellation of forces arises, is liable to turn into war.' He continued:

And when this hollow peace is achieved, how then do you think you'll be able to combat 'the spirit of militarism' when the leaders of the extreme nationalism will find it easy to convince the young that this kind of spirit is essential for the survival of the country? The battles will cease, but will suspicions cease? Will there be an end to the thirst for vengeance? Won't we be compelled, and I mean really compelled, to maintain a posture of vigilance forever, without being able to breathe? Won't this unceasing effort occupy the most talented members of our society?[2]

Unfortunately, for the bulk of the citizens of the new state, enjoying a position of military strength and internationally accepted statehood, the ethical concerns of the bi-nationalists seemed even more irrelevant and other-worldly.

The wars that Buber had predicted came to pass and after the second one in June 1967, the occupation of the West Bank and Gaza Strip brought about a change in the approach of the small minority of Israeli doves. From advocating a bi-national solution based on equality between the two peoples within the 1948 borders, support emerged for the division of the land. There was little consensus concerning the amount of land to be relinquished in the cause of peace however, and the different peace groups remained divided amongst themselves. Those that did campaign for withdrawal from the newly occupied territories remained lone voices for the first decade of occupation, as the more mainstream Zionist doves as a whole did little to arouse public interest in the question of withdrawal. There was still a widespread belief that the Labour-led government was actively pursuing the path of peace, whilst for most Israelis these were years of general satisfaction – there was employment, Israel was powerful, the Arab world was divided, and things were looking good. Far more prominent than any peace movement in the arena of extra-parliamentary activity during these years was the burgeoning settler movement *Gush Emunim* (The bloc of the faithful) whose members saw the victory of 1967 as Divine endorsement of their claim to the whole of the 'land of Israel'.

The sense of well-being began to crumble rapidly following yet another war, that of October 1973. However, in 1977 President Sadat of Egypt broke ranks with the Arab world and visited Jerusalem to start negotiations regarding Israel's withdrawal from Sinai and the future of the occupied territories. However, whilst the negotiations were taking place, the Likud-led government drew up plans to expand the settlement-building programme. Appalled at what they saw as a threat to the prospects for peace, 350 reserve officers and soldiers sent Prime Minister Begin a letter in the spring of 1978 which was published as a petition and eventually obtained some 250,000 signatures. In what became known as 'the officers' letter' they warned:

> A government that prefers the establishment of settlements across the Green Line to the ending of the historic conflict and to the establishment of a system of normal relations raises questions about the justice of our course. A government policy that leads to the continued rule over one million Arabs is liable to damage the Jewish democratic character of the State, and will make it difficult for us to identify with the basic direction of the State of Israel ... we know that true security will be achieved only with the advent of peace.[3]

The publication of the letter created a groundswell of support for what became Peace Now (*Shalom Achshav*). One of its first demonstrations in Tel Aviv in

March 1978 had some 30,000 participants, unprecedented numbers for Israel, and the movement continued to grow. Its main slogans were 'Peace is greater than Greater Israel', 'Occupation corrupts', and 'Settlements: an obstacle to peace'. This was as near to a programme that Peace Now went, no steps were proposed as to how to achieve an end to the occupation. Its aim was to pitch a 'peace message' as widely as possible amongst the Israeli public as a means of shifting public opinion. An early indication of the determination not to step beyond the boundaries of mainstream Israeli public opinion came in August 1978, when Peace Now denounced a declaration by reserve soldiers that they would refuse to defend Israeli settlements, which they considered to be 'an expression of annexationist aims and of the rejectionist policy of the government'. This refusal by Peace Now to support any kind of conscientious objection to military service continued throughout the Lebanon War. But following the complicity of the Israeli military forces in the massacre of Palestinian refugees by Christian Lebanese Falangists at the Sabra and Shatilla refugee camps, Peace Now held a mass protest in Tel Aviv on September 25, 1982 in order to pressurise the government to establish a national inquiry commission to investigate the massacres, as well as calling for the resignation of the Minister of Defense, Ariel Sharon. The demonstration was the largest in Israel's history, with some 400,000 people participating, approximately 10 per cent of Israel's population at the time.

Following the lead of earlier conscientious objectors, a group of reserve soldiers got together at the start of the Lebanon War to publish a letter declaring their reluctance to perform their military duty beyond the borders of the State of Israel on Lebanese land. They took the name *Yesh Gvul* (There is a limit/border). During the course of the war some 2,500 reserve soldiers signed the petition, and about 160 of them were tried and sentenced for their refusal to take part in the invasion. When the war in Lebanon ended Yesh Gvul lost much of its impetus, although a small number of activists kept the organisation alive as a support group for those few individuals who refused to serve in the occupied territories, a number which increased radically after the outbreak of the first intifada in 1987.

During the period of the first intifada there was a sense of hope shared by both Palestinians and Israeli solidarity activists that some kind of sea change was underway, and it was this mood that fed into the proliferation of Israeli peace groups. Some of these were composed of representatives from particular professions and sectors of Israeli society – such as Physicians for Human Rights established in 1988 and various women's organisations such as the Women's Network for Peace, Israeli Women Against the Occupation, and Women in Black. Other groups focused on particular types of activity – such as the Women's Organisation for Political Prisoners founded in 1988, shortly before the establishment of the human rights organisation *B'tselem* (In the image of God), to document human rights violations in the occupied territories, combat denial and help to create a human rights culture in Israel. A third category of peace groups created during this period were specifically aligned with particular leftist Israeli political movements and tendencies, each one distinguishing itself from the others in terms meaningful only to those who shared the vocabulary of the Israeli left.[4]

If the first intifada marked the high point in the relationship between Israeli peace and solidarity groups and Palestinians living under occupation, the second intifada marked its nadir. Activity had declined with the signing of the Oslo Accords, with many in the Israel peace movement seemingly of the view that this marked the end of the conflict rather than the start of a new phase requiring fresh forms of engagement. As one Peace Now activist recalled, 'For us, September 13, 1993 was the day when the goals to which we had aspired for so many years finally materialized.'[5] Moreover, the increase in the incidence of suicide bombings and other acts of violence targeted at Israeli civilians fed into the negative stereotyping of Palestinians as constituting a violent threat to security and a corresponding decline in support for the peace process amongst significant sections of the Israeli public. According to the *Peace Index* in 1997, 39 per cent of Israeli Jewish respondents viewed the Palestinians as violent, by the end of 2000 this proportion had risen to 68 per cent, with 78 per cent agreeing with the view that the Palestinians did not value human life whatsoever.[6] This image of the 'other' extended to the Palestinian citizens of Israel who had started demonstrating in solidarity with their cousins in the OPT, with 13 being killed as a consequence. As one observer noted, 'suddenly, in the minds of the Jewish majority, the Arabs seemed liked deeply disloyal citizens.'[7]

In the context of the second intifada, Peace Now was fundamentally lost and directionless. It felt it could not issue any statement of support for Palestinians as this would have alienated the mainstream Israeli Jewish public, which was its main target. This passivity was most noticeable with regard to the construction of the Wall, which was supported by an overwhelming majority of Israeli Jews with 84 per cent of respondents in a 2004 survey supporting its construction.[8] The opposition to the construction of the Wall was limited to new young radical small groups and some human rights groups that also challenged its legality, particularly with regard to the expropriation of Palestinian land beyond the Green Line of the pre-1967 border. These young newcomers brought new energy and creativity to the Israeli peace constituency, focusing on direct action and building links with Palestinian popular resistance networks and groups. They criticised the mainstream of the peace movement as old fashioned and 'establishment', challenging the left groups as Marxist, middle-aged and outdated. They were savvy in using social media and other forms of communication, including the organisation of cultural and musical events such as 'Rave against the occupation'. They brought a fresh perspective and dynamism to the Israeli peace constituency, but one thing did not change – their minority status on the margins of Israeli public opinion.

TYPES OF ENGAGEMENT

Offensive co-resistance and direct protest action

Several Israeli organisations have been engaged in different forms of direct action against the construction of the Wall and the ethnic cleansing of Palestinian populations in Areas B and C as a result of the Israeli occupation policy and attacks by settlers. Their activities have included solidarity visits, participation in demonstrations and confrontations with the army as part of the struggle against the construction of the Wall and related threats to the well-being of Palestinians living under occupation. Perhaps the best known group involved in this kind of action has been Anarchists Against the Wall (AATW). Initially the Israeli activists had tended to join the actions alongside Palestinians and internationals associated with the International Solidarity Movement, a Palestinian-led organisation started straight after the beginning of the second intifada that called especially for help from international activists.[9] The Israeli participants eventually came to the decision that their engagement as Israeli citizens alongside Palestinians resisting the construction of the Wall should be made known, and they came up with the name of Anarchists Against the Wall. AATW was thus created with the principle of joint struggle in mind, evidenced to some degree by the fact that their involvement is always organised through local Palestinian popular committees rather than unilaterally. As their website explains, *Why We Resist*:

> It is the duty of Israeli citizens to resist immoral policies and actions carried out in our name. We believe that it is possible to do more than demonstrate inside Israel or participate in humanitarian relief actions. Israeli apartheid and occupation isn't going to end by itself – it will end when it becomes ungovernable and unmanageable. It is time to physically oppose the bulldozers, the army and the occupation.[10]

It is also relevant to point out that by engaging in forms of co-resistance alongside Palestinians, the activists from AATW, like Israelis engaged in other forms of solidarity actions alongside Palestinians, were giving substance to their conviction that any sustainable future relationship between Israelis and Palestinians must be based on the principles of cooperation and equality. As someone from AATW expressed it:

Systems of segregation are very powerful. The idea of entering a Palestinian village seems to most Israelis dangerous and unthinkable. Breaking it with an ethos of cooperation and equality is critical to political reconstruction on both sides. Imagining a joint future and partnership is essential. The AATW has contributed to the creation of an ethos of popular struggle, an ethos of joint struggle with no fear of normalization since it doesn't ignore the power relations.

This sense of embodying in their actions an alternative pattern of relationship between Palestinians and Israelis was expressed particularly strongly by one of the women involved in directly challenging Israeli law through her involvement in the group *Lo Metsaylot* (Women Who Disobey) – a network of Israeli and Palestinian women who began taking day trips together to parks and the seaside, and in the process repeatedly broke the Israeli law restricting the entry of Palestinians into Israel. Based on the principle of rejecting the ideology that keeps Israelis and Palestinians apart and refusing to be enemies, our informant explained that through their activities, 'dozens of women experience a new reality of acquaintance, engaging in a joint political venture, overcoming fear and expressing solidarity. It is an act of civil disobedience … We are claiming the freedom to build an alternative reality.'

Solidarity through accompaniment

Palestinians living within Area C have very few basic rights under the Israeli occupation and consequently popular resistance in such circumstances takes on its own character, which includes a more manifest reliance on the support and solidarity of international and Israeli activists. Members of the Israeli group Ta'ayush have played an important role in working alongside the villagers of the South Hebron Hills since the first year of the second intifada.[11] Its members, Jewish and Arab, have worked fields, helped dig wells and repair damage caused by the army and extremist settlers. In the process they have experienced some of the violence and intimidation (including arrest) that is the everyday experience of the Palestinian residents.[12] As one of their founding members explained, 'We used the direct action of humanitarian-aid and solidarity to support Palestinians.' Appreciation of the work of Ta'ayush was expressed by one of the coordinators of the Hebron-based movement Youth Against Settlements during one of our conversations: 'Ta'ayush is doing a great job in the South Hebron Hills. Last Friday the settlers attacked us in our centre here. We phoned Ta'ayush and they came here at once.'

There is no hard and fast division of labour between Israeli peace and solidarity groups. Thus, our informant from Youth Against Settlements expressed his appreciation not only of Ta'ayush but also of activists with the Israeli Committee

Against House Demolitions when he noted how they had renovated the property they used as a centre with support from other Israeli peace and human rights group. In similar fashion, when homes were destroyed by the army in the village of Makhoul in the Jordan Valley and Israel prevented international humanitarian agencies from intervening, Israeli activists from *Machsom Watch* (Checkpoint Watch) with contacts in the village turned to other agencies for assistance, including Rabbis for Human Rights and Women Who Disobey: 'We put ads in the paper asking for donations to support the village and organised activity days to build new shelters.' In similar fashion organisations like Israeli Physicians for Human Rights have provided medical care for patients and secured passage for ambulances to reach Palestinian hospitals by accompanying them through checkpoints.

A number of Palestinian activists who we interviewed referred to the sense of empowerment they derived from the presence of Israeli activists alongside them in their struggle insofar as it helped to counter their sense of isolation. This view was expressed particularly clearly by an activist from Nabi Saleh who explained how the involvement with Israeli activists had helped build new bridges of trust with Israeli society: 'Before we had the example of the soldiers shooting and killing, the settlers stealing our land. This is the first time I have experienced the other side of Israel – as partners in our struggle against a common enemy. They also suffer.' By their preparedness to accompany Palestinians in their encounters with settlers and soldiers from the occupation force, Israeli solidarity activists have performed a significant protective and defensive function simply by their presence. The Israeli army's code of conduct is markedly different when Israelis are present and violence, while still severe, is significantly lower. Genuine appreciation was expressed by Palestinian activists for the 'defensive line' created by the Israeli and international activists during clashes. As one informant expressed it, 'They are a form of protection, they would be on the front line like a human chain against the army – like a shield.' An activist from Qalqilya District expressed a similar view: 'The foreign and Israeli activists act as human shields. The Israeli army does not shoot at them live bullets with the aim of killing or harming them badly, this also protects us.'

Addressing Israeli society

A number of our Palestinian informants expressed the view that whilst they appreciated the presence of Israeli activists alongside them in their actions, they felt that the prime role of such people should be directed towards influencing Israeli public opinion and discourse. As one Palestinian activist expressed it, 'They should become a real radio broadcasting on behalf of the Palestinians, speaking the truth about the occupation.' Of course, activists the world over see such advocacy as part of their *raison d'être* – to influence bystanders and publics. But it is not an easy task, particularly in societies such as Israel where the vast majority of the public just do not have the ears with which to hear the message. As one Israeli activist explained to us, 'The Israeli public has no interest in ending the occupation. It has no direct effect on their lives. They are not occupied. The occupation is irrelevant to them.' Despite this seeming indifference, the struggle goes on.

One of the groups that has had a public profile within Israel and internationally is Breaking the Silence. It is an organisation of veteran combatants who have served in the Israeli military since the start of the second intifada and have taken it upon themselves to expose the Israeli public to the reality of everyday life in the occupied territories. Their main method is the gathering of testimonies from soldiers serving with the occupation force documenting the 'reality' of occupation, publishing and distributing such testimonies as a means of informing the Israeli public that this is the price to be paid for occupation – there is no such thing as a gentle and humane occupation, by its very nature occupation rests on violence and the abuse of human rights. In January 2012 we interviewed one of the founders in a café near his home in Jerusalem. He prefaced his remarks by observing that Israeli society had no idea about the OPT. Sometime prior to our interview he had made a presentation to a class of former soldiers, he had been shocked that half of them thought the OPT was part of Israel. He continued:

> Our work is to increase the resistance to occupation. We are veterans of the second intifada that try to increase resistance to occupation through gathering testimonies and publishing them. We try to use our experience and testimony as an educational tool. ... We are not a membership organisation. Whoever testifies is a member. For many testifying is the first step in the right direction.
>
> We are not trying to promote specific outcomes. We are saying there is a price for the occupation. Our only line is that we don't want occupation. We don't talk about peace. We do not go into the question of East Jerusalem. We try not to lose focus on our added value as veterans.
>
> We are not 'shooting and crying'. During the first intifada some of the reservists cried with the shock of what they were required to do. We are not shocked by that. Don't be shocked. This is what is bound to happen. And we tell stories to illustrate this. We also give an approval stamp to what Palestinians have been saying for years.[13]

Whilst the movement has focused on influencing Israeli public opinion, they have also targeted Jewish communities overseas and diaspora Jews spending a year on study programmes in Israel. In Europe they have also focused on opinion leaders and decision makers, organising study tours of Hebron for such people in association with Youth Against Settlements.

Other groups focus not only on trying to influence Israeli public opinion but also to question the deeper cultural foundations of Israeli society that render the occupation of another people completely 'acceptable'. New Profile is one such network created in 1998 – a movement for the 'civilization of Israeli society'.[14] Israeli society is permeated throughout by different dimensions of militarism and a militaristic culture. The presence of so many armed soldiers in the Israeli streets, buses and cafés shocks many foreigners visiting Israel. Former senior army personal occupy the top positions in all spheres of life in Israel. But it goes far deeper into the interstices of social, political, cultural, economic and family life. The consequence is, according to New Profile, that 'Israeli culture generates an image of a world in which war was, is and will always be inevitable, a necessary and acceptable way of solving our problem'.[15] The members of New Profile have struggled to highlight and thereby challenge the pervasive influence of this militaristic culture, through various forms of public education – public exhibitions and presentations, alternative summer camps for children – and through advising and supporting Israeli 'refusers', those with a conscientious objection to serving in the Israeli military.[16] Their approach in the first place is to try and make militarism visible, primarily through highlighting the way militaristic values permeate the way the world is presented through the media and the formal educational processes in Israel. As one of their activists explained to us,

If you do not demilitarise, if you do not change peoples' mindsets, then you will not change things. ... We are not going to change the world in the here-and-now. We are involved in small processes. The last few years we have made more effort to talk to the Israeli public, creating a situation where people have to think. They might not agree with us but such encounters can resonate, generate interest.

One of the foundations upon which the Israeli militaristic culture is based is what might be termed the 'founding myths' around which the society's identity has been constructed. One such narrative has been the nature of the 1948 War of Independence which lay the basis for the Zionist state and which was also the occasion for the destruction of Palestinian villages and the ethnic cleansing of the land. One group that has sought to challenge this pillar of Israeli-Jewish self-identity has been *Zochrot* (Remembering) which was founded in 2002 with the aim of bringing knowledge of the Palestinian *Nakbha* to Israelis. One of the basic assumptions of their work has been that awareness and recognition of the *Nakbha* by Israeli-Jewish people, and their acknowledgement that they carry some responsibility for this tragedy, is a necessary condition for any meaningful process of reconciliation between the two peoples. Their activities include: 1. Exhibitions and other initiatives to raise the issue; 2. Tours to destroyed villages, along with booklets in Hebrew to explain what happened; 3. Posting signs in Hebrew and Arabic indicating the sites of destroyed villages and places; 4. Collecting oral histories and testimonies; and 5. Working with teachers to explore ways to introduce coverage of the *Nakbha* into the formal and informal curricula.[17] One of their members spoke to us at length about the challenges they face:

> How to speak the *Nakbha* in Hebrew is the core of our mission. ... We know Israelis know very little about the *Nakbha*. Knowing about it is to acknowledge it. And hopefully this would bring us to take responsibility for it. We have a responsibility for the future, to open the possibility for reconciliation between Jews and Arabs living here. ...
>
> Most of our actions are on the cultural level rather than petitions, to influence discourse. ... Nowadays there are so many Israelis without hope. They don't think any more about peace. But for those of us who retain hope, then we must address the *Nakbha*. We know that without addressing the roots of the refugees and Israel as a state of the Jews, then there is no real solution. When you learn about the *Nakbha* you understand that there were and are many morally wrong things done and attempts to resolve the conflict neglect this. You cannot have real peace without including those so wrongfully displaced. Palestinians will never give up this right to return.
>
> A Jewish state is a terrible thing for us Israelis – a state established on the ruined lives of Palestinians. If the state remains like this, we are sentenced to be colonisers forever. A democratic state with the right of return is my chance, for me and my family to be liberated. ... The biggest challenge is the reality of the Jewish state, it is in the 'nature of things'. Anything that challenges this is met with trauma. To acknowledge the *Nakbha* is to challenge this 'state of nature.'

Legal work

As was noted in Chapter 5, Palestinians over recent years have had most success in resisting the expropriation of their land due to the route of the Wall or the actions of settlers through using the Israeli legal system, for which they have relied upon Israeli partners. Particular mention was made in Chapter 5 of the role played by Rabbis for Human Rights in challenging the military expulsion orders imposed on villagers in the South Hebron Hills whilst Yesh Din (There is law) was closely involved in the case that resulted in the re-routing of the Wall near Bil'in. Both these organisations illustrate particular facets of the broader

Israeli peace and solidarity movement in their work challenging the threats to human rights posed by the occupation.

Rabbis for Human Rights (RFHR) was founded in 1988 during the first intifada. During its early years, according to one of its founding members, 'we saw ourselves as an *announcing tool* rather than a grass-roots organisation.' He explained, 'By our presence we could announce there was a more spiritual and moral approach to issues ... Five rabbis emerging from a taxi can create an impact!' By the 1990s RFHR's main focus had shifted to combating house demolitions, and its members were involved in the formation of the Israeli Committee Against House Demolitions (ICAHD). During the second intifada the emphasis shifted again to working in support of Palestinian farmers, and some of the members were involved in the formation of Ta'ayush. This focus continued through their involvement alongside Ta'ayush with the situation of the villagers of the South Hebron Hills, where they were instrumental in obtaining court orders affirming the right of Palestinians to have military protection from settlers when accessing their land. Our informant concluded the interview by reflecting on the particular character of RFHR and the challenges faced.

We have one foot in the grassroots and the other in the corridors of power. We are now trying to develop a third foot. We obtain court victories but these have no impact on the public. So now we are using social media at certain targeted sectors.

Also we are rabbis – we bring a different perspective from others.

In some ways we are the right-wing of the anti-occupation movement. There is a difference between human rights and peace organisations   we do not get involved in issues about final status etc. We say the occupation must end for the sake of human rights, peace is necessary for human rights – but not what kind of peace settlement.

We are rabbis and we are *Rabbis for Human Rights* – we have two Torahs. Our commitment is that the occupation must end in order for us to create a society embodying the fact that we are all made in God's image.

We are committed to nonviolence, although we do not have the same interest in civil disobedience we once had ... In 2001 we were dismantling road blocks – we would not do that now. We are becoming more of an institution. We are involved in educational work at the army academies. Our educational and legal work has grown. ... We have four mandates: prevent human rights abuses, develop a new way of understanding Judaism, breaking down stereotypes of Palestinians, and restoring hope.

After we had concluded our interview with the RFHR member we moved to an adjoining room to meet with a small group of Jerusalem-based peace activists from groups such as Sheik Jarrar Solidarity, Ta'ayush and Machsom

Watch (Checkpoint Watch).[18] It reminded us of how small the community of activists is in Israel, and in Jerusalem in particular. Indeed, if one was to map the different groups it would resemble something of a family tree – activists move from one group to another, creating new ones in response to a fresh challenge or opportunity. So, just as activists from RFHR participated in the establishment of ICAHD and Ta'ayush, so activists from Machsom Watch were involved in the establishment of another group involved in legal challenges to occupation practices and abuses – Yesh Din. This was in 2005 after they realised that in addition to reporting abuses and infringements at checkpoints there was a need to provide legal support for Palestinians.

Since then the work of Yesh Din has developed along three related tracks. Track one has focused on law enforcement in relation to the actions of Israeli settlers in the West Bank. By the end of 2013 they had handled over one thousand cases, each one involving documentation by volunteers, escorting Palestinians to police stations to report incidents, taking on power of attorney in order to follow up on complaints until the files were closed.[19] The second track has involved similar types of engagement but in relation to members of the Israeli occupation forces who stand idly by whilst abuses are perpetrated by settlers against Palestinians.[20] The third track has involved dealing with land confiscation and illegal seizures, usually by settlers but also by the state. Yesh Din's normal response is to complain to the police on behalf of the Palestinian landowners, petition the High Court to issue an administrative order to expel the settlers, and then petition the court to enforce its own orders. At the time of our meeting with staff and volunteers from Yesh Din (November 2013) they told us they had 20 cases active at that time relating to land seizures, with others in process that had not yet reached the court. In addition to this casework, Yesh Din has also published reports based on the information gathered by volunteers and the results of its casework, which have then been used to engage with decision makers and raise issues in the public domain.[21] We emerged from the meeting wondering how staff and volunteers managed to keep their heads above water, such was the extent of the demands and pressures they were facing. Our companion, an experienced Israeli peace activist we have known for several years, contextualised some of the challenges facing groups like Yesh Din:

> In earlier days of the struggle against the occupation, people thought there is not enough information about what is going on, we need to inform the Israeli public. This approach failed. There is a lot of information now, but the Israeli public doesn't want to see it. Also initiatives to promote dialogue have failed. So the legal channel is the most recent route – and as a consequence the government is trying to limit the powers of the court and undermine its relative autonomy. There is a huge struggle going on with attempts to limit the court powers and the politicisation of court appointments.

CHALLENGES FACING ISRAELI PEACE AND SOLIDARITY ACTIVISTS

As researchers and human beings we have been repeatedly moved and touched with admiration and regard for our Palestinian friends, contacts and activists who have managed to hold on to their humanity whilst summoning the courage to put their bodies and their livelihoods repeatedly at risk by openly defying the occupation regime under which they are forced to live. But we have also experienced the same feelings after spending time with our Israeli friends, contacts and activists who have also inspired us by the power of their example, by their courage in holding on to their moral and political convictions in the face of the incomprehension and animosity of their fellow citizens for whom they remain deviants, undesirables – even traitors. Often after spending time interviewing Israel activists in Tel Aviv or Jerusalem we would express our amazement to each other as to how they continued to summon the will to persist in challenging the taken-for-granted views of the 'moral majority' in Israel. To understand why we felt such regard it is important to understand the nature of the challenges they face in pursuing their vocation.

Public indifference to the occupation

Israeli peace activists are marginalised within their own society. Moreover, they are viewed as threats to the national interest by some of the more right-wing networks in Israel, with the offices of several organisations having been damaged on a number of occasions. As one of our informants, an active member of Machsom Watch, told us, 'Breaking the Silence – those who admit to having done terrible things, they are viewed as traitors. My friends distance themselves from anything to do with Machsom Watch.' Furthermore, as has been observed already the mainstream of Israeli Jewish society would seem to have little interest in the occupation or Palestinian popular resistance. As one activist informed us, 'The Israeli public has no interest in ending the occupation as it has no effect on their lives – they are not occupied. The occupation is irrelevant to them.' Another activist, a regular participant in Friday protests at places like Nabi Saleh and Al-Masara reflected ruefully on the lack of impact such actions had on the Israeli public, 'It is not so much that the protest actions are delegitimised, it is that they are virtually non-existent for the Israeli public. There is no reporting of the Friday protests' He told us of a discussion he had with a prominent television reporter,

> According to the journalist you could go to the editor of Channel Two news with the best possible story about the West Bank and they would not use it. No one is interested in stories about Arabs. If you ran it your ratings would decline. The Israeli media fosters ignorance about Palestinians and the Arab

world. Their position is 'We don't want to bring this kind of thing to the public, they are not interested.'

Furthermore, even when Palestinian protest actions are covered by the media, the actions are framed through the lens of the threat of violence. As one media specialist advised us,

> Bil'in, Al-Masara etc., they have become routine and they are portrayed as violent. The media consumers would not know what goes on there and what the protestors want. They are perceived as trying to disturb the soldiers, our children! This perception of the soldiers is very deep. ... The Israeli media covers the popular resistance as a security matter, with the focus on *how* to cope with the problem, not with *why* it happens, not the root of the matter. The protesters are seen as wild youngsters, *shabab*, who attack our children the soldiers.

Given that media coverage is the life blood of nonviolent resisters, who rely on it as a means of communicating and influencing target constituencies, at least one Israeli solidarity group (Women Who Disobey) resorted to taking out paid advertising space in order to get the word out about their activities.

Loss of hope

In circumstances of such political isolation and marginalisation it is perfectly understandable that one of the main challenges Israeli activists face is how to combat their loss of hope for the future. As one of their number explained, 'The main challenge we face is how to engage more Israeli activists. Despair and alienation prevent many activists from engaging with education and advocacy in Israeli society.' And, of course, once you start to lose hope you start to question the nature of your commitment to the 'cause', you start to lose the will to continue the struggle, especially when the cost in terms of social pressures from friends and family aligned with the stress of occupying a different moral universe from the majority of your fellow citizens takes its toll.[22] Some sense of this pressure was conveyed to us by a woman activist who we interviewed at a roadside café; she had agreed to interrupt her return journey after attending the funeral of a friend and fellow activist, who had been a founder of Machsom Watch and Yesh Din. Maybe it was this context that led her to express herself so forcefully:

> There was the second intifada – nothing came out of that and the buses being blown up. Now the buses are not being blown up and still nothing comes out of it. Israelis are comfortable with the situation. ... People look the other

way – it tears me to pieces seeing the conditions in the West Bank and then going into a shopping mall in Tel Aviv … I can get so angry. I bug people … people live with it.

Later in the interview we asked if she had any hope for the future?

Not really – maybe if there was real resistance. I fear that we are all sinking into a swamp. There will be an explosion someday. The responsibility is on Israelis to change. We are the masters. Resistance might help Israelis come to their senses. … The only hope is that the world really puts Israel in a position where she cannot live comfortably and ignore the occupation. Yes – the boycott. At first the Israelis will say this is anti-Semitic. But they will want the business – so what will be necessary for that?[23]

So how do such activists sustain themselves in their struggle? How do they keep their sanity and their will to resist? One way is by counting their 'small victories'. As one member of the Solidarity group that grew from the Sheikh Jarrah Solidarity Movement expressed it:

The forces we fight are very strong. The government, the wealthy, the Israeli public. We are very far from our ideal. For us a small success is a house not demolished, settlement plans frustrated. Also, when we bring Israelis who did not want to know to a demonstration and they experience the violence from the soldiers, for the first time they are victims of their own soldiers.

Another method that has been adopted by social, religious and politically deviant minorities throughout history has been withdrawal, whether this has been the spatial separation pursued by religious sects isolating themselves from the profane world or the social separation sought by radicals who only feel comfortable with folk of their own kind. So it is in Israel. In Jerusalem there is a particular bar where solidarity activists can meet and relax. More such venues exist in the secular city of Tel Aviv. Demonstrations can also be occasions for socialising and conviviality with your comrades. And increasingly there are the electronic networks, the social media, through which people can create their own virtual communities of people with shared views who can talk and interact together, albeit over the internet. Others survive through pure will and stoicism. As one veteran activist confessed, 'You never know in advance what is going to work – sometimes something might happen! … I have to confess I have given up on the Israeli public – we lost them along the way.' Others continue their struggle because each time they witness the abuses perpetrated on Palestinians in the name of Israel their anger, shame – and the desire to redeem their own society – galvanises them back into action. As one such activist explained to us:

I cannot not do it. It was Arundhati Roy who wrote, 'Once you have seen it, you cannot un-see it.' It touches me. I cannot live in Israel and know what is happening and not try to shout it out. ... The energy also comes from the people themselves – for me to say 'I can't take it anymore' is a luxury the Palestinians I work with do not have. I have such privileges. We can do whatever we want – we have all the rights and privileges. The people of *Makhoul* cannot say 'I can't take it anymore!' ... And we do have small successes – simple things like help someone who has been detained get home – this is also a source of energy.

Emerging from interviews with such people we invariably felt energised. But it is important to recognise that so many Israeli activists do get burned out. They devote so much time and energy and commitment to the struggle that their personal and professional lives suffer, and when the substantive achievements are so small and seemingly insignificant in the context of the wider picture, then it is not surprising that there is a high 'drop-out' rate as people become exhausted, dispirited and bone-tired and weary. Consequently, it is important to acknowledge the strength of will, the resilience and the moral stature of such people. Probably the bulk of Israeli solidarity activists would define themselves as secular Jews, but many of them would identify with the sentiments expressed by an activist from Rabbis for Human Rights:

What sustains me? Maybe it is like moving deckchairs on the Titanic but some changes have happened. In Judaism we say 'Save a life and you save the world'. Our work at the micro-level will not change everything, but it is important that we should play our part and have faith in God or whatever that things are moving and you never know what effect your actions might have.

8

AID, ADVOCACY AND RESILIENCE: THE ROLE OF INTERNATIONAL HUMANITARIAN AID AGENCIES

INTRODUCTION

Humanitarian aid involving the intervention of agencies across state borders has traditionally been justified by the mission to relieve suffering whether caused by natural disasters or by war. Agencies such as the International Committee of the Red Cross (ICRC) were guided by their founding principles of neutrality, impartiality and universality – humanitarian aid should be provided to all on the basis of need, irrespective of political allegiance or any other consideration. To fulfil this moral imperative the ICRC adhered to a strict policy of only intervening in a conflict zone with the consent of all parties, thereby avoiding allegations of partiality that might threaten its humanitarian work. Over the last decade or so, however, international humanitarian agencies (IHA) have been urged to extend their activities beyond the short-term relief of suffering into 'developmental relief' and 'peace-building', as donors have sought non-military modes of conflict management in different regions of the world. This has raised a range of dilemmas for IHAs – whereas traditionally they might have *worked around* conflict, that is avoided working in conflict-affected areas, they have come under pressure not only to *work in* conflict (continue to deliver aid in the midst of violent conflict) but also to *work on* conflict in the sense of linking their humanitarian aid to efforts to reduce the incidence and address the causes of violent conflict. This 'politicisation' of aid has called into question the adequacy of the old principles of neutrality and impartiality as guidelines for coping with the challenges faced by agencies intervening in internal wars and protracted violent conflicts.

POLITICISATION AND SECURITISATION OF AID TO THE PALESTINIAN TERRITORIES

Of course humanitarian aid has always been shaped in part by its geopolitical environment. In a commonly quoted observation Mary Anderson noted:

When international assistance is given in the context of a violent conflict, it becomes part of that context and thus also of the conflict. Although aid agencies often seek to be neutral or nonpartisan towards the winners and losers of a war, the impact of their aid is not neutral regarding whether the conflict worsens or abates.[1]

At no time has this been more apparent than in the years since the September 11, 2001 terrorist assaults on targets in the USA and the subsequent 'war on terror'. There has been an increasing trend for humanitarian aid delivery to be ever more closely integrated into national security agendas. Security is no longer just about targeting direct threats with bombs and bullets, it is also about social and economic development as a means of reducing the risk of new destabilising threats. Nowhere is this more true than in Israel/OPT where the delivery of aid has been closely aligned with the agendas of the donors.

Thus, in the years prior to the Oslo Accords of 1993 international aid was used to encourage both sides to the peace table. Following the signing of the Declaration of Principles international donors met in Washington and pledged to provide approximately $2.4 billion to the proposed Palestinian Authority (PA) as a means of fuelling Palestinian economic growth in order to ensure a tangible 'peace dividend' for Palestinians and thereby bolster support for the peace process. As it happened, throughout the 1990s the PA faced endemic economic and financial problems and many believe it was the influx of foreign aid that forestalled the collapse of the local economy, with foreign aid meeting the budgetary shortfalls of the PA and funding various housing construction and emergency employment generation programmes. The outbreak of the second intifada in 2000 brought an end to that phase of the 'peace process', which in turn resulted in a doubling of foreign aid to the PA from $500 million to $1 billion as a means of sustaining the administration until the peace process could be revived.[2]

The political agenda of the international donors became even more transparent after the electoral success of Hamas in 2006. Funding for the PA was halted whilst Israel refused to transfer the customs revenues on Palestinian goods entering via Israeli ports – the result was entirely predictable as poverty rates soared and the Palestinian economy fell into recession.[3] Refusing to direct funds to the coalition government and its administration insofar as Hamas was classified as a terrorist organisation, international donors (and here the key players were the USA and European Union) started to channel funding through the office of the President, Mahmoud Abbas, the leader of Fatah, and thereby participated quite directly in the fragmentation of the Palestinian political house. Throughout this period very little attention was given to international humanitarian law which quite simply affirms that the welfare of Palestinians is the obligation of Israel as the occupying state. From this perspective the charge could be levelled that foreign donors have been acting, however unintentionally, in a manner that reinforces the occupation insofar as it is foreign funds that help maintain the basic services which, according to international humanitarian law, should be the responsibility of Israel. It is foreign aid which funds the reconstruction of what Israel destroys and humanitarian aid that enables Palestinians to cope with the assault on their basic needs occasioned by Israeli restrictions on movement, access and other forms of repression that are an inevitable dimension of any occupation.[4]

It is the awareness of this dilemma that troubles many of the committed people working to deliver relief and development services to Palestinians in the occupied territories – this sense that whilst they are responding to the needs of the local population as best they can, they are in effect dealing with the symptoms and consequences of the occupation. As one aid worker told us: 'They [the Israelis] use us. This is a dilemma. If you see the inhuman conditions people are living in – do you talk about the right of return or try to change their circumstances?' By delivering services that under international humanitarian law are the responsibility of Israel as the occupying power they are, in effect, helping the occupation to be more bearable. The challenge they face is how to respond to the humanitarian needs of the Palestinians and help to strengthen Palestinian resistance and resilience without reinforcing the occupation. In the remainder of this chapter we shall explore the ways in which certain aid agencies have addressed this challenge and thereby sought to play a role in promoting a sustainable peace.

ABANDONING NEUTRALITY

Historically many humanitarian relief agencies were established in response to the horrors of war. Their forerunner was the International Committee of the Red Cross (ICRC) which was founded in 1863 to provide humanitarian help to people affected by conflict and armed violence. Over the years the ICRC has developed a number of key principles to guide its mission and its work.

Universality: the humanitarian imperative entails the preparedness to act to prevent and alleviate suffering wherever the need arises.

Impartiality: the provision of assistance must be based on need alone and not on distinctions of race, religion, or political persuasion.

Neutrality: humanitarian agencies such as the ICRC should not take sides in a conflict. This principle is necessary, according to the ICRC, 'In order to continue to enjoy the confidence of all, the Movement may not take sides in hostilities or engage at any time in controversies of a political, racial, religious or ideological nature.'[5]

Of these principles it has been the third one (neutrality) that has proven the most problematic for many agencies, particularly those involved in providing humanitarian assistance in the OPT. How can you remain neutral in relation to a conflict generated in a context where one side is occupying the land and inflicting suffering on the other? Yes, you can be impartial insofar as there is a humanitarian imperative to respond to suffering on whichever 'side' it occurs, but to be neutral in a situation where one side persists in contravening international law and the Geneva Conventions – that is more problematic. And one option is to abandon the commitment. This was most forcefully expressed by the director of the American Friends Service Committee commenting on their Middle East programme who was reported to have declared 'We are not neutral. We are for equality and justice.' A representative of an agency concerned with providing health care in the West Bank explained to us: 'Being completely neutral here is not acceptable. What does it mean? Does it mean turning a blind eye? The poor – why are they poor? It is because of the Israeli blockade.' At the same meeting a worker with a British agency commented, 'You cannot be neutral but you can be impartial.'

In other words, it would seem that one of the prerequisites of a conflict transformation approach to humanitarian assistance in the OPT is to abandon the traditional principle of neutrality – refraining from taking sides in the conflict – and acknowledging that the occupation is the prime reason for the suffering of the Palestinians in the occupied territories and this should be the prism through which one's intervention and delivery of humanitarian assistance is planned and evaluated.

AID TO SUPPORT RESILIENCE (*SUMUD*)

In the South Hebron Hills we met a local Palestinian, employed by an aid agency, who visited his hamlet at regular intervals to check on attendance at the school funded by his employers. The reason was to strengthen the resilience of the local people, to strengthen their will to resist pressures on them to leave their land. As he explained to us,

> The Bedouin area needs to change. Now we have nearly 42 children in the school. ... I am monitoring them and every month I go to organise after-school programmes for teaching the students that have lower marks in one subject. I cannot allow a single student to leave the school. If they want to leave the school I go to them, to the father, the mother of the student and say they must come back. ... If there is a family or student with low income and they cannot afford to study I have links with a university to try to do

something to keep this child in school ... They give us the computers, the chairs to improve the centre and do something for the community.

You are not allowed to do anything in this place. It is forbidden to dig a well. ... We have a demolition order for all the houses you can see in this place. They have forbidden electricity, forbidden water. All the time they are saying this area is for the settlement and they use the places where we used to take our sheep to graze. They are trying to make us leave our land. But despite all these things, with this bad situation, we are staying in our houses. ... Nowadays we do not think of moving from our place. They come to us and say go to another place, we will give you houses, with running water and electricity. ... We say no. No one in our community has said they want to leave.

This approach is an excellent illustration of how an activity that from one perspective can be viewed as humanitarian relief can also be seen as a means of strengthening community resilience in the face of enduring pressure and repression. It is an approach that has informed the work of a number of agencies whose representatives we met during our research.

A West Bank representative of a UK-based humanitarian agency told us how 'Our mission is not only to provide services for the needy but also to advocate by doing – to improve livelihoods so that people can continue to live and remain on their land.' He gave an example – when they provided kidney dialysis equipment for a Bedouin community, that enabled the people to remain on their land and resist Israeli pressure to dislodge them. A representative of a German agency explained how they supported the Israeli group Community Electricity and Technology Middle East (COMET-ME) in providing solar power for Bedouins in the South Hebron Hills: 'It is not so much about development as supporting the fight for space and to remain.' In similar vein one agency worker described how they were providing aid to help villagers construct a road to improve access to their fields and thereby strengthen local resilience. He explained, 'Settlers approached our bulldozer and threatened the driver. We don't say we are doing this to help the local villagers to stay on their land and so prevent loss to settlers – we say we are improving access to land to enhance their livelihoods.'

A more difficult decision for agencies than engaging in slight subterfuge is what to do in the face of the virtual blanket refusal of the Israeli authorities to grant building permits for any kind of structure throughout the large tracts of land that have been designated as Area C, covering over 60 per cent of the West Bank, and which is under Israeli control and where the writ of the Palestinian Authority does not run.[6] According to the UN Office for the Coordination of Humanitarian Affairs (OCHA), between January 2000 and September 2007, over 94 per cent of applications submitted by Palestinians to the Israeli authorities for building permits in Area C were denied. Shir Hever, author of *The*

Political Economy of Israel's Occupation, has argued that Western governments and NGOs need to be more active in opposing such restrictions that are an integral part of the Israeli occupation regime, claiming that 'donors put 99 per cent of their work in doing what is allowed and 1 per cent in protesting conditions.'[7] Sensitive to the charge that adhering to the permit regime helps legitimise the occupation, some agencies have proven themselves prepared to face the challenge, the representative of one of them informing us that:

> In the Jordan Valley using private donations – we have built two kindergartens without permits. So far there have been no demolition orders. ... The Israeli civil administration has provided us with a list of locations where they say we have a higher chance of obtaining a permit – but how can we allow ourselves to be dictated to in such a manner?[8]

PRIORITISING HUMAN RIGHTS AND THE PRINCIPLE OF UNIVERSALITY

Up until the late 1980s the spheres of development and human rights were deemed to be separate. In part this was due to the rhetoric of the Cold War period when the Western powers championed civil and political rights whilst the state socialist regimes prioritised economic rights, with the result that the relationship between the two was obscured. This began to change with the end of the Cold War and the two fields began to move closer together. During this period there was a questioning of the stance of the development community that had heretofore considered economic development to be the way to address all basic human needs. As this school of thought and practice came to lose credibility in the context of the ongoing marginalisation of the poor and excluded, so there grew an awareness that participation and the rights of citizenship (including non-discriminatory practices and accountability) were necessary elements of any poverty-alleviation programme. This achieved more widespread recognition in 1993 at a UN conference on Human Rights held in Vienna where it was acknowledged that 'Development and respect for human rights and fundamental freedoms are interdependent and mutually reinforcing'. That same year the UN Secretary-General also acknowledged that 'human rights are inherent to the promotion of peace, security, economic prosperity and social equality'. In 1999 the Overseas Development Institute attempted to delineate the key features of this approach which informs the programmes of those agencies seeking to incorporate a conflict transformation dimension to their work in the OPT.

A rights-based approach to development sets the achievement of human rights as an objective of development. It uses thinking about human rights as the scaffolding of development policy. It invokes the international apparatus of human rights accountability in support of development action. In all of these, it is concerned not just with civil and political (CP) rights (the right to a trial, not to be tortured), but also with economic, social and cultural (ESC) rights (the right to food, housing, a job).[9]

The implications of this approach for agencies working in the OPT are significant. The Palestinians are denied so many of their basic human rights by the occupying power, and consequently – from the perspective of a rights-based approach – they should be empowered to make legitimate claims on those whose responsibility it is to protect their entitlements. And indeed when one examines the claims made by representatives of a number of agencies working in the region one finds clear reference to their rights-based approach. Thus on the Christian Aid website we can read:

> *Christian Aid* has been working with the poorest in the region since the early 1950s, when we provided help to Palestinian refugees. Today we are working with more than 20 Israeli and Palestinian organisations to protect human rights, access to services and resources, and to build a peace based on justice for all.

DanChurchAid (DCA) has used comparable language to portray the nature of its approach:

> *DCA* is committed to promoting rights-based development and gender equality in all of our programmes. ... The drive to promote the interests and rights of the poorest, most marginalised and discriminated men and women is interlinked with our core values.

Oxfam UK has also adopted the language of human rights:

> Ensuring the basic rights for ordinary women, men, and children is fundamental to the success of any peace process. Oxfam is against the use of violence against civilians in any form and calls on all parties to protect civilians from harm ... We work directly with partners, allies and communities and we seek to influence the powerful to ensure that poor people can improve their lives and livelihoods and have a say in decisions that affect them. We believe that respect for human rights will help lift people out of poverty.

Perhaps the most explicit statement by an agency regarding its commitment to a rights-based approach has been articulated by the Swiss faith-based agency HEKS. In their strategy paper for the period 2008 to 2012 they explained:

> The rights enshrined in the Universal Declaration of Human Rights, the UN agreements on civil, political, economic, social and cultural rights, are also ground-breaking. *HEKS* constantly endeavours to ensure that people know their rights and are in a position to claim them. It strives to ensure that all people can live in dignity.

It is axiomatic that human rights are inherent to all human beings, whatever their race, religion or gender. This principle of universality was enshrined in the first article of the 1948 Universal Declaration of Human Rights: 'All human beings are born free and equal in dignity and rights.' The recognition of this principle – that what holds for one side in the conflict also holds for the other – is quite central to the approach of agencies pursuing a conflict transformational approach in the region. What it means in practice is a preparedness to work not only with Palestinian but also with Israeli partners. As one agency expressed it, 'Our work is shaped by its recognition of Israelis' and Palestinians' shared humanity and the importance of working with both peoples to end the conflict, based on the principles of equality, rights and justice.'

WORKING WITH ISRAELI PARTNERS

Aid agencies that believe it is important to work with Israeli partners in addition to Palestinians have found that it provokes serious problems in their working relationship with their Palestinian partners, exposing them to allegations of 'normalization' which can undermine their legitimacy and credibility in the eyes of their partners and wider Palestinian publics.

To understand this challenge a little background analysis is necessary. Following the Oslo Accords and the attendant hopes of a sustainable peace process unfolding between Israel and Palestinians, there was a flood of initiatives funded by international donors to promote dialogue and other forms of 'people-to-people' encounters between Israelis and Palestinians. Indeed, it has been estimated that between September 1993 and October 2000 there were about 500 people-to-people projects involving over 100 organisations and a total budget of $20–30 million.[10] Whilst these encounters were taking place, the Israeli occupation was deepening. The confiscation of land and the expansion of settlements continued at an accelerated pace and the West Bank and Gaza Strip (prior to Israeli withdrawal) were divided into cantons separated from each other by Israeli-controlled territory. Innumerable checkpoints and barriers had been set up throughout the territories controlling the movement of Palestinians and enabling the Israelis to lock them into their particular enclaves, with disastrous consequences for economic activity and general living standards. Moreover, as Sara Roy has observed, 'In these policies Israel relied on the Palestinian Authority and its vast security apparatus to maintain control of the population, suppress any visible forms of opposition, and provide protection for Israeli actions.'[11]

As a consequence of these developments 'peace' became a dirty word for many Palestinians insofar as it was associated with 'pacification'. This was accompanied by a deepening disgust and distrust of any initiative that appeared to be an attempt to promote superficial 'normal relationships' between Israelis and Palestinians within the context of a deepening occupation. The term 'normalization' was used to refer to this practice, described by one source as:

> Economic, political, cultural and institutional normalization legitimize Israel's oppression of the Palestinian people by giving the appearance of normalcy to the relationship between oppressor and oppressed. This relationship is hardly one between equals as Israel continues to violate our inalienable rights, steal our land, and prevent refugees from our right of return in contravention of international law and numerous UN resolutions.[12]

From this perspective any initiative can be deemed to be an example of normalization if it 'is designed to bring together – whether directly or indirectly – Palestinians with Israelis (whether individuals or institutions) and is *not* explicitly designed to resist or expose the occupation and all forms of discrimination and oppression inflicted upon the Palestinian people.[13] It follows from this that any agency seeking to integrate a conflict transformation approach into their humanitarian interventions needs to be very clear about the principles underpinning such a strategic choice, being particularly clear about the ways in which their partnership with Israeli groups and organisations does not constitute 'normalization'.

The principles informing the agencies that seemed to us to be pursuing a conflict transformation agenda appeared to be twofold.[14] First was that of universality – human rights are *human* rights, not Palestinian or Israeli. So, just as work with Palestinian partners might be premised on empowering the beneficiaries to claim their entitlements as human beings, so there are sections of the population within Israel who are also marginalised, discriminated against and denied equal rights – especially the Palestinian citizens of Israel. Second, there was an awareness that any move towards transforming the ongoing conflict in the direction of a sustainable peace required significant changes in Israeli attitudes and practices in relation to the Palestinians and the occupation. As the representative of one agency explained to us, 'The objective of our work in Israel is to strengthen Israeli civil society working for change in the OPT. ... We recognise that changes in Israeli policy are the ones that will have the most effect on Palestinian lives, the idea is to strengthen Israeli civil society through different entry points.'

This support for Israeli peace groups and organisations that challenge the consensus within Israeli society could also be informed by an awareness that such oppositional groups face sustained threats of persecution on account of their minority views and as such need support and solidarity from outside. As one of our informants representing a small US-funded agency in Jerusalem phrased it, 'There is tension between the pressure from the US to work with Israelis and the pressure from Palestinian partners to avoid normalization ... But we do see importance in unmasking the occupation and supporting groups that are persecuted here in Israel.'

Our research revealed that international agencies that attempted to 'work across the divide' with Israeli and Palestinian partners tended to support the work of Israeli groups and organisations that fell into one or more of four categories.[15]

1. Those focusing on promoting and defending the human rights of particular sections of the Israeli public – particularly the Palestinians citizens of Israel

The Arab Association for Human Rights: Founded in 1988 by lawyers and community activists to promote and protect the political, civil, economic and cultural rights of the Palestinian Arab minority in Israel from an international human rights perspective.

Association for Civil Rights in Israel: Established in 1972 with a mandate to ensure Israel's accountability and respect for human rights, by addressing violations committed by the Israeli authorities in Israel, the Occupied Territories, or elsewhere.

Adalah: ('Justice' in Arabic) Established in 1996 to promote and defend the rights of Palestinian Arab citizens of Israel.

ADRID: Established to represent Palestinian Arabs in Israel who were displaced from their homes during the 1948 war and *Nakbha*.

Baladna Association for Arab Youth: Based in Haifa, working with Palestinian Arab youth in Israel on issues of concern to them such as discrimination in education and youth provision, the question of identity, and countering state initiatives 'aimed at making us good Arab-Israelis under Jewish hegemony.'

Druze Initiative Committee: Established in 1971 to support those from the Druze community in Israel who refuse military service.

Kayan: Established in 1999 to promote and defend the human rights of Palestinian Arab women in Israel.

2. Those seeking to change the dominant attitudes and practices towards the Palestinians and the occupation

Breaking the Silence: Established by combatants who have served in the Israeli military since the start of the second intifada, who try to use their experience and testimony to expose the Israeli public to the reality of occupation and the price to be paid when young soldiers are engaged in controlling the everyday life of a people.

Coalition of Women For Peace: Established in 2000 after the start of the second intifada as a coalition of feminist peace organisations but now exists as a 'free-standing organisation'. 'We are trying to understand what is a feminist opposition to the occupation. ... We are trying to find connections between feminist thinking and the occupation.'

Gun-free Kitchen Tables: Established in 2010 by women activists from Machsom Watch, campaigns for small-arms control in Israel, which can be used as a way of raising critical questions about the linkage between domestic violence and militarism in Israel society – 'We are getting a wedge in the door of militarist consciousness.'

Israeli Committee Against House Demolitions: Established in 1997 to campaign to end the occupation, mainly by resisting Israeli policy of demolishing Palestinian homes in the OPT and within Israel.

New Profile: A feminist movement of men and women seeking to challenge and undermine the militarisation of Israeli society and culture in all its many manifestations, focusing in particular on conscription and the 'right to refuse'.

Zochrot: Established in 2002 to promote awareness in Israeli society of the Palestinian *Nakbha* of 1948, thereby raising questions about the moral foundation of the State of Israel. 'We are revealing hidden pasts that make possible different futures. ... We are working for a sustainable future.'

3. Those seeking to use the space they have within Israel to promote and defend the human rights of Palestinians living under occupation

B'tselem (Israeli Information Centre for Human Rights in the Occupied Territories): Established in 1989, seeks to document and inform the Israeli public and policy makers about the human rights violations in the OPT.

Gisha: Founded in 2005, works to protect the rights of Palestinians, particularly Gaza residents, with regard to freedom of movement – especially to facilitate access to education, employment, family members and health care.

Yesh Din: Established in 2005, seeks to protect the human rights of Palestinians living under occupation by taking up individual cases through the Israeli legal system and publishing reports as a means of advocacy.

4. Those groups in Israel that apply their expertise and resources to enhance the well-being, human rights and resilience of Palestinians living under occupation

Comet-ME: Provides renewable energy service (solar and wind-powered) for off-grid Palestinian communities in the South Hebron Hills.

Physicians for Human Rights: Established in 1988 is to promote a more fair and inclusive society in which the right to health is applied equally for all within Israel and the Palestinian occupied territories, informed by the belief that the occupation is the basis of human rights violations.[16]

ADVOCACY

Any humanitarian agency seeking to exercise an influence in transforming the conflict between Palestinians and Israelis must define its role not only in terms of promoting human rights, the delivery of aid and the facilitation of development in support of Palestinian resilience, but they must also take seriously the more overtly 'political role' of seeking to influence policy makers and publics – advocacy. This can be conducted by a variety of means – lobbying policy makers at national and international levels, issuing press releases and position statements, placing articles and op-ed pieces in the media, circulating sponsors and supporters with information sheets and appeals, sponsoring and supporting public demonstrations and petitions. But advocacy need not take on an oppositional or confrontational form – influence over policy makers can be exercised by agency specialists acting as consultants and expert witnesses for government committees and commissions. One of the most effective forms of advocacy is through witnessing: agency workers and their partners telling stories of their experiences living and working in the OPT.[17]

But should it be the role of humanitarian agencies to engage in the kind of overtly political manner entailed in advocacy? For those that do take their advocacy role seriously there are two main answers to this question. First of all, they point out that in the OPT the humanitarian need to which they try to respond has been created by political decisions, it follows therefore that if politics is recognised as one of the root causes, then humanitarians cannot ignore addressing it in their search for solutions. This reasoning has been evident at the time of writing, with Israel waging war on the Gaza Strip for the third time in five years in 'Operation Protective Edge', with a death toll exceeding 1,000 in Gaza (predominantly civilians) and over 50 Israeli fatalities. Many aid agencies issued moving appeals for an immediate ceasefire on humanitarian grounds – the slaughter must stop. But a number of these appeals were also linked with a recognition that the root causes of the recurring violence must be addressed for a sustainable ceasefire to be achieved. For example, this is the call issued by DanChurchAid on July 16, 2014:

> We now appeal to the international community to spare no effort to bring the parties in conflict to end military operations, and to ensure the firm application of International Humanitarian Law as well as International Human Rights Law. ... However a cease fire will not be enough. Long-term solutions must found, based on security for Palestinians as well as Israelis, Palestinian right to self-determination, and respect for international humanitarian and human rights law.[18]

A similar tone was adopted by Christian Aid in the UK:

> *Christian Aid* urges the international community to act immediately to bring about a ceasefire and address the root causes of the Israeli–Palestinian conflict to prevent this happening again. ... The current crisis is a result of decades of political failure. Without genuine dialogue and a determination from all sides to achieve a just peace, Palestinians and Israelis will be destined to live through the horrors of violence again and again.[19]

A second answer one receives when querying the legitimacy of humanitarian agencies engaging in political advocacy is the acknowledgement that pressure from their partners has been a factor. For many of the partners of international aid agencies the delivery of humanitarian aid is hollow without the political engagement deemed necessary to tackle the root causes of the humanitarian problems. Their demand is that the agency goes that extra step beyond saying the right things in their face-to-face encounters with partners and takes a public stand with the intention of influencing policy makers and publics at home and internationally.[20]

But whilst the focus on political advocacy has been increasing, it has also brought with it accusations that humanitarian charities are partisan, political and anti-Israel, particularly from the Israeli government, which operates with a very narrow definition of 'humanitarian'. According to one spokesperson '*Humanitarian* means they want to help in a humanitarian way, either in the field of health, or food, or welfare, if it is done without political judgement. ...

But when they take sides and start giving out political opinions, that's already non-humanitarian.'[21] Agencies have to try and negotiate a fine line between the risk of having restrictions placed on their work by the Israeli authorities and the moral and practical need to speak out. An illustration of how the Israeli occupiers can pressurise humanitarian agency staff was provided in an interview by someone working for a German-based aid agency.

> Our organisation had put its name to a report on settlement products in relation to the EU that was published in October 2012. I was called in to the Civil Administration for a 'friendly discussion' – but then there was an attempt at intimidation. We appealed to our own government regarding the kind of pressure being exerted on us by the Civil Administration – but there was no response. There was no pressure from the German government on Israel.[22]

The sharing of this experience at a round-table discussion of aid workers in East Jerusalem in November 2013 provoked a lengthy exchange about the manner in which Israeli authorities also use visa restrictions to exert pressure on expatriate humanitarian aid workers. This in turn led into criticisms of the participants' own governments for their apparent failure to act on the reports generated by the diplomatic staff based in the region. As one of the participants complained:

> The diplomats see the same things we see – and they produce reports for their desk officers in the capital cities. But something happens to them when they become desk officers. The desk officer at that time, he had worked here so he was familiar with how things are on the ground but … We were advised to be careful about the terms we used in relation to demolitions.

The reference to what language to use is significant, because agencies have to take into account not only the problems of provoking the Israeli authorities but also the risk of losing the support of their funders at home. It is this awareness that leads to a level of what might be termed 'self-censorship' on the part of agency staff when compiling their reports for 'home consumption'. As one worker with a church-based agency explained, when engaged in advocacy within their church, 'We do engage in some self-censorship – we do not want to upset our constituencies. We stress that we are working with partners who work non-violently for human rights.' Another participant in the discussion explained the constraints they faced in dealing with their constituencies in the USA:

> We do have to guard against criticisms of anti-Semitism, especially when we are calling for a boycott of those who are profiting from occupation. So we censor ourselves. We try to emphasise that we are criticising particular state policies, not the state itself. Also we tend to quote Israeli NGO sources to

support our position, but this has the unintended result of valorising Israeli sources over and above Palestinian ones. But it is the case that Israeli sources have legitimacy in certain parts of the world compared with Palestinian.

Our own research would seem to bear out this observation. Talking with a left-wing German member of parliament sympathetic to the Palestinian struggle in 2012, she recalled how impressed she had been by presentations by spokespeople from Breaking the Silence with their message that as long as Israeli soldiers could continue to act with impunity as occupiers, the atrocities and human rights abuses would continue to escalate. Unfortunately, it has also been our experience that Palestinians are not necessarily the best advocates of their own cause, certainly in the context of generating support in Europe. Too often when appearing in front of European audiences Palestinian spokespeople seem to think that it is sufficient to present their stories as victims and recount the horrors of living under occupation, and on occasion that emphasis on Palestinian victimhood can lead to comparison of their contemporary suffering with that of European Jewry in the Second World War. This is not the way to generate support from European constituencies – particularly in northern Europe. What does seem to have worked in terms of swaying audiences has been joint presentations by Palestinians and Israelis – groups like Combatants for Peace seem able to convey a particular credibility through their joint witnessing, storytelling and advocacy. But in a situation where the level of division, mistrust and bitterness towards the 'other' has escalated over the years, it has become increasingly difficult for Palestinians and Israelis to work together for peace.

This growing divide between Israeli and Palestinian activists for peace and justice is what makes the achievement of some international humanitarian agencies particularly significant, insofar as they have been able to create frameworks within which activists from the two sides can come together and even collaborate on joint projects. We have particular insight into the principles and practice of one such agency which has pursued the path of integrating a conflict transformation approach into its programmes in Israel/Palestine and we conclude this chapter with a brief overview of its main features.

HEKS-EPER: AN EXAMPLE OF A CONFLICT TRANSFORMATIONAL APPROACH TO HUMANITARIAN INTERVENTION IN ISRAEL AND PALESTINE

What is the key characteristic of your conflict transformation approach to developing partnerships in Palestine and Israel?
We try to address the factors that contribute to producing conflict. We try to empower civil society organisations so that they can help overcome the

▶

existing situation of conflict and inequality by non-violent means. ... We are concerned with structural violence, not just 'open violence'. Justice also has a big priority, which links with our human rights driven approach.

How does your approach differ from that of other humanitarian agencies?
Most do not have a conflict transformation perspective, most have a perspective that emphasises conflict sensitivity – being aware of the extent to which the conflict impacts on the capacity to fulfil their humanitarian mission. We say we are addressing some of the root causes – we are trying to at least. The civil society organisations being supported by HEKS are analysing the causes of conflict such as racism and inequality within Israel, the militarisation of Israeli society, and the unresolved refugee problem, in order to tackle them from a human rights standpoint.

In addition, HEKS and its partners are helping to protect the civilian population as well as human rights advocates and peace activists, for example, through accompaniment by international human rights observers under the Ecumenical Accompaniment Programme in Palestine and Israel (EAPPI).

The Ecumenical Accompaniers (EAs) are very important in our advocacy programme – particularly in outreach to church-goers and the general public. In 2014 we had a travelling exhibition to mark ten years of our involvement – it was very suitable for a church environment, it was part of our efforts to strengthen support within the churches. The EAs do a lot of local media work and get lots of responses. We send 12–14 EAs every year, so now we have a body of 120 people who have been EAs – and about half of them are still active.

You have Palestinian and Israeli partners. You have also developed a mechanism whereby they work together on certain projects ...
We established the Open Forum – a network for Jewish and Palestinian organisations in Israel as well as organisations in the occupied Palestinian territories and East Jerusalem. Over the years we have created a platform for these partner organisations to interchange ideas, and plan and implement joint projects. Through the framework of the Open Forum we focus on improving access to land, developing alternatives to the current unjust practices.

Also nowadays we are working directly with communities affected by lack of access to land, not just with partner NGOs. We are working with village councils directly in the area between Hebron and Bethlehem – a community-based approach. Normally HEKS works with local organisations but there are no Palestinian organisations that are strong on working with community-based organisations ... so we are working directly with the popular committees, the women's committees, the farmers.

▶

As we understand it your partners have been urging you to enhance your advocacy role in Switzerland and Europe.
Yes. It is becoming more difficult for us because one of our three strands is a focus on settlement products and trade. We were instrumental, with others, in getting a major supermarket chain in Switzerland to require its suppliers to label settlement products properly. This took place in 2013 after two years of dialogue, and we showed our support by placing an advert in a newspaper. This resulted in severe criticism from various churches and pro-Israel organisations and individuals.

A second important strand has been to focus on the Swiss churches – to strengthen the pressure for a just peace. We have organised study trips for key members of the Swiss protestant churches, made representations to the Federation of Swiss Protestant Churches and attempted to generate a broad discussion of the Kairos Document issued by the Palestinian Christian leadership endorsing the campaign for boycott, divestment and sanctions. The Ecumenical Accompaniers have played an important role in this programme.

The third main strand of our advocacy activities is membership of the Forum for Human Rights in Palestine and Israel. This is a working group of Swiss development and human rights organisations that attempts to keep the public informed about the human rights situation in Israel and Palestine, and suggests strategies to strengthen the position of human rights in the political process. The forum lobbies to persuade the Swiss authorities to take a more active role in pushing for a peace agreement based on the principles of international law insofar as Switzerland is the depositary state of the Geneva Conventions. As part of this work we secured the funding necessary to organise a study tour in Palestine and Israel for selected members of the Swiss parliament in 2012.

In addition we have an advocacy worker in Zurich and another one in Jerusalem, who is working to enhance the advocacy capacities of our partners, particularly to improve their advocacy of issues relating to refugees and access to land. We plan to have more delegations – when people see for themselves at first hand it makes a huge difference to what they are prepared to do. But it is a huge workload.

Will the 2014 war in Gaza affect your programmes because of a diversion of funding towards relief?
We are not so involved in relief so maybe we shall lose some funding. We hope it will not be a big problem but there are a lot of appeals for funding relief work at the moment and our sense is that private donors do respond to such appeals. …. And we are also competing with humanitarian crises in Syria and Iraq, and when there is no light at the end of the tunnel in terms of an end to the conflict, it is a challenge …

▶

Also in Switzerland there seemed to be reduced solidarity and support for Palestinians with the rockets being fired from Gaza, and there is a lack of trust in Hamas ... There is an anti-Islamist element, but also the feeling that they (Hamas) are responsible for the escalation ... this gets linked with Jihadist elements like ISIS, and of course Israel can play on this very easily. I think this is a European-wide phenomenon. Moreover, around the campaign over settlement products there have been charges of anti-Semitism, and HEKS has been mentioned in this context, so we have to be very cautious.

9

LINKS IN THE CHAIN –
INTERNATIONAL LEVERAGE?

*Without the internationals we would be like one hand clapping – they are the
other hand that we need.*

INTRODUCTION

One of the most significant (and discouraging) findings of our research is
that Palestinian popular resistance since the second intifada appears to have
exercised virtually no significant influence on large sections of the Israeli
public. Protests were not covered by the Israeli media, and it was reported to us
that if events were covered on news programmes people might switch channels
in order to avoid exposing themselves to such unwanted items. Despite this
lack of impact on the Israeli public and decision makers, it has touched and
affected a wide network of activists throughout the world – links in the
chain of nonviolence with the potential to act as significant intermediaries
and points of leverage in relation to the Israeli public and decision makers.
In other words the popular resistance has fed and nurtured the growth of
a burgeoning movement of international solidarity in favour of ending
the occupation and associated abuse of Palestinian human rights and civil
liberties. The growth of this movement can be attributed to a whole range of
factors which has led to an increasing international awareness of the brutality
of the Israeli occupation and the everyday oppression and humiliation suffered
by Palestinians. Undoubtedly the development of new forms of media and
communications technology has played an important part in this spread of
international awareness and concern, but there has been another significant
driver – the growth of advocacy for the Palestinian cause carried out by
individuals and groups who have personally witnessed the everyday reality of
what the occupation means to Palestinians during solidarity visits to the OPT.
The aims of this chapter are: first, to review the different forms of engagement
on the ground carried out by international activists and representatives of
civil society networks from around the world and second, to examine how

the different forms of engagement have fed into the growth of a transnational movement of movements campaigning for Palestinian human rights and an end to the occupation.[1]

FORMS OF ENGAGEMENT: DELEGATIONS AND STUDY TOURS

The phenomenon of what some might term 'political tourism' whereby interested people have been escorted on study tours to Palestine and Israel has been common for decades, but it seems to have increased in popularity since the outbreak of the second intifada in 2000. Typical of such programmes has been the North American Interfaith Peace-Builders (IFPB) that was established by the Fellowship of Reconciliation in 2001.[2] Since that time the IFPB has organised over 50 study tours involving over a thousand participants. Their initiative was based on the premise that by having a first-hand experience participants' understanding of the conflict would be deepened such that they would be able to participate more effectively in movements for peace and justice in Israel/Palestine on their return to the USA. According to their prospectus:

> Delegations to Israel/Palestine are designed to begin a process of experiential learning and personal transformation. Our delegations expose participants to perspectives that are not readily available in North America. Meetings are held with diverse representatives of Palestinian and Israeli society, focusing particularly on the voices of those working nonviolently for a resolution to the conflict and an end to the occupation. Delegates see the Wall, checkpoints, and demolished homes and learn how these and much more affect Palestinians. Likewise, delegates hear from Israelis about the effects of the conflict on Israeli society. The experiential learning that the delegation fosters is intended to motivate action for change when delegates return. *IFPB provides materials, support, and mentoring to help returning delegates make the most of their experience.*[3]

Organisations like IFPB arrange the visits for everyday people rather than politicians or faith leaders, which is more the preserve of international humanitarian aid agencies who see such initiatives as integral to their advocacy work. As one worker with a European agency that has sponsored a number of visits to Israel and Palestine by parliamentarians and church figures observed to us, 'These are key people for us in terms of our advocacy programme, and when they see for themselves first hand, it makes a huge difference to what they are prepared to do on their return.'

FORMS OF ENGAGEMENT: DIRECT INTERVENTION TO CHALLENGE ISRAEL

Over recent years there have been a number of direct physical interventions by internationals travelling to Israel and the OPT in order to express their solidarity with the Palestinian people, shame the Israeli government and attract international media attention as a means of influencing international publics. Perhaps the best known was the Freedom Flotilla of May 2010.

The Freedom Flotilla

In the early hours of May 31, 2010 Israeli commandos boarded the vessels that constituted the 'Freedom Flotilla' sailing to deliver much needed humanitarian aid to the civilians of the Gaza Strip suffering under the ongoing Israeli blockade. A violent confrontation occurred in which nine activists were killed and dozens of other passengers injured along with several Israeli soldiers. It was a dramatic encounter which resulted in widespread condemnation of the Israeli use of lethal violence against what was proclaimed to be a nonviolent humanitarian mission to relieve suffering and show solidarity. Civilian protests erupted around the world, and a number of countries downgraded their diplomatic relations with Israel.[4]

Despite the loss of life and the failure to deliver the humanitarian aid, the Freedom Flotilla could be judged to have been a powerful 'performance of opposition' that touched the hearts and minds of many people. It was presented to audiences around the world as symbolic of the asymmetry of the struggle between the State of Israel and the suffering civilians besieged in the Gaza Strip. Large numbers of those who witnessed it through the various media that covered the clash found themselves feeling anger, indignation, shock, alarm and shame.[5] The communicative power of the performance lay not just in the actual encounter, but also derived from the setting in which it took place. The confrontation was in some ways the high point in a drama that had unfolded over an extended period. The first stage had been the assembly in Cyprus of the convoy of six vessels coming from Greece and Turkey. Then on May 30 the ships set sail. First contact was made with Israeli forces at 11pm that evening. Around 4.30am in the morning of the next day the assault was launched. Throughout this drama there had been global media coverage, no doubt due in part to the participation in the action of a number of well-known figures.[6] After they had been released by the Israeli authorities, such personalities were able to use their status to reproduce the narrative of Israeli aggression and thereby further undermine Israel's standing amongst significant international audiences.

The Freedom Flotilla was not the first attempt to deliver aid by sea to the besieged population of the Gaza Strip, and it has not been the last. The Free

Gaza movement succeeded in delivering aid to Gaza on a number of occasions in 2008.[7] In July 2011 a significant convoy of vessels ('Freedom Flotilla 2') organised by an international coalition of groups was due to sail from Greece to Gaza, but the exercise was aborted, primarily because the Greek government forbade the vessels from leaving its ports, citing safety concerns.[8] In October 2012 the Swedish organisation, Ship to Gaza, sailed the Finnish-flagged vessel *Estelle* towards Gaza but was intercepted by Israeli forces.[9]

Welcome to Palestine: the 'flytilla'

'Welcome to Palestine' was an initiative of Palestinian civil society organisations who invited hundreds of internationals to come and visit them in the OPT via Tel Aviv Airport. The aim was to draw attention to the restrictions Israel places on anyone seeking to gain entry in order to visit the OPT. On July 8, 2011 the solidarity activists planned to present themselves at Ben Gurion Airport and declare their intention to travel on to the West Bank. Many intending travellers were not allowed on their scheduled flights after Israel had warned the airlines that the passengers would not be allowed entry on arrival, whilst others were refused entry on landing and were either flown back to their country of origin immediately or kept in Israeli prisons until their deportations would be arranged. A similar event was organised for April 2012 with much the same outcome – only three participants made it to their intended destination in Bethlehem. Both these actions failed to generate the level of international interest occasioned by the sea-borne attempts to breach the Gaza blockade. It was clear from the beginning that Israel would not allow the people to enter, and one has to wonder whether it was really worth it to spend so much money on an action that failed to generate any significant media coverage at the international level. The fact that it took place over a weekend, when fewer people read the newspapers or watch the news, and presented very limited 'photo opportunities' for the media meant that it must be classed as a 'weak performance of protest'. Evidence of this is that the main item reported by the correspondent of the British newspaper *The Guardian* in Jerusalem that weekend was about a Danish member of a European pro-Palestinian cycling party being clubbed by an officer with the Israeli occupation forces in the Jordan valley, with only the briefest mention of the fact that only three of the intended participants in the 'flytilla' had made it to Bethlehem.[10]

FORMS OF ENGAGEMENT: PROTEST AND SOLIDARITY ON THE GROUND

Volunteers have been going to Israel and Palestine for decades in one capacity or another and for a variety of purposes. However, following the outbreak of the second intifada a relatively new pattern emerged of solidarity activists from different countries (but mainly Europe and North America) going to the OPT in order to actively support and participate in the popular resistance. One of the main conduits for this flow was the International Solidarity Movement (ISM) which was launched in August 2001 with the declared aim of 'supporting and strengthening the Palestinian popular resistance'. This would be achieved by volunteers who would be 'immediately alongside Palestinians in olive groves, on school runs, at demonstrations, within villages being attacked, by houses being demolished or where Palestinians are subject to consistent harassment or attacks from soldiers and settlers as well as numerous other situations.'[11]

It would seem clear from our interviews that the presence of international volunteers has been appreciated by popular resistance activists. The most frequently mentioned contribution was their protective function – Israeli soldiers seemed more restrained in their responses to Palestinian protest when foreigners were present. As one activist from a village outside Jenin put it, 'They are a form of protection – they would be on the front line like a human chain against the army, like a shield.' Another important function referred to was that through their solidarity actions the internationals empowered the Palestinians by reassuring them that they were not alone in their struggle. As an activist from Bethlehem district phrased it:

I also feel motivated by the foreigners who come here and support our struggle. When I see them I know that I am not alone. Sometimes we think that people in the rest of the world ignore us or don't care about us. But when we see people from other countries trying to learn about Palestine and participating with us in the demonstrations side by side we feel more strong.[12]

In addition the internationals have proven their importance in acting as witnesses – monitoring and documenting what they have experienced and sharing this throughout their global networks. This was emphasised particularly strongly by a community leader in the village of Nabi Saleh where international solidarity activists have been a very visible presence in the community struggle to protect their land from settlement expansion. He informed us:

The internationals are important because Israel makes the link between our struggle and violent resistance – suicide bombings, terrorists – it harms our image. So when people (the international solidarity activists) see the reality, they can act as messengers to their own societies. ... We must use all creative methods to expose the ugly face of the occupation. We must utilise the information technology to capture the minds and hearts of the international community and to use that against the occupation. We have a fight with Israel to get international support. This is crucial keeping in mind the Israeli public media machinery, it is very sophisticated and we have to be aware of this and find ways to address this demagogy. The international solidarity groups and human rights activists and all our allies and friends should become a real radio broadcasting on behalf of the Palestinians – speaking the truth about the occupation.

Certainly it would seem as if organisations like the ISM have taken their advocacy/broadcasting function very seriously. According to Véronique Dudouet who studied the ISM during its earlier years 'militant tourism' constituted only 50 per cent of their activity, the other half was what took place in volunteers' home countries developing support for the Palestinian struggle through lobbying, educational and public awareness campaigns.[13] This has been appreciated by Palestinian activists, as one of them explained:

> The internationals? This is a big difference from the first intifada when the only internationals were journalists. Since 2002 we have been using the international community. I realised the significance of this when on a speaking tour in Sweden and in one place a pro-Israeli member of the audience raised a point, and before I could answer someone else in the audience rebutted him. This showed how Europeans are better informed about the situation here, especially compared with Americans who can have no idea that there is an occupation. Without the internationals we would be like one hand clapping – they are the other hand that we need.

But the experience of international solidarity activists has not proven completely positive. Véronique Dudouet noted that during her research there were times when she observed ISM activists taking over the planning of an action without waiting for Palestinian initiatives. Moreover, just like anyone who intervenes in a conflict situation there is the possibility of outsiders, knowingly or not, aligning themselves with a particular faction within a divided community and thereby exacerbating the fractures as they seek to coordinate with a group that does not enjoy the support or the trust of the community as a whole.[14] Dudouet also noted that sometimes the internationals exercised a determining influence over the timing and sequencing of protest actions, which tended to peak during the vacation periods when there was a more pronounced international presence. This was experienced by one of our informants who commented:

> Internationals come with an agenda and sometimes they want to impose it on us. For example we had discussion in the committee about whether or not to cut the fence around the settlement, and the decision was not to. The

Israeli and international activists wanted to cut the fence, and this created a split in the committee and we become two committees. We also had a disagreement about the closure of the settlers' road. The internationals and the Israeli activists wanted to close the road on Saturday and we wanted to do in on another day. The reason was that Saturday was good for them and they wanted to get attention from their action.

Concern was also expressed by some Palestinian activists regarding the manner in which certain protest sites became dependent on the participation of internationals. As an activist from the Bethlehem district remarked, 'The internationals (and the Israelis) can play a positive role, but there are risks. They can cause harm. They want to have confrontations with the settlers every day. But they come for a short while … a month … and then they go, and we pay the price.' This view was echoed by a community leader from one of the neighbourhoods in Silwan, just outside the walls of the old city in Jerusalem:

> It is a difficult situation in Silwan. … We do not want weekly demonstrations like in Bil'in and other places. We do not have the resources for that. … We do not want to rely on Israelis and internationals who might leave one day. When there is an issue and a need we call on them. It is important to have their support but the resistance must be grounded in the community.

Moreover, whilst the presence of internationals as accompaniers proved in general to have a restraining influence on Israeli soldiers, this is not something that could be taken for granted. Thus, during the second intifada the ISM organisers decided to halt their practice of internationals accompanying ambulances as experience seemed to show that negotiating passage through the Israeli checkpoints was more problematic when internationals were present.[15] A similar kind of problem was experienced by volunteers with the International Women's Peace Service (IWPS) operating south-west of Nablus where they were accompanying farmers during the olive harvest in October 2012. They found that the soldiers were turning them off land close to 'aggressive settlements' with the result that they could not help with the harvesting. As one of them noted in her report, 'This raises the whole issue of whether some farmers feel that internationals are a liability rather than a help because they too may be prevented from picking when accompanied.'[16]

The members of the IWPS teams, unlike many international volunteers in Palestine associated with ISM, remain based in a particular community throughout the length of their stay in the OPT, and their focus has been very much upon accompaniment as a form of protection for the Palestinian inhabitants of the villages located in an area where there are several settlements populated by highly aggressive 'ideological' settlers. As described on their website,

> The *International Women's Peace Service (IWPS)* is a team of human rights volunteers, based in the village of Deir Istiya, Salfit district, occupied Palestine. We provide international accompaniment to Palestinian civilians, document and non-violently intervene in human right abuses and support acts of non-violent resistance to end the illegal Israeli occupation and building of the apartheid wall.

FORMS OF ENGAGEMENT: LONG-TERM ACCOMPANIMENT

A number of international organisations have initiated long-term 'residencies' in different locations of the OPT in an effort to give expression to their solidarity with the suffering of the Palestinians by seeking to act as a protective presence in their midst. The longest established has been the Christian Peacemaker Team (CPT) which started its work in Hebron in 1995.

Christian Peacemaker Teams in Hebron

Christian Peacemaker Teams was founded in 1986 by three of the North American peace churches (Mennonite, Church of the Brethren and Quakers) and subsequently attracted support from a wide range of Christian denominations. A number of teams have been located in different conflict zones around the world, with the team in Hebron being established in July 1995, following a formal invitation from the Palestinian mayor of the city.[17] In their 'statement of conviction' issued by the three women and three men who constituted this first intervention, they emphasised that those committed to nonviolence should be prepared to take the same risks for peace that soldiers were willing to take in the course of a violent war. Their initial activities involved establishing relations with local Palestinian journalists and youth, and working with Israeli human rights organisations trying to document the experiences of Palestinians living near the settlements. They also began accompanying local children to school in an attempt to provide protection against assaults from settlers.[18]

Much of the team's time was devoted to monitoring the incidents and clashes that were (and have continued to be) a regular feature of everyday life in Hebron's old city, and sending reports back to their networks in North America and beyond. In the late 1990s, as Israel increased the rate of house demolitions and land confiscations, they launched a 'Campaign for Secure dwellings' with members of their support networks and church congregations 'twinning' with

Palestinian families whose dwellings were under threat. A sense of their activities during this time is conveyed in the following account by one of their number:

> By 1998, the team's work had expanded to include visiting dozens of other families who belonged to the CSD network. The team was also conducting regular tours for Israeli, Palestinian, and international delegations and individuals seeking to understand the situation in Hebron and the rest of Palestine. They had to visit regularly with families affected by soldier and settler violence and conduct regular patrols past military checkpoints in their neighborhood. Daily meetings and writing required a significant block of time. Team members had also begun establishing relationships with Palestinians, Israelis, and internationals in Jerusalem and Bethlehem and taking Arabic lessons … in Bethlehem.[19]

It should be noted that some of the families whose case was taken up by CPT came to the conclusion that their interests would be better served without the attention that CPT attracted from settlers and the occupying power. Furthermore, with the escalation of violent clashes that marked the second intifada the team members faced further challenges to their morale and resolve. They learned early on that interposing themselves between the military and the Palestinian stone-throwers had no effect, just as their attempts to 'protect' people living in neighbourhoods by staying in their homes overnight proved futile, and also attracted a level of animosity from local youth who saw them as United States citizens whose government carried ultimate responsibility for the continuation of the occupation.[20] As links with local Palestinians deteriorated, members of CPT strengthened their relationship with other international solidarity groups. They began providing two days of training to new ISM volunteers and also participated with the volunteers in popular resistance activities against the Wall. In 2001 they hosted a delegation from the World Council of Churches that came to learn from the experience of the team, an initiative that led to the establishment in August 2002 of the Ecumenical Accompaniment Programme in Palestine and Israel (EAPPI).

Ecumenical Accompaniment Programme in Palestine and Israel (EAPPI)

One of the messages the delegation from the World Council of Churches took back with them after their exploratory visit of 2001 was that Palestinians wanted international solidarity groups who offered concrete support and did more than write reports. As a consequence, whilst participants in the programme (Ecumenical Accompaniers – EAs) do monitor and report violations of human rights and international humanitarian law perpetrated by the settlers and occupation forces, they also actively support acts of nonviolent resistance by standing alongside Palestinian and Israeli activists struggling against the occupation, and offer protection to vulnerable individuals and communities by their presence. A major element in their role as EAs is also a commitment to engage in public advocacy on their return to their home communities after their three-month placement in the West Bank.

Like the CPT and the international humanitarian agencies examined in Chapter 8, the EAPPI rejects the principle of neutrality but not that of impartiality. Its code of conduct states:

> We do not take sides in the conflict and do not discriminate against anyone, but we are not neutral in terms of principles of human rights and international humanitarian law, we stand with the poor, the oppressed, the marginalised and the dispossessed and aim to serve all parties in the conflict in a fair and unbiased way.

By 2014 there were 16 countries participating in the programme, each sending volunteers through their national coordinating agency. There is no standardised process for the selection and training of volunteers, but in the UK volunteers who have been short-listed go through a one-day selection process before being accepted for the two-week training programme. According to one who had been through this process:

> Volunteers are selected according to different criteria – it is not just you as a person. It is you as someone who can do a job on the ground and it is also your advocacy base, what networks you have got. They try to cover different churches, different areas of the country, ... gender ... Your advocacy base is so important because your work as an EA is multifold. It is the nonviolent presence, the working alongside Israeli and Palestinian peacemakers, and it is your advocacy.

This particular volunteer from the UK joined a team based in the village of Yanoun in the Jordan Valley. Other teams have been based in Jerusalem, Hebron, Bethlehem, Tulkarem and Jayyous. Their responsibilities on the ground include:

- Being visibly present in vulnerable communities and locations.
- Monitoring the conduct of settlers and soldiers and contacting relevant organisations and authorities to intervene if necessary.
- Reporting on violations of human rights and attempting to engage non-violently with the perpetrators.

There can be little doubt that through their activities the EAs, like the members of the CPT, have contributed to strengthening the resilience of Palestinians, particularly those located in Area C who face unceasing pressure from settlers and soldiers to drive them off their land. Our friend who was based in Yanoun told of how the villagers she accompanied confessed to her that if the EAs were to leave, then the villagers would have to leave also in the face of the settler assaults that would be launched in the absence of the internationals.

Whilst the solidarity work of the EAs has been significant, of equal importance has been the advocacy work they are required to do on their return, whether this be in the public sphere of talks and presentations to local groups and associations, writing letters to the media and to politicians, lobbying policy makers, or organising public events of one kind or another.[21] There is also the advocacy work that goes on in the private sphere with returnees talking to their friends, families and networks expressing their sympathies and convictions with a new language borne from their direct experience of life under occupation. In a number of countries 12 or more volunteers have been recruited each year for the EAPPI programme by participating organisations. This means that in each of these countries there are now somewhere between 100–150 people who have engaged in some form of public advocacy to bring an end to the occupation. As someone associated with coordinating, the Swiss programme informed us:

The EAs are very important in our advocacy programme – particularly in outreach to church-goers and the general public. They have been very important over the years. We had a travelling exhibition to mark ten years of our involvement – it was very suitable for a church environment, it was part of our efforts to strengthen support within the churches. The EAs do a lot of local media work and get lots of responses. We send 12–14 EAs every year, so now we have a body of 120 people who have been EAs – and about half of them are still active.[22]

A number of EAs have established links with local groups with twinning arrangements with Palestinian communities. One such group is the Antonine Friendship Link based in the Scottish town of Falkirk and linked with the Palestinian village of Jayyous which has lost open access to the bulk of its agricultural land due to the construction of the Wall and where EAs monitor the checkpoints through which farmers have to transit in order to cultivate their land.[23] Such solidarity groups are becoming increasingly common, and constitute one more dimension of the burgeoning international movement into which international solidarity activists feed.

Operation Dove: South Hebron Hills

The third example of long-term accompaniment – by the Italian movement Operation Dove in the South Hebron Hills – is included in order to illustrate the manner in which internationals and Israeli solidarity activists can work together with local people in order to strengthen and support their resistance and resilience in a part of the West Bank that has been designated as Area C and where the Israelis have made no secret of their intention to evict the local Palestinians from their land and resettle them in urban centres, thus leaving the land free for the expansion of settlements. The area itself is semi-desert and the local Palestinian way of life revolves around their sheep and livestock.

In 1996 members of the Hebron-based CPT began making occasional visits to villages to the south of the city that were being targeted by settlers. CPT members would help the villagers to rebuild animal pens and other structures destroyed by settlers and, of course, document what they had witnessed. Then in November 1999 the inhabitants of Al-Tuwani, the main village close to the settlement of Maòn, were issued with an eviction order and the confiscation of their land. At that point they were approached by Israeli solidarity activists (who were later to found Taàyush) who offered to try and help by challenging the order in the Israeli courts. In the words of one of the village activists:

> We were confused – Israelis offering to work with us and at the same time the Israelis destroy homes and confiscate land. They are not the same Israelis. But little by little we established good relations with them. Now they help us in following up legal cases in the Israel court. They had very good lawyers, and four months after our eviction we were allowed to return to our villages. ...
>
> After the 2000 decision we started organising ourselves, how to resist. ... We have had some important successes – Palestinians staying on the land is the main success. Al-Tuwani has been targeted, but we have met the challenge. Every time they demolish something, we rebuild. Media attention also puts pressure on the Israelis.

Some of the media pressure referred to can be attributed to the long-term presence and work of international solidarity teams. In 2003 members of Taàyush approached the CPT in Hebron to convey a request from the villagers that they accompany their children to and from school where their route went close to the fence of the Maòn settlement and the settlers threatened and attacked the children aiming to prevent them from using the road. A year later, in 2004, the Italian peace initiative Operation Dove visited the villages following up on links they had with Taàyush. A few weeks after this visit, in September 2004, Operation Dove and CPT began their joint accompaniment programme, escorting the local children to and from school. Within two days of its commencement masked settlers attacked them, throwing stones at the children, breaking the elbow of one of the accompaniers and puncturing the lung of another – one more example of the manner in which the well-intentioned peace-keeping intervention of international solidarity activists can provoke settler violence. However, the assault did generate a significant amount of media coverage both nationally and internationally.[24]

In 2011 CPT ceased its involvement and Operation Dove took over sole responsibility for the international presence. On our visit to talk with them in November 2013 we had just sat down to enjoy our cup of Italian coffee freshly made for us by the young volunteers when a mobile phone rang – an Israeli jeep had been seen approaching a local encampment of pastoralists so everything was dropped as they grabbed their camcorders and raced off to monitor and record the anticipated encounter. Ta'ayush has continued its solidarity visits and along with Rabbis for Human Rights continued to provide the links to Israeli legal resources, which remains one of the key ways to combat the expropriation of land and livelihoods. Every week and after every incident a press release is issued, with the volunteers working with the Jerusalem-based Alternative Information Centre that acts as its main media channel. Their work continues to be challenging. At the time of writing (September 15, 2014) a press release was issued headed 'Israeli settlers attacked internationals and a Palestinian shepherd'. The report continued:

> Al Tuwani – On September 14, two Israeli settlers attacked a Palestinian shepherd and two internationals near the Israeli outpost of Mitzpe Yair, South Hebron hills area. During the aggression the settlers stole from the internationals their video-cameras and broke one of their phones. Israeli police detained the Palestinian shepherd and one of the internationals for 6 hours. There were no consequences for the settlers.[25]

Being realistic we have to acknowledge that such reports will not impact in any direct manner on those immediately responsible for such assaults. But they do ensure that there is an international network that is kept briefed and informed about the abuses of basic human rights perpetrated in out-of-the-way locations such as Al-Tuwani and – it needs to be emphasised – in so many other places throughout the OPT. And as such they all feed into a growing international voice demanding an end to the occupation for the sake of the Palestinians and the Israelis themselves.

THE BOOMERANG PATTERN

The argument underpinning the previous section has been that the growth in international grass-roots/civil society engagement with the Palestinian popular resistance has not only strengthened the resilience of the Palestinians, but also fed into and nurtured growth in transnational movements of solidarity and support. From this perspective, the accompaniers and solidarity activists have performed the crucial function of providing credible counter-information to global networks, an essential role in what Margaret Keck and Kathryn Sikkink have termed the 'boomerang pattern': 'Where governments are unresponsive to groups whose claims may none the less resonate elsewhere, international contacts can "amplify" the demands of domestic groups, pry open space for new issues, and then echo these demands back into the domestic arena.'[26]

In other words, the boomerang pattern refers to processes that occur when local movements, such as the Palestinian popular resistance in the OPT, feel that their influence on their targets is too limited and so they 'throw a boomerang' out to external actors and networks naming and shaming their oppressors, in the hope that the boomerang will return and hit their target with international pressure, particularly from international allies of the targeted regime. Most boomerang throwers operate with a model of 'links in the chain of nonviolence/ influence' whereby they communicate in the first instance with networks of grass-roots supporters in other countries, who in turn exercise influence on their governments and policy makers.[27] As Howard Clark noted, 'In its flight the boomerang might pass through NGOs and activist constituencies, media, government departments and intergovernmental institutions before returning to make a difference at the point from where it was thrown.'[28] Thus, by producing authoritative eye-witness accounts of human rights violations the international accompaniers in the OPT 'feed' their international networks of support with the kind of stories and case material that can be used to move decision makers higher up the vertical ladder of influence.

Perhaps the most significant exercise in boomerang throwing by Palestinian civil society in recent years emerged out of a meeting of Palestinian organisations in July 2005 – the call for a worldwide boycott, divestment and sanctions (BDS) campaign against Israel. Based on the simple premise that Israel must be made to realise that continued occupation and disregard for international humanitarian law carries with it a price, the campaign has gone from strength to strength in the years since its launch.[29] In December 2009 the campaign received the endorsement of leading Palestinian Christians with the publication of the 'Kairos Palestine Document' entitled *A Moment of Truth*.[30] The authors condemned the occupation as: 'a sin against God and humanity because it deprives the Palestinians of their basic human rights, bestowed by God. It distorts the image of God in the Israeli who has become an occupier just as it distorts the image in the Palestinian living under occupation.' They then went on to urge support for the BDS campaign with an appeal that drew on a significant element in the nonviolent philosophy of many activists throughout history – the goal was not solely the liberation of the oppressed Palestinians but the emancipation of the oppressors from their evil:

Palestinian civil organisations, as well as international organisations, NGOs and certain religious institutions call on individuals, companies and states to engage in divestment and in an economic and commercial boycott of everything produced by the occupation. We understand this to integrate the logic of peaceful resistance. These advocacy campaigns must be carried out with courage, openly sincerely proclaiming that their object is not revenge but rather to put an end to the existing evil, liberating both the perpetrators and the victims of injustice. The aim is to free both peoples from extremist positions of the different Israeli governments, bringing both to justice and reconciliation. In this spirit and with this dedication we will eventually reach the longed-for resolution to our problems.

But even the authors of such resounding words and possessed with such a wonderfully inclusive vision acknowledged that they lacked 'even a glimmer of positive expectation', but they lived in hope.[31]

However, since the Kairos Appeal was issued in 2009 the broader BDS movement has experienced a quite dramatic growth in support around the world. Many of those involved with the campaign have drawn parallels between the BDS call and the boycott campaign directed against South Africa during the anti-apartheid struggle, likening the white-minority regime in South Africa and the apartheid system on which it was based to the oppression of the Palestinians living under Israeli occupation. There seems to be a confidence amongst activists that global pressure worked in the case of the freedom struggle in South Africa, and so the model is there to be followed in the case of Palestine. However, it would seem that if the boycott of South Africa that was such an integral part of the overall anti-apartheid struggle is to be used as a model of the Palestinian BDS campaign, then it is important to identify the similarities and the differences between the two contexts and cases – it is not sufficient to claim 'It worked in the case of South Africa therefore it is important for us to follow the same pathway!' In the next section we shall examine how and why the boycott campaign was so significant – if it was – in the South African case, and explore whether or not the same factors can be seen to apply in the case of the BDS movement in particular and the Palestinian solidarity movement in general.

COMPARING THE ANTI-APARTHEID STRUGGLE WITH THAT AGAINST THE ISRAELI OCCUPATION

Research shows that there are key differences between the two cases and it is only by taking these differences into account, and addressing the challenges they embody, can the transnational movement in support of Palestinian human rights make substantive progress.

1. The global anti-apartheid movement took its lead from the African National Congress (ANC) which was recognised as the unified and legitimate leadership of the liberation struggle in South Africa. In the Palestinian case, the PLO is weak and there is not a unified leadership to be followed. There is the ongoing division between Fatah and Hamas that remains a significant handicap despite the 2014 'reconciliation' between the two and the formation of a unity government.

2. The aim of the anti-apartheid movement was clear and unambiguous – a free democratic political system that would lead to the end of white minority rule in South Africa. In the case of the Palestinian solidarity there is not the same clear vision beyond ending the occupation. Is the aim one state or two?

3. The ANC had its armed wing, but in general it used violence in a controlled manner targeting mainly physical installations and property and eschewing attacks that would result in civilian deaths. This enabled campaigners around the world to claim the moral high ground, contrasting the actions of the ANC with those of the South African government and its involvement in torture, disappearances, deaths in custody, the violent suppression of internal protest and armed intervention in civil war situations in neighbouring states. By contrast the Palestinian solidarity movement faces a much greater struggle to lay claim to the moral high ground in the context of the terror campaign of a decade ago when hundreds of Israeli civilians were killed by suicide bombers and the more recent launching of rocket attacks from Gaza that terrorised citizens in Southern Israel and beyond, not to mention the public execution of alleged collaborators by Hamas security personnel in August 2014 during Operation Protective Edge.

4. The South African government tried to taint the ANC and its supporters as part of an international communist threat to the established order. It is true of course that there were dedicated communists in key positions within the ANC, but all remained committed to the Freedom Charter which had been adopted in June 1955 and remained the guiding document of the ANC and its supporters right through to the drawing up of the new constitution in 1996. By contrast those seeking to undermine the Palestinian liberation struggle find it all too easy to portray them as 'Jihadists'. From this perspective people such as Iran's former president, Mahmoud Ahmadinejad were an absolute God-send to those seeking to delegitimise the Palestinian solidarity movement.[32] A former Israeli ambassador to the USA once described Ahmadinejad's hate-filled rhetoric as 'the gift that keeps on giving'.[33] In similar vein the Netanyahu government tried to deflect criticism of Israel's 2014 war on Gaza with a new public relations mantra, 'Hamas is ISIS, ISIS is Hamas', whilst the military affairs analyst Yoav Limor writing a post-mortem to the war observed:

The event that was most helpful to Israel in its public relations battle that it waged alongside the military battle in Gaza took place thousands of kilometres from here – the execution of American journalist James Foley. … The Islamic State group is giving us a rare opportunity to tell an attentive audience in the West something that it has thus far refused to hear: Israel is not the problem, but the solution.[34]

5. One factor that contributed to Washington's eventual withdrawal of support from the apartheid regime was the realisation that through the 1980s South Africa's strategic role as a bulwark against communism sweeping through the African continent was no longer significant. However, it would seem that international trends are not so favourable for the Palestinian solidarity movement. From the perspective of Washington (and elsewhere) Islamic Jihadism has replaced communism as the major threat to the status quo, in relation to which Israel seeks to portray itself as an important bulwark. There is, of course, a counter-argument that it is Israel's occupation and the abuse of Palestinian basic human and civil rights that is one of the main drivers of Jihadism, and that the delegitimisation and outlawing of Hamas as an elected party has contributed to radicalisation but it would appear that this argument has yet to obtain any purchase in Washington, which remains Israel's staunchest supporter.

6. The apartheid system was so monstrously inhuman – a privileged white minority dominating and exploiting a black majority – that it was indefensible in the eyes of the vast majority of people who became aware of the situation. Hence the anti-apartheid movement around the globe could draw on wide swathes of support and mobilise people on the basis of a simple morality tale of good and evil which resonated loud and clear. By contrast, and particularly for Europeans and people from European backgrounds, the target of the BDS movement appears to be a significant section of the Jewish people – those living in Israel – and the Jews historically have been a vulnerable and persecuted minority. So we can see that the transnational Palestine solidarity movement does not have the resource of a simple morality tale that people can grasp and identify with in the manner that they could in the case of South Africa.

7. People of all political persuasions could support the struggle for free non-racial elections in South Africa. Unfortunately for the Palestinians and their international supporters their situation is not so clear-cut. In the South African case, only those who supported the regime could be castigated as racist, but Palestinian solidarity activists are always vulnerable to the standard accusation of being anti-Semitic. Of course this charge is used repeatedly to delegitimise criticisms of Israel from any quarter. But, particularly in Europe and North America, the accusation can act as a powerful deterrent to people openly expressing their support for the Palestinians, and activists need to be ever-alert to initiatives that can spark charges of anti-Semitism. As Norman

Solomon expressed it: 'The failure to make a distinction between anti-Semitism and criticism of Israel routinely stifles public debate.'[35]

8. No organisation is more adept at manipulating the anti-Semitic slur than the American Israel Public Affairs Committee (AIPAC) and other pro-Israeli groupings elsewhere in the world. The anti-apartheid movement never had to face such a transnational network of well-funded and organised opponents with such a level of influence over policy makers as those who continue to confront the Palestinian solidarity movement.

9. Up until the 1980s the USA lagged behind Europe in mobilising around apartheid. But through the 1980s the pressure from below grew, involving Black human rights groups, universities, churches and trade unions campaigning for disinvestment, and receiving sympathetic media coverage which reached its peak during 1984–86. According to some analysts, one factor in this growth was the elevation into positions of influence within the USA of African-American politicians. Certainly the parallels between the struggle for majority rule in South Africa and the Black freedom struggle in the USA were so clear that the campaign was able to draw on the language of the civil rights movement to mobilise people. The Palestinian solidarity activists have no such comparable narrative resource upon which to draw.[36]

10. Sport and cultural boycotts were significant elements in the anti-apartheid struggle. South Africa was excluded from the 1964 and 1968 Olympics and expelled from the International Olympic Movement in 1972. This followed the widely publicised protests in the UK against the tour of the South African cricket team in 1970. The campaign against sporting links with South Africa became a significant mobilising issue for anti-apartheid campaigners, particularly in rugby- and cricket-playing countries, and by the later 1980s South Africa was effectively excluded from international sporting activities. This sporting isolation had a profound impact on white South Africans, forcing them to acknowledge the degree to which they were isolated from the rest of the world. Once again, however, the global Palestinian solidarity movement does not have the same resource around which to mobilise. Sport does not occupy the same place in Israeli culture as it did in South Africa, and the only sport at which Israel ranks amongst the world's best is basketball. At the same time the campaign for a cultural and academic boycott of Israel has achieved a degree of prominence and in many ways is comparable to the arts and entertainment boycott of apartheid South Africa that was observed by many throughout the 1980s.

11. The sport and cultural boycott added to the sense of isolation experienced by white South Africans consequent upon their withdrawal from the Commonwealth, their expulsion from the UN and other world organisations. Although hard to measure, there is no doubt that this sense of isolation was one of the factors leading to South Africans agreeing to engage in negotiations to end the apartheid system. Unfortunately for the Palestinian solidarity activists

around the world, there is no consensus around the morality and the political efficacy of a total economic, cultural and academic boycott of Israel.[37]

12. Determining the precise impact of the international moves against apartheid is difficult. Perhaps the most significant impact was on the morale of black and white South Africans. Outside pressure encouraged internal opposition to apartheid, reassuring protestors that they were not alone. It also weakened the resolve of the white minority who, despite protestations to the contrary, had a deep fear of total international isolation and their abandonment by erstwhile friends such as the USA. As Alan Hirsch insightfully observed, 'The power of the US was never its ability to talk to Pretoria, and always its ability to stop talking.'[38] Once again we come back to what many see as the major obstacle to ending the Israeli occupation and making substantive steps towards a sustainable peace – the solidarity that successive United States governments extend to Israel.

13. Another factor that played a part in bringing South Africa to the negotiating table was the fact that the white minority in South Africa needed the Black majority as a workforce. Indeed the Black trade unions under COSATU – Congress of South African Trade Unions – became a powerful instrument of resistance and pressure from inside for dismantling apartheid. By contrast, the Israelis do not need the Palestinians as a workforce, in fact they are trying to drive them from their land.

14. One of the most significant factors in the vulnerability of South Africa to external pressure was the economic and financial difficulties the state was facing before the international divestment campaign came to its peak in 1984–86. Calls for disinvestment had little impact during the years of South Africa's economic growth (1960s through to mid-1970s). But by the mid-1970s returns on investment had begun to fall, and these reduced rates of return influenced decision makers in the financial institutions so that by the 1980s they began to take heed of the calls for disinvestment. The continuing pressure from below and reaction to the Black uprising in the townships during 1984–86 led to an increased rate of withdrawal. As Kenneth Grundy commented, 'More than half the U.S. firms with direct investments in South Africa withdrew between 1984 and 1989. ... Although many European firms were also forced to disinvest (e.g. Barclays Bank) and to reconsider their involvement, the impact of the campaign to isolate South Africa was not nearly so compelling in Europe.'[39]

Pretoria was forced to rethink its policies. Prospects for economic growth were minimal, and without growth there would be escalating protest and pressure from the townships, with a consequent deepening of the socio-economic and political crisis. As Rory Ewins concluded, 'In the end the informal sanctions implemented by the international private sector – prompted by events within South Africa, and by popular and government anti-apartheid moves in the West

– probably had the greatest impact of all international moves directed against apartheid.'[40]

By contrast to South Africa in the 1980s, Israel at the time of writing (December 2014) would appear to have remained in reasonable economic and financial health. However, it might not remain so if it continues to wage recurrent wars on the Palestinians in the Gaza Strip and its prime international sponsor in Washington begins to question whether it should continue bank-rolling right-wing Israeli governments that make little pretence of their lack of interest in pursuing what the majority of the world would consider to be a substantive peace process.[41]

TOWARDS AN UNCERTAIN FUTURE

The comparison between the anti-apartheid movement and the broad movement for a sustainable peace between Israel and Palestine based on an end to the occupation reveals what can only be described as a depressing and pessimistic outlook. As the preceding analysis makes clear, there are significant differences between the case of the South African boycott and the contemporary BDS movement, which means that however significant the South African boycott was as a factor in bringing an end to apartheid, it does not follow that the Palestinian BDS movement will be able to play the same role in bringing an end to the occupation.

Perhaps most crucial of all the differences is the contrast between the 'organic relationship' in South Africa between the ANC on the outside and the UDF as its internal manifestation within the country, which was able to organise and coordinate internal protest and resistance on such a scale that it imposed a heavy economic and financial cost on the regime and which energised the third key player – social movements in key countries, especially in the USA. These actively encouraged people to support the economic and cultural boycott of South Africa, pressuring corporations and financial institutions to disinvest from South Africa, and urging their governments to impose sanctions on the minority white regime. All this contributed to a burgeoning economic, financial and security challenge to the white regime, allied with a crisis of confidence nurtured by a growing sense amongst the white population and their leadership of their international isolation. All this led to a preparedness to engage in substantive negotiations to end minority rule.

By contrast there is no such Palestinian 'organic leadership' within or outside the occupied territories with the will or the capacity to coordinate any sustained movement of popular protest comparable to that which brought about change in South Africa. Indeed, without the genuine commitment of all political factions within the Palestinian political domain to work together to mobilise people inside and outside the OPT as part of a sustained movement to raise the financial, economic, political – and moral – costs of occupation such that the Israelis will sue for peace under mounting international pressure from their key allies, particularly the USA, then what we shall undoubtedly witness is 'more of the same'. By this we mean a deepening loss of hope on the part of the Palestinian public, which will in turn manifest itself in a willingness for individuals to contemplate acts of personal violence against Israeli civilians out of a sense of despair and desperation and a concomitant desire to inflict at least some suffering on the oppressors. Writ on a larger scale these same feelings will lead to repeats of the latest war in Gaza, a direct result of an imprisoned people forced to live in inhuman conditions, feeling they can stand it no more.

Consequently the challenge for the Palestinian political leadership is to build on the experience of the popular resistance of the last few years, drawing on the experience and expertise of the activists, in order to create a situation where the occupation cannot continue as normal, where the violence on which it is based becomes ever more visible to widening constituencies of concerned people around the world, and where political leaders within the states that make the occupation possible find it increasingly difficult to refrain from exercising pressure on Israel to sue for peace. And the evidence from South Africa is that this will only come about through all elements – the Palestinians, the global networks of support and solidarity, the corporations and financial institutions, and the governments – working to bring an end to an intolerable and unsustainable situation whereby a whole population is subjugated by an occupying force that continues to deny it the most basic of human and civil rights. In Chapter 10, we shall try to give some pointers to how such a scenario might come about.

INTERVIEW WITH DIANE EDWARDS – ACTIVIST

Diane was politically active in the anti-apartheid movement, the Jubilee 2000 debt campaigns and more recently has been a dedicated campaigner for Palestinian human rights and the end to the occupation.

In 2003 I joined a Pax Christi (Holland) solidarity visit to Palestine. That was my first visit and it was just mind-blowing. ... I was staggered at how much I did not know, although I had been a religious studies teacher I knew nothing about modern Israel and that here was a situation of insane injustice and inhumanity. ... Once again I listened to people's stories. We were there for ten days but it was like a lifetime's visit, a kind of total immersion. So when I came back I started reading. I learned a lot and started to tell stories

▶

about the people I had met there, particularly the people I had lived with. Mostly to church groups but also local political parties invited me as well. This would have been in 2004. I went again in 2007.

When I tell their stories there is a purpose. I always want to leave a group of people knowing a bit more about what is happening, feel a link with the person whose story I have been telling and through that understand the political situation, without giving a load of statistics and all the rest of it, so that they can do something. I always want them to feel that no matter how big and complicated the situation is, there is something that they can do. I believe this even though I get to a stage sometimes where my head is flattened from banging it against brick walls ... and of course you can't always tell what effect you have had. You give people a bit of information that they could not have got from anywhere else, and they can identify then with other ordinary people. That gives them a link that makes them want to do something without feeling overwhelmed by the situation.

A friend of mine in Pax Christi had been an EA (ecumenical accompanier) and it began to grow as an idea. In Britain people are selected according to different criteria – it is not just you as a person. It is you as someone who can do a job on the ground and it also your advocacy base, what networks have you got, different churches, different areas of the country, looking at England, Ireland, Scotland and Wales, gender, church membership. Your advocacy base is so important because your work as an EA is multi-fold. It is the nonviolent presence, the working alongside Israeli and Palestinian peacemakers, and it is your advocacy.

There are people who do their thing and they give their required number of talks on their return and that is it. But other people do much more. I know that many of the people who have listened to my stories will be championing Palestine when they are talking with friends in a way that they would not have done before, or maybe they will come and offer to help with the Palestinian produce stall. I say to people that you going home to talk to your family or anything else that you do is significant. You are spreading the word. They watch the news in a different way. They might start writing letters to the local newspaper – because they know, they have seen the photos I took.

There is a growing movement. Many of us are doing political advocacy. I have been to Brussels doing advocacy there, and I know that we changed the opinions of some European parliamentarians – they told us so. We did loads of meetings over five days with different parliamentarians from different countries – and they said that they never got this kind of insight and information when they went on their Friends of Israel sponsored fact-finding trips. The same is happening here. My MP is very supportive. His tactic is to ask questions in parliament. If I ask him he will raise an issue with the minister responsible and also ask a question in parliament. I know others whose MPs will not meet with them, which is scandalous.

10

CONCLUSION

We ended the previous chapter on a pessimistic note, and any rational analysis of the dynamics of the Israeli–Palestinian conflict will inevitably lead to a pessimistic view of the short-to-medium term future as long as the Israeli political leadership remain committed to their strategy of maintaining the status quo of occupation and as long as the Palestinian political leadership place their narrow personal and factional interests above the national interest of their fellow Palestinians. So, perhaps now is the time to abandon narrow conceptions of rationality/realism and engage in some optimism of the imagination, envisioning a pathway towards a situation where the Palestinians can be liberated from occupation and the Israelis liberated from their role as occupiers and jailers. But before we take on this challenge, it is time to address the elephant in the room – the topic that has not been addressed so far in this book: Gaza.

THE GAZA STRIP

It is a tragic, perhaps criminal, situation, but it seems that Gaza only enters the international news when there is a war going on. And there have been no shortage of them – in 2008 there was Operation Cast Lead, in November 2012 there was Operation Pillar of Defence, and in July 2014 Operation Protective Edge. As a direct result of these wars somewhere in the region of 3,689 Palestinians were killed, of whom approximately 68 per cent (2,503) were civilians. Israel bore a considerably lighter toll – 87 killed, of which 15 per cent (13) were civilians. To understand the dynamic behind this escalating violence we need to go back at least to February 2006 when Hamas decided to participate in Palestinian legislative elections, and to the surprise of everyone won a clear majority: 76 of the 132 seats. The following month a Hamas-led government was formed, only to be accompanied by persistent clashes between Fatah- and Hamas-affiliated militias and security personnel. As a consequence, a compromise national unity government was formed in March 2007, but two months later in June of that year fighting broke out once again and Hamas took the opportunity to seize control in Gaza. Driven by their fear of an Islamist 'terrorist' regime being established in the Middle East, the USA and other members of the international community withdrew development aid from Gaza, tacitly supporting Israel's shutdown and blockade of the territory, and refused to work directly with Hamas. Their hope was to force Hamas' collapse and bring Fatah back to power.

The consequence for the Gazan population has been an unceasing nightmare of unemployment, accelerating rates of impoverishment, unmet basic needs – all endured under an authoritarian regime in a 365-square-kilometre prison compound surrounded by buffer zones, sensors and a wire fence guarded by Israeli soldiers with rules of engagement allowing them to fire at anyone seen adjacent or attempting to cross the barrier.[1] In such a context, resentment against their Israeli gaolers escalated, as did the rhetoric of Hamas.

In such circumstances most civil society organisations within the Gaza Strip focused on the provision of basic services, many of them working as partners of international aid and relief agencies tasked with reconstructing the basic societal infrastructure after each of the wars. There was little or no space for popular resistance against what many saw as their mass incarceration by Israel, other than the usual Hamas-orchestrated marches and demonstrations. More prominent have been the activities of international solidarity activists to highlight the plight of the Gazan population through attempting to deliver aid by sea in contravention of the Israeli-imposed blockade. International volunteers based in Gaza have also suffered injury and death alongside Gazans. On March 16, 2003, an American student and activist with the International Solidarity Movement, Rachel Corrie, was killed by an Israeli occupation force bulldozer in Rafah at the southern tip of the Gaza Strip. She had been accompanying Palestinians for just two months when she was killed. A month later Tom Hurndall, a British student and activist also based in Rafah with the ISM, was shot in the head by an Israeli soldier whilst trying to care for some children caught in a crossfire. He died nine months later on January 13, 2004. Some years later, on April 14, 2011, an Italian ISM activist, Vittorio Arrigoni, was kidnapped and murdered by a rogue Salafist group in Gaza. Arrigoni had arrived in Gaza in August 2008 on one of the first boats to break the Israeli blockade. Over the next few months, he suffered injuries and arrest by the Israelis in the course of his work accompanying Palestinian fishermen at sea off the Gazan coast. An anarcho-pacifist activist and journalist, Arrigoni condemned the Israeli government as one of the worst apartheid regimes in the world, but he also made no secret of his critical stance vis-à-vis the Hamas administration in Gaza, alleging that 'they have deeply limited human rights since they have won the elections.'[2]

As an internationally known blogger, Arrigoni enjoyed a certain freedom to express views that Palestinians within Gaza would have been hesitant to express in the open, unless they were prepared to accept arrest, rough treatment and imprisonment at the hands of Hamas security personnel. Perhaps the denial of the basic rights of free expression and assembly have been no harsher in Gaza than in other parts of the Middle East and Arab world, but in December 2010 the carapace was broken when unprecedented protests broke out in Tunisia following the self-immolation of Mohammed Bouazizi in protest at police corruption and abuse. The protests spread like a wave to Algeria, Jordan, Egypt, Yemen and beyond. And Palestinians were not immune to the new spirit. One Palestinian activist confessed to us that the overthrow of the Egyptian President Hosni Mubarak in February 2011 was the occasion when he could honestly say that he was proud to be an Arab – something he had not felt for many years. So this was the context within which a group of young Gazans issued their own appeal, their own 'manifesto for change' in the name of Gaza Youth Break Out (GYBO). It was an immensely powerful cry from the heart which they posted on Facebook, and by early January 2011 it had gone viral. It still resonates today with all the passion, the anguish, the frustration and the yearning that drove those that composed it.

Fuck Hamas. Fuck Israel. Fuck Fatah. Fuck UN. Fuck UNWRA. Fuck USA! We, the youth in Gaza, are so fed up with Israel, Hamas, the occupation, the violations of human rights and the indifference of the international community! We want to scream and break this wall of silence, injustice and indifference like the Israeli F16's breaking the wall of sound; scream with all the power in our souls in order to release this immense frustration that consumes us because of this fucking situation we live in; we are like lice between two nails living a nightmare inside a nightmare, no room for hope, no space for freedom. We are sick of being caught in this political struggle; sick of coal dark nights with airplanes circling above our homes; sick of innocent farmers getting shot in the buffer zone because they are taking care of their lands; sick of bearded guys walking around with their guns abusing their power, beating up or incarcerating young people demonstrating for what they believe in; sick of the wall of shame that separates us from the rest of our country and keeps us imprisoned in a stamp-sized piece of land; sick of being portrayed as terrorists, homemade fanatics with explosives in our pockets and evil in our eyes; sick of the indifference we meet from the international community, the so-called experts in expressing concerns and drafting resolutions but cowards in enforcing anything they agree on; we are sick and tired of living a shitty life, being kept in jail by Israel, beaten up by Hamas and completely ignored by the rest of the world.

There is a revolution growing inside of us, an immense dissatisfaction and frustration that will destroy us unless we find a way of canalizing this energy into something that can challenge the status quo and give us some kind of hope … We are really living a nightmare inside a nightmare. It is difficult to find words for the pressure we are under. We barely survived the Operation

Cast Lead, where Israel very effectively bombed the shit out of us, destroying thousands of homes and even more lives and dreams. They did not get rid of Hamas, as they intended, but they sure scared us forever and distributed post-traumatic stress syndrome to everybody, as there was nowhere to run.

We are youth with heavy hearts. We carry in ourselves a heaviness so immense that it makes it difficult for us to enjoy the sunset. How to enjoy it when dark clouds paint the horizon and bleak memories run past our eyes every time we close them? We smile in order to hide the pain. We laugh in order to forget the war. We hope in order not to commit suicide here and now. During the war we got the unmistakable feeling that Israel wanted to erase us from the face of the earth. During the last years Hamas has been doing all they can to control our thoughts, behaviour and aspirations. We are a generation of young people used to facing missiles, carrying what seems to be a impossible mission of living a normal and healthy life, and only barely tolerated by a massive organization that has spread in our society as a malicious cancer disease, causing mayhem and effectively killing all living cells, thoughts and dreams on its way as well as paralyzing people with its terror regime. Not to mention the prison we live in, a prison sustained by a so-called democratic country.

History is repeating itself in its most cruel way and nobody seems to care. We are scared. Here in Gaza we are scared of being incarcerated, interrogated, hit, tortured, bombed, killed. We are afraid of living, because every single step we take has to be considered and well-thought, there are limitations everywhere, we cannot move as we want, say what we want, do what we want, sometimes we even can't think what we want because the occupation has occupied our brains and hearts so terrible that it hurts and it makes us want to shed endless tears of frustration and rage!

We do not want to hate, we do not want to feel all of these feelings, we do not want to be victims anymore. ENOUGH! Enough pain, enough tears, enough suffering, enough control, limitations, unjust justifications, terror, torture, excuses, bombings, sleepless nights, dead civilians, black memories, bleak future, heart aching present, disturbed politics, fanatic politicians, religious bullshit, enough incarceration! WE SAY STOP! This is not the future we want!

We want three things. We want to be free. We want to be able to live a normal life. We want peace. Is that too much to ask? We are a peace movement consistent of young people in Gaza and supporters elsewhere that will not rest until the truth about Gaza is known by everybody in this whole world and in such a degree that no more silent consent or loud indifference will be accepted.

This is the Gazan youth's manifesto for change!

We will start by destroying the occupation that surrounds ourselves, we will break free from this mental incarceration and regain our dignity and self-respect. We will carry our heads high even though we will face resistance. We will work day and night in order to change these miserable conditions we are living under. We will build dreams where we meet walls.[3]

How could such an impassioned appeal/confession/proclamation not touch the spirit of anyone reading it who could identify to some degree with the imprisoned bodies, minds and spirits to the pain of which it gave expression? One of the founders of GYBO explained to a journalist how it came about:

I started reading books about non-violent resistance, Mahatma Gandhi, Nelson Mandela, all these people. I had a new understanding. And I talked about it with my friends. We were sitting in a coffee shop, we started thinking about GYBO, how to do it. We wrote the manifesto in 30 minutes. We put it online. Then we started planning for the future. Before the creation of GYBO, before March 15, we had this phenomenon in Gaza: you never criticise the political movements. If you criticise Hamas you're always gonna be called a collaborator. If you criticise Fatah you're never going to have a job. If you criticise Israel you'll never be able to leave Gaza. You never criticise anyone. But when we created GYBO we thought of breaking this wall of silence. To say what we have in mind without taking into consideration what other people think of us.[4]

The group decided to take things further in their efforts to break out of the walls of silence, moving from social media initiatives to organising something substantive on the ground. They Skyped with youth in the West Bank and in the Palestinian diaspora around the world and consulted with activists in Egypt, and started to plan a 'day of rage' demanding political unity between Hamas and Fatah.[5] On Tuesday March 15, 2011 tens of thousands of Palestinians, the majority under the age of 30, demonstrated at different locations within the West Bank and the Gaza Strip.[6] It was an unprecedented public display of the desire felt by so many Palestinians for an end to the divide and the enmity between Fatah and Hamas. It was also a manifestation of public disgust at the cronyism, corruption and abuse of human rights that was a feature of both regimes – Fatah in the West Bank and Hamas in the Gaza Strip. It was a heartfelt call for a new chapter, a fresh start – a spring-cleaning of the Palestinian house. And, as might have been expected, the die-hards of both parties did not sit idly by and do nothing. In Ramallah security forces tried to break up the 3,000 strong gathering and at least 20 people were reported injured. Fatah thugs also tried to hijack the demonstration by shouting their own anti-American slogans and burning the American flag, whilst forcing journalists to delete photos of the protest from their cameras. Protesters in Gaza encountered similar opposition. Hamas supporters flooded the Square of the Unknown Soldier in Gaza City with their green flags and forcibly dispersed the demonstrators who had to regroup in an alternative space at Brigade Square where they continued to sing national songs and chant their slogans calling for an end to the political division. The hounding of the protesters continued for several days, with police and security forces entering Gaza City's Al-Azhar University, beating up students and arresting several of them.[7] A young Gazan blogger voiced her shock, dismay and disgust at witnessing such scenes:

Dear Hamas
May God forgive you, as I do not have the capacity to do so. … I am deeply disgusted, disappointed, and infuriated by the way in which you have handled – or, rather, mishandled – the situation. The course of action that you have, so stupidly and callously, been undertaking is not in the slightest justified. Where is your so-called Islam??? Perhaps I am in no position to judge, but … beating up kids, girls, and elderly is by no means Islamic. Beating up university students for merely calling for the end of division is by no means Islamic. Preventing ambulances from reaching the wounded inside the university is by no means Islamic. Beating up journalists and confiscating all cameras, brutally and recklessly, and so explicitly lying to the public are by no means Islamic. The policy of silencing your people is also far from Islamic.[8]

Perhaps some of the protesters had dreams that their action would launch a wave of similar protests throughout the West Bank and the Gaza Strip, but it was not to be and the action petered out – an outcome that could be explained in part by the grip exerted by the respective regimes in the West Bank and Gaza Strip but also by the exhaustion of the Palestinian population after so many decades of trying to survive under occupation. And it is this exhaustion which has drained from all but the most optimistic and committed any sense of their own agency and its prerequisite – hope for the future.

TOWARDS A SCENARIO OF HOPE

The challenge for the Palestinians is to develop a unified resistance strategy, one that envisions a role for all, whatever their gender, political persuasion, location or age. At the core of such a strategy must be a sustained commitment by political leadership at all levels to build on the experience of the popular resistance of the post-second intifada period in order to create a situation where the occupation cannot continue as normal. This requires creating a situation where:

- The financial, human and diplomatic costs incurred by Israel in maintaining the occupation becomes increasingly burdensome to wide sections of the public and their political leaders;
- The violence on which the occupation is based becomes ever more visible to widening constituencies of concerned people around the world;
- Political leaders within the states that make the occupation possible find it increasingly difficult to refrain from exercising pressure on Israel to sue for peace.

And the evidence from South Africa is that this will only come about through all elements – the Palestinians, the global networks of support and solidarity, the corporations and financial institutions, and the governments – working to bring an end to an intolerable and unsustainable situation whereby a whole population is subjugated by an occupying force that continues to deny it the most basic of human and civil rights.

So, what would be the necessary preconditions for such a situation to take shape? What would be the key elements in such a scenario of hope?

1. The deepening of the process initiated in 2014 towards political reconciliation between Fatah and Hamas, the establishment of a unity government and the agreement to pursue a new diplomatic offensive with the aim of bringing an end to the occupation focusing on the international community rather than pursuing empty 'negotiations' with an Israeli government that manifests no interest in making the concessions necessary for a sustainable peace process.[9]
2. The recognition that a powerful popular resistance movement can act as a significant lever in such a diplomatic offensive and create a new power relationship.
3. The political factions making up the Palestinian political domain agreeing to use all their organisational resources to mobilise people for popular resistance such that all sections of Palestinian society within the OPT and outside feel they have a role to play in the struggle to end the occupation.
4. Experience shows that the major powers in the world only take notice of popular struggles when they create some kind of crisis situation that demands their attention. Therefore the strategic challenge for Palestinians (and their allies within the transnational solidarity movements) is to develop modes of popular resistance that impose significant economic, financial, social and diplomatic costs on Israel such that 'normal service is no longer possible'.
5. A significant part of such a campaign must be to coordinate with Israeli activists with a view to mobilising grass-roots international participation in a global boycott of settler produce and other forms of boycott and

disinvestment from companies profiting directly from the ongoing occupation. An important role in such a campaign could be played by Jewish peace groups in the diaspora – their active participation would strengthen the resonance of the campaign amongst many constituencies.

6. Serious attempts should also be made to obtain financial support from as many sources as possible in order to finance the popular resistance movement with regard to training, salaries for organisers, compensation for those Palestinians who answer the call to cease working in settlement enterprises, and care and sustenance for the direct and indirect victims of the struggle.

7. Throughout this campaign every effort should be made to reassure the Israeli public that the aim of the resistance is the ending of the occupation as the basis for substantive negotiations to lay the foundations for a shared future for Palestinians and Israelis.

This is, we freely admit, a scenario of hope for change – and hope is something that has been in very short supply in the Middle East for several decades. But without hope despair rules, and as long as despair dominates there is no possibility of creating a worthwhile future for Palestinians and Israelis. A Rabbi in a Nazi death camp is reported to have pronounced, 'To despair is to betray the future'. More recently the Israeli novelist David Grossman reflected on the failure of Israelis to overcome their fears and existential despair in order to take substantive steps towards peace, whilst reaffirming his own refusal to relinquish hope for the future:

> What hope can there be when such is the terrible state of things? The hope of nevertheless. A hope that does not disregard the many dangers and obstacles, but refuses to see only them and nothing else. A hope that if the flames beneath the conflict die down, the healthy and sane features of the two peoples can gradually be revealed once more. The healing power of the everyday, of the wisdom of life and the wisdom of compromise, will begin to take effect. The sense of existential security. Of being able to raise children without abject fear, without the humiliation of occupation or the dread of terrorism. The basic human desires for family and livelihood and study. The fabric of life.[10]

A Palestinian activist in the current popular resistance movement and former activist in the first intifada reflected on the situation and the struggle to end the occupation:

> We are aware of the imbalance of power, the financial and the political support for Israel from the USA and internationally. But we have hope and belief

that the situation will change. It is our right to live in freedom on our land. We deeply believe in it. We believe the Israeli occupation will end someday like those before it. Also we see that the younger generation is very active and they are a source of hope for older generations. They have energy. The younger generation has overcome the fear of the army and settlers, not like us the older generation. Israel has not succeeded in suppressing the resistance.

NOTES

1. Introduction

1. Quoted in Andrew Rigby, *Living the intifada*. London: Zed Books, 1991, p. 41.
2. Some of our key informants were interviewed on more than one occasion over the period of the fieldwork. We also convened a number of round-table meetings to report our findings to activists and others to receive their observations.
3. Kurt Schock, for example, defines nonviolent action as 'non-routine political acts that do not involve violence or the threat of violence'. See Kurt Schock, 'The practice and study of civil resistance', *Journal of Peace Research*, vol. 50, no. 3 (2013), p. 277.
4. Quoted in Rigby, *Living the intifada*, p. 40.
5. See discussion on stone-throwing in Chapter 4.
6. This draws in particular on definitions suggested by Adam Roberts, Kurt Schock and Jacques Semelin. See Adam Roberts, 'Introduction', in A. Roberts and T. Garton Ash (eds), *Civil resistance & power politics: The experience of non-violent action from Gandhi to the present*. Oxford: Oxford University Press, 2009, pp. 1–24; Schock, 'The practice and study of civil resistance'; Jacques Semelin, *Unarmed against Hitler: Civilian resistance in Europe, 1939–1943*. Westport, CT: Praeger, 1993, p. 2.
7. For an overview of the development of civil resistance during the twentieth century, see Peter Ackerman and Jack DuVall, *A force more powerful: A century of nonviolent conflict*. New York: St Martin's, 2000.
8. April Carter, *People power and political change: Key issues and concepts*. London: Routledge, 2012, p. 10.
9. Gene Sharp, *The politics of nonviolent action*, (3 volumes). Boston, MA: Porter Sargent, 1973.
10. Erica Chenoweth and Maria J. Stephan, *Why civil resistance works: The strategic logic of nonviolent conflict*. New York: Columbia University Press, 2011.
11. Sharon E. Nepstad, *Nonviolent revolutions: Civil resistance in the late 20th century*. New York: Oxford University Press, 2011.
12. Semelin, *Unarmed against Hitler*, p. 3.
13. Ibid., p. 27.
14. Ibid., p. 49.
15. Werner Rings, *Life with the enemy: Collaboration and resistance in Hitler's Europe 1939–1945*. Garden City, NY: Doubleday, 1982.
16. Mazin B. Qumsiyeh, *Popular resistance in Palestine: A history of hope and empowerment*. London: Pluto Press, 2011.
17. See Gene Sharp, *Social power and political freedom*. Boston, MT: Porter Sargent, 1980.
18. See Peter Ackerman and Christopher Kruegler, *Strategic nonviolent conflict: The dynamics of people power in the twentieth century*. Westport, CT: Praeger, 1994, especially pp. 21–53.
19. One important dimension of nonviolent struggle with regard to the erosion of a repressive regime's pillars of support is holding out a future role for those who are today's opponents. As Gandhians have emphasised – the target is the system, not the people.

20. See Brian Martin, *Justice ignited: The dynamics of backfire*. Lanham, MD: Rowman & Littlefield, 2007. Earlier writers identified such processes as moral and political ju-jitsu (Richard B. Gregg, *The power of non-violence*. Nyack, NY: Fellowship Publications, 1959), whilst in 1989 Johan Galtung coined the term 'shame power' (J. Galtung, *Nonviolence and Israel/Palestine*. Honolulu, HI: University of Hawaii, 1989, p. 19). More recently attention has been focused on 'dilemma actions' – creating situations to which any reaction by the regime will be costly. See, for example, Srdja Popovic et al., *A guide to effective nonviolent struggle*. Belgrade: Centre for Applied Nonviolent Action and Strategies, 2007, pp. 142–51.

21. Galtung, *Nonviolence and Israel/Palestine*. See also Howard Clark (ed.), *People power: Unarmed resistance and global solidarity*. London: Pluto Press, 2009, p. 215.

22. See G. Sharp, *Waging nonviolent struggle: 20th century practice and 21st century potential*. Boston, MA: Extending Horizon Books, 2005, especially pp. 49–68.

23. Rings did not have a category of 'constructive resistance'. Our understanding of this mode of resistance draws on the insights developed by Bob Overy in his study of Gandhi's mode of resistance and mobilisation. See B. Overy, 'Gandhi as Political Organiser: An Analysis of Local and National Campaigns in India 1915–1922', unpublished Ph.D. thesis, University of Bradford, 1982.

24. Other key sources in addition to those cited above include Michael Randle, *Civil resistance*. London: Fontana, 1994; and Adam Roberts (ed.), *The strategy of civilian defence: Non-violent resistance to aggression*. London: Faber & Faber, 1967.

25. Doug McAdam has argued that a major factor in the success of the US civil rights movement was their continuous 'strategic innovation'. See D. McAdam, *Political process and the development of black insurgency, 1930–1970*. Chicago, IL: University of Chicago Press, 1999.

2. Palestinian resistance to the establishment of the State of Israel

1. Some of this chapter is based on work previously published in Andrew Rigby, *Palestinian resistance and nonviolence*. East Jerusalem: PASSIA, 2010.

2. Neville J. Mandel, *The Arabs and Zionism before World War I*. Berkeley, CA: University of California Press, 1976, p. xxiv.

3. Abdul-Wahhab S. Kayyali, *The Palestinian Arab reactions to Zionism and the British mandate, 1917–1939*, University of London, doctoral thesis, February, 1970, p. 10.

4. Kayyali, *Palestinian Arab reactions*, p. 20.

5. Ibid., p. 21.

6. Ibid., p. 32.

7. Ibid., p. 61.

8. See Ilan Pappe, *A history of modern Palestine*. Cambridge: Cambridge University Press, 2006, p. 47.

9. Correspondence between Sir Henry McMahon, British High Commissioner in Egypt, and Hussein, 14 July 1915–30 January 1916.

10. Albert Hourani, *A history of the Arab peoples*. London: Faber & Faber, 1991, p. 318.

11. Kayyali, *Palestinian Arab reactions*, p. 76.

12. Yehoshua Porath, *The emergence of the Palestinian-Arab national movement, 1918–1929*. London: Frank Cass, 1974, p. 96.

13. Porath, *Emergence of the Palestinian-Arab national movement*, p. 96.

14. Ibid., p. 97.

15. After four days of disturbances, the toll was four Arabs and five Jews dead, 22 seriously wounded (including 18 Jewish victims) and 193 Jews slightly wounded; see Kayyali, *Palestinian Arab reactions*, p. 118.

16. The San Remo Conference awarded France the mandate for Syria. They expelled Faisal from Damascus in July 1920. A year later the British installed him as ruler of Iraq.

17. Rosemary Sayigh, *Palestinians: From peasants to revolutionaries*. London: Zed Books, 1979, pp. 14–15.

18. Ibid., p. 50.

19. According to Emile Touma this was the first expression of Palestinian nationalism, see E. Touma, *The roots of the Palestinian question*, (Arabic), Jerusalem: n.p., 1976. p. 144.

20. There were reports that Arab members of the police force were directly responsible for some of the violence inflicted against Jews.

21. Quoted in Porath, *Emergence of the Palestinian-Arab national movement*, p. 200.

22. Kayyali, *Palestinian Arab reactions*, p. 201.

23. Porath, *Emergence of the Palestinian-Arab national movement*, p. 135. It is also worth noting that at this stage Haj Amin Husayni was amongst the most forceful opponents of any suggestion of resorting to violence, as he sought the support of the British in building up his power base within the SMC.

24. It is important to record that 19 local Arab families in Hebron saved 435 Jews by hiding them in their houses during the pogrom. See Eli Ashkenazi, 'Survivor of 1929 Hebron Massacre recounts her ordeal', *Haaretz*, August 10, 2009, at: http://tinyurl.com/qxse7w9 (accessed March 14, 2015).

25. Kayyali, *Palestinian Arab reactions*, p. 217.

26. This watering down of the resolution was due in part to Haj Amin Husayni's fear of jeopardising his relationship with the British High Commissioner (Kayyali, *Palestinian Arab reactions*, p. 252).

27. This practice was encouraged by the *Histadrut* which had been established in 1920 to look after Jewish workers' interests.

28. Touma, *Roots of the Palestinian question*, p. 194.

29. Yehoshua Porath, *The Palestinian Arab national movement, 1929–1939: From riots to rebellion*. London: Frank Cass, 1977, p. 45. Porath also claims that at this stage people were establishing secret arms caches and engaging in clandestine military training delivered by former members of the Ottoman forces under the guise of sports clubs and Boy Scout camps. See Porath, *Palestinian-Arab national movement*, pp. 130–32.

30. See Mary E. King, *A quiet revolution: The first Palestinian intifada and nonviolent resistance*. NY: Nation Books, 2007, pp. 45–49.

31. King, *A quiet revolution*, p. 49.

32. See Wendy Pearlman, *Violence, nonviolence, and the Palestinian national movement*. New York: Cambridge University Press, 2011, p. 43.

33. See Kayyali, *Palestinian Arab reactions*, pp. 168–69.

34. As a substitute for striking, officials were required to pay a percentage of their salaries into a strike fund. They were also expected to pass on to the resistance any confidential information that came their way, and senior officials were required to sign a declaration expressing solidarity with the aims of the strike. (Porath, *Palestinian-Arab national movement*, p. 170).

35. It was the awareness of the risk to their jobs from Jewish workers that caused the Arab dock workers of Haifa to refuse to heed the call to strike until early August

1936, when they finally succumbed to sustained pressure. (Porath, *Palestinian-Arab national movement*, p. 166)

36. Porath claims that this practice was approved by the Palestinian boycott committee. (Porath, *Palestinian-Arab national movement*, p. 220).

37. Quoted in Kayyali, *Palestinian Arab reactions*, p. 292.

38. Haj Amin Husayni evaded arrest and eventually escaped to Syria.

39. Quoted in Porath, *Palestinian-Arab national movement*, p. 238.

40. Kayyali, *Palestinian Arab reactions*, p. 293.

41. Porath, *Palestinian-Arab national movement*, p. 249.

42. At: http://tinyurl.com/ojtlpuw (accessed January 12, 2014).

43. See Charles Townshend, 'The First Intifada: Rebellion in Palestine 1936–39', *History Today*, vol. 39, no. 7 (July 1989), at http://tinyurl.com/nfdy3kb (accessed March 14, 2015).

44. The Nashashibis had aligned themselves with the British and were supportive of the partition proposal.

45. Quoted in Porath, *Palestinian-Arab national movement*, pp. 254–55.

46. One example was the Passfield White Paper published by the British in October 1930 in the wake of the August 1929 riots, which recommended the establishment of a legislative council and heavy restrictions on Jewish immigration, land acquisitions and settlement. It provoked outrage in Zionist circles. Large sections of the Jewish population in Palestine went on strike and the British Prime Minister, Ramsay MacDonald, came under strong domestic pressure so that he felt obliged to distance himself from the White Paper. See Gudrun Krämer, *A history of Palestine: From the Ottoman conquest to the founding of the State of Israel*. Princeton, NJ: Princeton University Press, 2008, pp. 234–45.

47. Krämer, *History of Palestine*, p. 310.

48. Pappe, *History of modern Palestine*, pp. 128–30.

49. Krämer, *History of Palestine*, p. 313.

50. Pappe, *History of modern Palestine*, p. 130.

51. Krämer, *History of Palestine*, p. 315.

52. Pappe, *History of modern Palestine*, p. 131.

53. This section is based on the unpublished MA dissertation of Jawad Botmeh, *Civil resistance in Palestine: The village of Battir in 1948*, Coventry University, September 2006, at: http://tinyurl.com/qarfy4y (accessed October 14, 2014).

54. Hasan Mustafa, *Welcome to Battir* (Battir, Jordan, July 1959), quoted by Botmeh, *Civil resistance in Palestine*, p. 35.

55. Botmeh, *Civil resistance*, p. 45. A number of villagers were killed by Israeli troops during the early 1950s. See Benny Morris, *Israel's border wars, 1949–1956*. Oxford: Clarendon Press, 1988, p. 138.

56. See Benny Morris, *1948: A history of the first Arab–Israeli war*. New Haven, CT: Yale University Press, 2008, p. 83. See also Sayigh, *Palestinians*, pp. 64–66.

3. Palestinians in Israel: from quiet resistance to audible protest and political mobilisation

1. Extracts from a story written by Ghassan Fawzi, and an interview with his mother Ifat Sharef.

2. Asef Bayat, *Life as politics: How ordinary people change the Middle East*. Stanford, CA: Stanford University Press, 2013, p. 5.

3. Bayat, *Life as politics*, p. 15.
4. We will use the terms Palestinians in Israel and Arabs in Israel interchangeably throughout the book.
5. For an exploration of how such activities differ from the 'hidden resistance' studied by James C. Scott, see Asef Bayat, 'Un-civil society: the politics of the "informal people"', *Third World Quarterly*, vol. 18, no. 1 (1997), pp. 53–72.
6. Bayat, *Life as politics*, p. 20. Bayat makes the point that it is because such noncollective activities are part and parcel of everyday life that 'nonmovements' are able to enjoy a degree of resilience in the face of repressive regimes. See Bayat, *Life as politics*, pp. 20–12.
7. See Benny Morris, *The birth of the Palestinian refugee problem revisited*. Cambridge: Cambridge University Press, 2003, p. 604. See also Walid Khalidi (ed.), *All that remains: The Palestinian villages occupied and depopulated by Israel in 1948*. Washington, DC: Institute for Palestine Studies, 1992, pp. 224–25.
8. Sarah Graham-Brown, *Education, repression and liberation: Palestinians*. London: World University Service, 1965, p. 37.
9. *Waqf* property is an inalienable religious endowment under Islamic law, typically held by a charitable trust.
10. Sami Khalil Mar'i, *Arab education in Israel*. Syracuse, NY: Syracuse University Press, 1978, p. 18.
11. Ian Lustick, *The Arabs in the Jewish state*. Austin, TX: University of Texas Press, 1980, p. 189.
12. The strategy of the Zionist political parties was to create their own 'Arab lists' in order to gain votes in the Knesset elections. In the 1959 elections, for example, five Arabs affiliated to the Labour Party were elected to the Knesset.
13. Quoted in J. Wajdi, *In the state of the Jews: 1949–2006. Umm al-Fahim and Lajjun. A journey through time*. Jerusalem: Al Resala Press, 2007, (Arabic).
14. Pappe, *History of modern Palestine*, p. 170.
15. Ben White, *Palestinians in Israel: Segregation, discrimination and democracy*. London: Pluto Press, 2012, p. 75.
16. Traditionally *mukhtar*s enjoyed significant social status but under the military regime they came to be seen by many as corrupt collaborators.
17. Lustick, *Arabs in the Jewish state*, p. 187.
18. Emile Touma, 'The history of Rakah in Israel', *Leviathan*, (Boston) vol. 3 (Fall 1980), p. 4.
19. Quoted in White, *Palestinians in Israel*, p. 76.
20. For an analysis of the basis of the ethnic division within Israel, see Yiftachel Oren. 'Israeli Society and Jewish–Palestinian Reconciliation: "Ethnocracy" and its Territorial Contradictions', *Middle East Journal* vol. 51, no. 4 (1997), pp. 505–519. Also Marwan Darweish, 'Human Rights and the Imbalance of Power: The Palestinian–Israeli Conflict', in V. Dudouet and B. Schmelzle (eds), *Human rights and conflict transformation: The challenges of just peace*. Berlin: Berghof Conflict Research Centre, 2010, pp. 85–94.
21. In May 1977 the PLO leadership and representatives of the Palestinians inside Israel met for the first time in Prague. These meetings continued for several years.
22. By 1993 over 80 per cent of the lands owned by Palestinian Arabs living in Israel had been confiscated and placed at the exclusive disposal of Jewish citizens. Arjan El Fassad, 'What is it that Palestinians commemorate on Land Day?', *The Electronic Intifada*, March 30, 2001, at: http://tinyurl.com/opvjhhn (accessed March 14, 2015).

23. Souad A. Dajani, *Ruling Palestine: A history of the legally sanctioned Jewish-Israeli seizure of land and housing in Palestine*. Geneva and Bethlehem: Centre on Housing Rights and Evictions (COHRE) and BADIL Resource Center for Palestinian Residency and Refugee Rights, 2005, p. 61.

24. The new parties included Progressive List for Peace (PLP) and Abna al-Balad, and the Democratic Arab Party (1988).

25. See M. Darweish and A. Rigby, *Palestinians in Israel: Nationality and citizenship*. Bradford: University of Bradford, 1995, pp. 8–11.

26. Darweish and Rigby, *Palestinians in Israel*, p. 43.

27. *Al-Ittihad*, December 20, 1987.

28. See Darweish and Rigby, *Palestinians in Israel*, pp. 48–51.

29. The Oslo Accord, also known as the Declaration of Principles, was an attempt to establish a framework for a sustainable peace agreement between the Israeli government and the Palestine Liberation Organisation. See Graham Usher, *Palestine in crisis: The struggle for peace and political independence after Oslo*. London: Pluto Press, 1995.

30. Graham Usher, 'Uprising wipes off Green Line', *Al-Ahram*, no. 503, October 12–18, 2000, at: http://weekly.ahram.org.eg/2000/503/re6.htm (accessed March 14, 2015).

31. See White, *Palestinians in Israel*, pp. 80–81.

32. Ilan Pappe, *The forgotten Palestinians: A history of the Palestinians in Israel*. New Haven, CT: Yale University Press, 2011, p. 234.

4. From the Nakbha to the Separation Wall: 1948–2002

1. The June 1967 war was fought between Israel and the neighbouring Arab states of Egypt, Syria and Jordan. After six days of fighting Israel had captured the Gaza Strip and Sinai Peninsula from Egypt, the West Bank (including East Jerusalem) from Jordan, and the Golan Heights from Syria. See Michael B. Oren, *Six days of war: June 1967 and the making of the modern Middle East*. New York: Oxford University Press, 2002.

2. In the words of Frantz Fanon, 'Violence alone, violence committed by the people, violence organised and educated by its leaders, makes it possible for the masses to understand social truths and gives the key to them.' Frantz Fanon, *The wretched of the earth*. Harmondsworth: Penguin, 1967, p. 118.

3. Rashid Khalidi, *Palestinian identity: The construction of modern national consciousness*. New York: Columbia University Press, 1997, p. 196.

4. Ibid., p. 195.

5. Ibid.

6. Quoted in Khalidi, *Palestinian identity*, pp. 198–99. Sartarwi was subsequently murdered in Lisbon in 1983, an act that was presumed to be the work of the dissident Abu Nidal group.

7. Pappe, *History of modern Palestine*, p. 195.

8. By 1972 almost 28 per cent of the West Bank had been confiscated, see Pappe, *History of modern Palestine*, p. 200.

9. Salim Tamari, 'What the uprising means', *Middle East Report*, May–June 1988, p. 26.

10. The Camp David Accords of 1978 between Israel and Egypt led directly to the 1979 Egypt–Israel Peace Treaty. As part of the framework agreement it was determined the West Bank and Gaza Strip would have a level of autonomy under a 'self-governing authority' for a period of up to five years, during which negotiations would take place to determine their final status. No mention was made of the status of Jerusalem or

the Palestinian right of return, and there was no consultation with the PLO. As a consequence the proposals were vehemently opposed by Palestinians. See William Quandt, *Camp David: Peacemaking and politics*. Washington, DC: Brookings Institution Press, 1986.

11. See Robin L. Bidwell, *Dictionary of modern Arab history*. Abingdon: Routledge, 2010, pp. 323–24. See also Alain Gresh, *The PLO: The struggle within*. London: Zed Books, 1988.

12. Galtung, *Nonviolence and Israel/Palestine*, p. 19.

13. Israel had requested $10 billion loan guarantees from the USA so that they could fund the absorption of the Russian Jews who were flooding into the country.

14. A similar pattern had already been imposed in the Gaza Strip, with Jewish settlements divided into three blocs covering about one third of the territory, with the remaining two thirds cut into cantons for the 1.1 million Palestinians.

15. In 1995 there might have been grounds for such an optimistic scenario, but as events unfolded it became increasingly clear that Israel had no intention of transferring territory of any significant scale over to the PA. At the time of writing Area C, over which Israel exercises complete control, covers over 60 per cent of the West Bank.

16. The organisational infrastructure of popular committees that had directed and guided the first intifada had been superseded by the agencies of the PA.

17. See Michael Ellman and Smain Laacher, *Migrant workers in Israel – A contemporary form of slavery*. Euro-Mediterranean Human Rights Network and International Federation for Human Rights, 2003, at: http://tinyurl.com/pbk8ovv (accessed February 3, 2015).

18. It has been estimated that between September 1993 and October 2000 there were about 500 people-to-people projects involving over 100 organisations and a total budget of $20–30 million. Shira Herzog and Avivit Hai, 'What do people mean when they say "People-to-People"?', *Palestine–Israel Journal*, vols 12–13, no. 4 (2005–06), at: www.pij.org/details.php?id=395 (accessed July 28, 2014).

19. Sara Roy, *Failing peace: Gaza and the Palestinian–Israeli conflict*. London: Pluto Press, 2007, p. 245.

20. For a discussion of some of the points of contrast, see Ghassan Andoni, 'A comparative study of intifada 1987 and Intifada 2000', in R. Carey (ed.), *The new intifada*. London: Verso, 2001, pp. 209–218.

5. The resurgence of popular resistance: 2002–13

1. See Nigel Parsons, *The politics of the Palestinian authority: From Oslo to Al-Aqsa*. London: Routledge, 2005, p. 265.

2. Some observers claim that the violent response of the Israeli military to the initial protests was to 'fan the flames' of anger so that the protesters would resort to arms and the confrontations could then be dealt with militarily rather than politically. See Michael Bröning, *The politics of change in Palestine: State-building and non-violent resistance*. London: Pluto Press, 2011, p. 135.

3. Quoted in Laetitia Bucaille, *Growing up Palestinian: Israeli occupation and the Intifada generation*. Princeton, NJ: Princeton University Press, 2004, p. 125.

4. It has been estimated that 45 per cent of arable land in the West Bank is planted with olive trees. See Marwan Darweish, 'Olive Trees: Livelihoods and Resistance', in A. Özerdem and R. Roberts (eds), *Challenging post-conflict environments: Sustainable agriculture*. Ashgate: Farnham, 2012, p. 183.

5. Along much of its length the barrier consists of an electronic fence flanked by paved pathways, barded-wire fences, security cameras and control towers and trenches. The

average width of the barrier is 60 meters. Along the remainder of its route it consists of a concrete wall six metres or more in height. Different terms are used to depict the structure; it remains a highly contested concept. We have decided to follow the term used by most of our interviewees and call it 'the Wall'.

6. This sabotage continued after the barrier had been completed. As an activist from the village of Tourah recounted, 'The youth went out and sabotaged equipment during the construction of the wall, and after the construction they continued to sabotage the security cameras and cut the electric wires.'

7. Some international solidarity organisations supported small development projects for education and youth. In Taybeh village they organised a 'football match' with the Palestinians playing on the eastern side of the fence and Israeli activists on the western side.

8. Shuhada Street is located in the old city of Hebron, access by Palestinians is severely restricted.

9. It was also our impression that activists engaged in very little sustained evaluation of their actions.

10. Quoted in Jody McIntyre, 'Interview: Budrus "built a model of civil resistance"', *The electronic Intifada*, November 4, 2010, at: http://tinyurl.com/qbbut6b (accessed March 13, 2015).

11. Quoted in Arundhati Roy, 'Gandhi, but with guns: Part One', *The Guardian*, March 27, 2010, at: http://tinyurl.com/olz8g6v (accessed March 14, 2015).

12. 'Twenty years after Berlin, Palestinians crack Israel's wall', *Ma'an News Agency*, November 6, 2009, at: http://tinyurl.com/mb5fwv6 (accessed March 14, 2015).

13. Invariably such clashes are filmed and photographed not just by the Israeli security but also by activists for release on websites as a polemical form of resistance.

14. See report by B'Tselem, October 28, 2009, at: http://tinyurl.com/6zumw6f (accessed March 14, 2015).

15. Interviews, Tel Aviv, November 20, 2013.

16. See Haggai Matar, 'Palestinian women take back spring as settlers, soldiers look on', *+972 Magazine*, April 22, 2012, at: http://tinyurl.com/qx6x6yl (accessed March 14, 2015).

17. Since 2010 there has been a decline in coverage of Palestinian popular resistance in Israeli media. According to one Israeli activist, 'You go to news editors with the best possible story about the West Bank and they would not use it. No one is interested in stories about Arabs. Because if you ran it your ratings would decline.' (Interview, Tel Aviv, November 2013).

18. A more significant way of addressing this challenge has been the targeting by Palestinians of wider publics and constituencies of potential support internationally. See Chapter 9.

19. Quoted in 'Palestinians block Route 443 to protest settler violence', *+972*, October 17, 2012.

20. Abir Kopty, quoted in Mya Guarnieri, 'Palestinians beaten, arrested during protest at settlement supermarket', *+972*, October 24, 2012.

21. Interview with the national coordinator of the Karama Fund, July 20, 2010.

22. The threatened sanctions included refusal to issue travel permits to those endorsing such a campaign and to impose restrictions on Palestinian international financial transactions which passed through Israeli banks. In addition Israel has regularly threatened to withhold the customs duties collected on goods headed to the OPT through the border crossings Israel controls.

23. The role of internationals in accompaniment programmes is examined in Chapter 9.

24. For an authoritative analysis of this process, see Meron Rapoport, *Shady dealings in Silwan*. Jerusalem: Ir Amin, 2009.

25. Sources include report from Alternative Information Centre, '900 Palestinians detained in East Jerusalem', October 27, 2014, at: http://tinyurl.com/not8qvd (accessed March 14, 2015); Bradley Burston, 'A special place in Hell', *Haaretz*, October 28, 2014 and Ben Caspit, 'Jerusalem's silent intifada', *Al-Monitor*, October 23 2014, at: http://tinyurl.com/n3ne2xp (accessed March 14, 2015).

26. Extracts from interviews with activists carried out in November 2013.

27. Equivalent to 4,275 acres.

28. In June 2001 Al Aqaba won a legal battle when the Israeli High Court recommended the army remove its military camp from village land and find an alternate site. Two years later in June 2003 the military finally complied and removed themselves from the village.

29. For details of aquaponics, see http://tinyurl.com/mxtgkfk (accessed October 22, 2014).

30. Irene Nasser, 'In Bab Al-Shams, Palestinians create new facts on the ground', *+972 Blog*, January 25, 2013, at: http://tinyurl.com/pjbl554 (accessed March 14, 2015).

6. Challenges facing Palestinian popular resistance

1. Semelin, *Unarmed against Hitler*, p. 3.

2. B. Michael, *Ha'aretz*, August 21, 1988.

3. Joost R. Hiltermann, *Behind the Intifada: Labor and women's movements in the occupied territories*. Princeton, NJ: Princeton University Press, 1991, p. 12.

4. For a few months in the latter half of 1988 the leadership of the uprising was contested by Hamas, but by early 1989 an understanding had been reached between the PLO and Hamas that they would try to coordinate their activities as much as possible.

5. Quoted in Rigby, *Living the intifada*, p. 41.

6. According to Hiltermann, it was the interlocking network of community-based organisations and civil society organisations that provided 'the local institutional infrastructure as well as leadership for the uprising that began in December 1987.' Hiltermann, *Behind the intifada*, pp. 5–6.

7. Daoud Kuttab, *Washington Post*, September 4, 1988.

8. Rigby, *Living the intifada*, p. 197.

9. Ibid., pp. 197–98.

10. We were informed that the incomers were labelled 'Thais' by the Ramallah elite – placing them in the same category as the migrant labour from Thailand to be found in Israel.

11. Salah Abdel Shafi, 'Diversity in Unity? Fragmentation of the Palestinian People and the Fight for Unity', March 12, 2010, at: http://tinyurl.com/pulnt99 (accessed March 14, 2015).

12. Benoit Challand, 'Looking Beyond the Pale: International Donors And Civil Society Promotion in Palestine', *Palestine–Israel Journal*, vol. 12, no. 1 (2005), at: www.pij.org/details.php?id=330 (accessed March 14, 2015).

13. Ibid.

14. 'Despite threats Israel transfers tax moneys to Palestinian Authority', *Alternative information centre*, May 7, 2014, at: http://tinyurl.com/l9cdwxv (accessed March 17, 2015).

15. Fatah remains the dominant secular nationalist tendency within Palestinian politics. But whilst many of its members are now occupying positions within the PA, others

still consider themselves part of a liberation movement. In the West Bank Hamas had discouraged its members from participating in the popular resistance. According to one informant speaking a few months prior to the political reconciliation of summer 2014, 'Hamas does not participate – their leaders do not want them to be active with popular resistance as for them the PA is a greater enemy than Israel.'

16. It became apparent during our research that in a number of locations there was more than one popular resistance committee, each one aligned to a different coordinating network. These locations included Ni'lin, Beit Ummar, Al-Masara, Hebron and in the Jordan Valley.

17. A number of informants attributed economic hardship and consequent low rates of participation in popular resistance to the liberalisation of the local economy and the ready availability of loans that has led to an increasing level of personal debt. As one activist put it, 'It is all part of the package of the peace process, so that people worry about what they will have to sacrifice, so they are reluctant to take action that might result in them losing their home.'

18. See Rigby, *Living the intifada*, pp. 167–68.

19. See the website of the Palestinian BDS National Committee (BNC), at: http://bdsmovement.net for updates on the campaign.

7. The role of Israeli peace and solidarity activists

1. See Simha Flapan, *Zionism and the Palestinians*. London: Croom Helm, 1979, pp. 168–73. Magnes was a pacifist and first chancellor of the Hebrew University in Jerusalem, which he envisaged as a place for Arab–Jewish cooperation.

2. Quoted in Dan Leon, 'Binationalism: A Bridge Over the Chasm', *Palestine–Israel Journal*, vol. 6, no. 2 (July 1999), at: www.pij.org/details.php?id=929# (accessed March 14, 2015).

3. Quoted in Adam Keller, *Terrible days: Social divisions and political paradoxes in Israel*. Amstelveen: Cypres, 1987, pp. 167–68.

4. See Rigby, *Living the intifada*, pp. 182–83.

5. Tzali Reshef, *Peace now: From the officers' letter to the peace now*. Jerusalem: Keter Publishing House, 1996, p. 10. (September 13, 1993 was the day the Oslo Accords were signed in Washington, DC).

6. The Peace Index is an ongoing public opinion survey on the effects of the Israeli–Palestinian conflict on Israeli society. *Peace Index: December 2000*, at: http://tinyurl.com/q4l9bjw (accessed March 14, 2015).

7. Quoted in International Crisis Group, 'Back to Basics: Israel's Arab minority and the Israeli–Palestinian Conflict', *Middle East Report*, no. 119, March 14, 2012, p. 2.

8. *Peace Index: May 2004*, at: http://tinyurl.com/o5rpfag (accessed March 14, 2015).

9. See Chapter 9, pp. 153–4.

10. www.awalls.org/about_AATW (accessed March 14, 2015).

11. The tagline of Ta'ayush is 'Israelis and Arabs striving together to end the Israeli occupation and to achieve full civil equality through daily non-violent direct action.'

12. See Michael Omer-Man, 'Breaking down barriers in the South Hebron Hills', *Common ground news service*, 5 April, 2011, at: http://tinyurl.com/kjm35to (accessed March 14, 2015).

13. See the website for Breaking the Silence: Israeli soldiers talk about the occupied territories, at: www.breakingthesilence.org.il/

14. See the website for New Profile: The Movement for the Demilitarization of Israeli Society, at: www.newprofile.org/english/

15. New Profile leaflet, *We want peace, don't we? After all nobody wants war.* (2002).
16. Another group which works with 'resisters' is the Druze Initiative Committee. See Budour Hassan, 'New Palestinian campaign to support Druze conscientious objectors', *Middle East Monitor*, March 20, 2014, at: http://tinyurl.com/orv3tlj (accessed March 14, 2015).
17. See the website for Zochrot, at: http://zochrot.org/en. At the time of writing Zochrot were about to issue a *nakbha* app for android devices to enable people to learn about Palestinian localities destroyed in 1948.
18. Machsom Watch was formed in 2001 when a group of 'mature, professional women' started to visit the checkpoint at Bethlehem to observe and monitor the behaviour of the occupation forces. Their numbers have grown to cover significant areas of the West Bank. They report their findings to decision makers and the wider public, and will also intervene when they witness inappropriate action by personnel from the occupation forces. See Joshua Hammer, 'Grandmothers on Guard', *Mother Jones*, November–December 2004, at: http://tinyurl.com/m7zjb5 (accessed March 14, 2015).
19. According to Yesh Din's records over 90 per cent of cases are closed by the police due to 'lack of evidence'.
20. We were informed that research by Breaking the Silence has revealed that soldiers are not aware that whilst they are expected to protect settlers, they also have a responsibility to protect Palestinians.
21. Yesh Din is a 'hybrid' organisation insofar as it has a professional staff and a volunteer body who participate in the collection and checking of information, and serve on the organisation's steering committee, which is composed entirely of active volunteers.
22. There can also be real costs in terms of arrests, fines and imprisonment. It was the challenge of finding the funds to cover mounting legal costs due to the increased state assault on anti-occupation activists within Israel that led to the establishment of a Human Rights Defenders Fund. See www.hrd.org.il/ (accessed March 14, 2015).
23. It should be noted that not all Israeli activists are in favour of the BDS movement. As one close friend and activist observed: 'The problem with BDS is that it does strike a sensitive nerve in us, that the whole world is against us. We carry that sensitivity … We have been persecuted throughout history, we are suffering from anti-Semitism as Jews, the world is against us. This is the danger. This is the risk. It brings out such a reaction – we are the victims once again!'

8. Aid, advocacy and resilience: the role of international humanitarian aid agencies

1. Mary B. Anderson, *Do no harm: How aid can support peace–or war.* London: Lynne Rienner, 1999, p. 1.
2. Shearer and Pickup have estimated that foreign aid at this stage amounted to about 25 per cent of the PA's total budget. David Shearer and Francine Pickup, 'Dilemmas for aid policy in Lebanon and the occupied Palestinian territories', *Humanitarian Exchange*, no. 37 (March, 2007), pp. 4–6, at: http://tinyurl.com/k366nb5 (accessed March 14, 2015).
3. According to Shearer and Pickup customs revenues constituted somewhere in the region of half the PA's total revenue, see Shearer and Pickup, 'Dilemmas for aid policy'.
4. See Mary B. Anderson, 'Do no harm – the impact of international assistance in the Occupied Palestinian Territory', in M. Keating, A. Le More and R. Lowe (eds), *Aid,*

diplomacy and facts on the ground: The case of Palestine. London: Chatham House, 2005, pp. 144–45.

5. 'The fundamental principles of the Red Cross and Red Crescent', at: http://tinyurl.com/oof3xbd (accessed March 14, 2015).

6. Ninety per cent of the Jordan Valley is under full Israeli civil and military control as part of Area C. Other areas falling under the same designation include the South Hebron Hills, the central area of Hebron city and neighbourhoods of East Jerusalem, including Silwan.

7. Quoted in *IRIN News*, 'Israel-OPT: Aid agencies tread gingerly in Area C', January 11, 2013, at: http://tinyurl.com/o7tb6bz (accessed March 14, 2015). In May 2012, the European Union (EU) Council of Foreign Affairs called on Israel to meet its obligations to communities in Area C, 'including by accelerated approval of Palestinian master plans, halting forced transfer of population and demolition of Palestinian housing and infrastructure … and addressing humanitarian needs'. The Council stated that the 'social and economic developments in Area C are of critical importance for the viability of a future Palestinian state'.

8. Apparently the agency had to promise its national government not to use state funds for construction without permits, hence the reference to using private donations for the construction of the kindergartens.

9. 'What can we do with a rights-based approach to development?', *ODI Briefing Paper*, September 1999, at: http://tinyurl.com/qcjr6np (accessed March 14, 2015).

10. Herzog and Hai, 'What Do People Mean When They Say "People-to-People"?'.

11. Roy, *Failing Peace*, p. 245.

12. Adapted from 'Palestinian youth against normalization with Israel', *Palestinian youth against normalization*, April 28, 2010, at: http://pyan48.wordpress.com/ (accessed March 14, 2015).

13. Ibid.

14. It is relevant to note that amongst those agencies working with Israeli and Palestinian partners there is an over-representation of faith-based (Christian) agencies, reflecting the pressures from their supporters and constituencies at home that the agency should work on both sides of the divide.

15. In presenting some of the Israeli partners of agencies attempting to work on the conflict 'across the divide' we are not making claims to present a comprehensive listing – this is a selection to illustrate the range and types of partners.

16. It should be noted that at least one agency with Physicians for Human Rights as its partner only provides funding for its work with Palestinians in the OPT, not for its work on the right to health within Israel.

17. According to some informants the most powerful 'witnessing' has been from people associated with Breaking the Silence; it would seem that for European audiences at least they carry more legitimacy than Palestinians.

18. DanChurchAid, 'Statement on Gaza', July 16, 2014, at: http://tinyurl.com/oaesnat (accessed March 14, 2015).

19. 'Christian Aid launches Gaza Appeal', *Christian Aid*, July 22, 2014, at: http://tinyurl.com/pnfxkpu (accessed March 14, 2015).

20. For double-mandate agencies such as Medical Aid for Palestinians (MAP), it is part of their mission to provide humanitarian assistance while also advocating politically for one side in the conflict.

21. Quoted in IRIN, 'Politics and humanitarianism in Israel-oPt', November 29, 2012, at: http://tinyurl.com/lsewn6e (accessed March 14, 2015).

22. The October 2012 report, *Trading away peace: How Europe helps sustain illegal Israeli settlements*, called for banning the import of settlement products from entering European Union markets, at: www.fidh.org/IMG/pdf/trading.pdf (accessed March 14, 2015).

9. Links in the chain – international leverage?

1. The unprecedented wave of international grass-roots protest unleashed against the Israeli war on the Gaza Strip in July–August 2014 reflected the growth of international support for the Palestinian struggle to end the occupation.
2. One of the founders was Scott Kennedy, who led more than 36 delegations to the Middle East before his untimely and tragic death in November 2011, by which time IFPB had become an independent organisation.
3. See Interfaith Peace-Builders, at: www.ifpb.org/delegations/upcoming.html (accessed March 14, 2015).
4. Over 50 countries condemned or protested the Israeli action. See *CNN* report, May 31, 2010, at: http://tinyurl.com/mxy6vzc (accessed March 11, 2013).
5. This would seem to be an excellent example of what has been termed 'dilemma actions' when demonstrators create a situation in which the opponent will pay a cost whatever they do. If they use force, as in the case of the Freedom Flotilla, this can backfire and lead to public outrage and a consequent loss of legitimacy. If they allow the action to proceed, the demonstrators gain by achieving their nominal goal. (See George Lakey, *Strategy for a living revolution*. San Francisco, CA: W. H. Freeman, 1973, pp. 103–08.) For a discussion of the conditions under which counter-measures against demonstrators can backfire, see Brian Martin, *Justice ignited: The dynamics of backfire*. Lanham, MD: Rowman & Littlefield, 2007.
6. Probably the best known was the Swedish author Henning Mankell.
7. See www.freegaza.org (accessed October 27, 2011). See also, Greta Berlin and Bill Dienst (eds), *Freedom sailors: The maiden voyage of the free Gaza movement and how we succeeded in spite of ourselves*. Free Gaza, 2012.
8. See http://en.wikipedia.org/wiki/Freedom_Flotilla_II (accessed February 21, 2013).
9. See http://shiptogaza.se/en (accessed February 22, 2013).
10. Harriet Sherwood, 'Israeli soldier clubs Danish protester with rifle', *The Guardian*, April 16, 2012, at: http://tinyurl.com/pe9v6w5 (accessed March 14, 2015). It is also relevant to point out that a 'flytilla' cannot compare with a 'flotilla' in terms of drama.
11. Quoted from http://palsolidarity.org/about (accessed March 14, 2015).
12. Hasan Brijia, quoted in 'Interviews from Al Ma'asara resistance', *ISM*, June 13, 2011, at: http://tinyurl.com/o53zwes (accessed March 14, 2015).
13. Véronique Dudouet, 'Cross-border nonviolent advocacy during the second Palestinian intifada: The International Solidarity Movement', in Clark (ed.) *People Power*, p. 132.
14. Ibid., pp. 128–29.
15. Ibid., p. 131.
16. 'Olive harvest: Issues and challenges', November 1, 2012, at: http://iwps.info/2012/11/01/olive-harvest-challenges/ (accessed March 14, 2015).
17. At that time there were also teams in Haiti, Chiapas (Mexico), Colombia and Iraq.
18. After a short while the headmistress became fearful that the CPT presence might provoke the settlers and asked them to stop the formal accompaniment. This was the first of a number of occasions when local Palestinians declined the 'accompaniment' of the team members.

19. Kathleen Kern, *As resident aliens: Christian peacemaker teams in the West Bank, 1995–2005*, Eugene, OR: Cascade Books, 2010 (Kindle edition), Kindle loc. 1717–1723.

20. Ibid., Kindle loc. 2625–2643.

21. In the UK volunteers are contracted to do a certain number of public speaking engagements on their return.

22. Interview, August 13, 2014.

23. The name of the group stems from the fact that Falkirk is situated near the site of an old Roman Wall (the Antonine Wall) constructed across the central belt of Scotland to mark the northernmost frontier of the Roman Empire.

24. Kern, *As Resident aliens*, Kindle loc. 6001–6028.

25. Email from Operation Dove (operationdove@gmail.com). For images of the assault, see 'Operazione Colomba – Photogallery', September 14, 2014, at: http://tinyurl.com/p3cub9x (accessed March 14, 2015).

26. Margaret E. Keck and Kathryn Sikkink, 'Transnational advocacy networks in international and regional politics', *International Social Science Journal*, vol. 51, no. 159 (March 1999), at: http://tinyurl.com/ohyxcaa (accessed March 14, 2015).

27. According to Sidney Tarrow the boomerang works best when thrown upwards in terms of global hierarchies of power, rather than horizontally towards solidarity campaigns that are equally distant from metropolitan power centres. See Sidney Tarrow, *The new transnational activism*. Cambridge: Cambridge University Press, 2005, pp. 157–59.

28. See Clark, *People power*, p. 15.

29. For up-to-date information, see the website of the Palestinian BDS National Committee (BNC), at: http://bdsmovement.net

30. The document, 'Kairos Palestine: A moment of Truth', is at: http://tinyurl.com/yedtppq (accessed September 22, 2014).

31. Modest grounds for such hope has been evidenced by the fact that Christian groups and networks in the USA, Brazil, Philippines, South Africa and the UK have responded to the challenge by engaging with the Kairos Appeal and issuing their own calls for nonviolent means of bringing peace with justice to Israel and Palestine.

32. Ahmadinejad was a vocal supporter of the Palestinian cause who queried whether the holocaust had ever taken place and questioned Israel's right to exist.

33. Quoted in Connie Bruck, 'Friends of Israel', *The New Yorker*, September 1, 2014, at: http://tinyurl.com/kmdah6z (accessed March 14, 2015).

34. Quoted in Larry Derfner, 'Israel's watershed moment that wasn't', +972, September 12, 2014, at: http://tinyurl.com/mhzxpua (accessed March 14, 2015).

35. Quoted in Edward C. Corrigan, 'Is Anti-Zionism Anti-Semitic? Jewish Critics Speak', *Middle East Policy Journal*, vol. 16, no. 4 (Winter 2009), at: http://tinyurl.com/k9jsdzf (accessed March 14, 2015). An interesting source is *How to criticize Israel without being anti-Semitic*, at: http://tinyurl.com/b9sda9r (March 17, 2015).

36. Interestingly, in November 2014 comparisons started being made (and linkages drawn) between the shooting of unarmed young African-Americans by white police officers and the killing of Palestinians by Israeli occupation forces and settlers. See, for example, this report by Jenn Selby, 'NFL player Reggie Bush compares Ferguson "racial injustice" to Palestinian casualties after the Israel-Gaza conflict', *The Independent*, November 28, 2014, at: http://tinyurl.com/lnfumh6 (accessed March 14, 2015).

37. See for example Noam Chomsky's reservations, 'On Israel–Palestine and BDS', *The Nation*, July 21–28, 2014, at: http://tinyurl.com/p6e46de (accessed March 14, 2015).

38. Alan Hirsch, 'The United States and South Africa since 1948.' *Social Dynamics*, vol. 15, no. 2 (1989), p. 75.
39. Kenneth Grundy, *South Africa: Domestic crisis and global challenge*. Boulder, CO: Westview Press, 1991, p. 60.
40. Rory Ewins, 'International Moves Against Apartheid', *Textuary*, 1995, at: http://tinyurl.com/pj73wyj (accessed March 14, 2015).
41. See Porter Speakman, 'Netanyahu's party platform "flatly rejects" establishment of Palestinian state', *Mondoweiss*, November 3, 2011, at: http://tinyurl.com/mxxtrwc (accessed March 14, 2015).

10. Conclusion

1. One of the roles of internationals has been to accompany farmers trying to cultivate their land adjacent to the buffer zone. See Tiffany Ornelas de Tool, 'Farmers in the Gaza buffer zone', *Mondoweiss*, December 4, 2012, at: http://mondoweiss.net/2012/12/farmers-in-the-gaza-buffer-zone (accessed March 14, 2015).
2. See interview with Vittorio Arrigoni in 'Gaza, eliminate il pacifista Arrigoni', *Peace reporter*, January 14, 2009, at: http://tinyurl.com/ogfp2kx (accessed March 14, 2015), in Italian. See also Matthew Kalman, 'Idealistic blogger "was more Palestinian than the criminals who killed him"', *The Independent*, April 16, 2011, at: http://tinyurl.com/3z2ocvo (accessed March 14, 2015).
3. For full text, see 'Gaza youth breaks out with a "manifesto for change"', *Mondoweiss*, January 2, 2011, at: http://mondoweiss.net/2011/01/gaza-youth-breaks-out-with-a-manifesto-for-change (accessed March 14, 2015).
4. Quoted in Tom Dale, 'The right to speak up in Gaza', *Red Pepper*, April 2012, at: www.redpepper.org.uk/the-right-to-speak-up-in-gaza/ (accessed March 14, 2015).
5. For a full list of the demands, see Adam Horowitz, 'Gaza "March 15" protests continue amidst ongoing crackdown', *Mondoweiss*, March 18, 2011, at: http://tinyurl.com/otjye3c (accessed March 14, 2015).
6. Demonstrations also took place in Nazareth and different locations around the world.
7. A hard core of protesters continued with a hunger strike in a tent in Manara Square in Ramallah for some time, despite being subjected to assaults by PA security.
8. Jehan Al-Farra, 'To my beloved Palestine, I am sorry. I love you.' *Mondoweiss*, March 20, 2011, at: http://tinyurl.com/q9kmun4 (accessed March 14, 2015).
9. At the time of writing, there is evidence that the Palestinian leadership have decided to focus their efforts on international diplomacy rather than 'empty' peace talks with Israel. In his speech to the United Nations on September 23, 2014 Abbas posed the question: 'It is a moment of truth and my people are waiting to hear the answer of the world. Will it allow Israel to continue its occupation, the only occupation in the world?', Chris McGreal, 'Abbas defies US with formal call for Palestinian recognition by UN', *The Guardian*, September 23, 2014, at http://tinyurl.com/ld9mzmh (accessed March 14, 2015).
10. David Grossman, 'On hope and despair in the Middle East', *Haaretz*, July 8, 2014.

BIBLIOGRAPHY

Abdel Shafi, S., 'Diversity in unity? Fragmentation of the Palestinian people and the fight for unity', March 12, 2010, at: http://tinyurl.com/pulnt99 (accessed March 14, 2015).

Abdul-Hadi, M. (ed.), *Palestinian personalities: A biographic dictionary*. Al Quds/ Jerusalem: PASSIA, 2006.

Ackerman, P. and DuVall, J., *A force more powerful: One hundred years of nonviolent conflict*. New York: St Martin's, 2000.

Ackerman, P. and Kruegler, C., *Strategic nonviolent conflict: The dynamics of people power in the twentieth century*. Westport, CT: Praeger, 1994.

Al-Farra, J., 'To my beloved Palestine, I am sorry. I love you.' *Mondoweiss*, March 20, 2011, at: http://tinyurl.com/q9kmun4 (accessed March 14, 2015).

Al-Jubeh, N. *et al.*, *Old Hebron: The charm of a historical city and architecture*. Hebron: Hebron Rehabilitation Committee, 2009.

Anderson, M. B., *Do no harm: How aid can support peace–or war*. London: Lynne Rienner, 1999.

Anderson, M. B., 'Do no harm – the impact of international assistance in the Occupied Palestinian Territory', in M. Keating, A. Le More and R. Lowe (eds), *Aid, diplomacy and facts on the ground: The case of Palestine*. London: Chatham House, 2005, pp. 144–45.

Andoni, G., 'A comparative study of intifada 1987 and intifada 2000', in R. Carey (ed.), *The new intifada: Resisting Israel's apartheid*. London: Verso, 2001, pp. 209–18.

Arrigoni, V., in 'Gaza, eliminate il pacifista Arrigoni', *Peace reporter*, January 14, 2009, at: http://tinyurl.com/ogfp2kx (accessed March 14, 2015), in Italian.

Baransi, S., 'The story of Palestine under occupation', *Journal of Palestine Studies*, vol. 11, no. 1 (Autumn 1981), pp. 3–30.

Barghouti, O., *BDS: Boycott, divestment, sanctions – The global struggle for Palestinian rights*. Chicago, IL: Haymarket Books, 2011.

Bar-On, M., *In pursuit of peace: A history of the Israeli peace movement*. Washington, DC: United States Institute of Peace Press, 1996.

Bayat, A., 'Un-civil society: the politics of the "informal people"', *Third World Quarterly*, vol. 18, no. 1 (1997), pp. 53–72.

Bayat, A., *Life as politics: How ordinary people change the Middle East*. Stanford, CA: Stanford University Press, 2013.

Berlin, G. and Dienst, B. (eds), *Freedom sailors: The maiden voyage of the Free Gaza movement and how we succeeded in spite of ourselves*. Free Gaza, 2012.

Bidwell, R. L., *Dictionary of modern Arab history*. Abingdon: Routledge. 2010.

Botmeh, J., 'Civil resistance in Palestine: The village of Battir in 1948'. Dissertation: Coventry University, September 2006.

Bröning, M., *The politics of change in Palestine: State-building and non-violent resistance*. London: Pluto Press, 2011.

Bruck, C., 'Friends of Israel', *The New Yorker*, September 1, 2014, at: http://tinyurl.com/ kmdah6z (accessed March 14, 2015).

Bucaille, L., *Growing up Palestinian: Israeli occupation and the intifada generation*, trans. Anthony Roberts. Princeton, NJ: Princeton University Press, 2004.

Burston, B., 'A special place in Hell', *Haaretz*, October 28, 2014.

Carey, R. (ed.), *The new intifada: Resisting Israel's apartheid*. London: Verso, 2001.

Carter, A., *People power and political change: Key issues and concepts*. London: Routledge, 2012.

Carter, A., Clark, H. and Randle, M. (eds), *A guide to civil resistance: A bibliography of people power and nonviolent protest: Volume One*. London: Green Print, 2013.

Caspit, B., 'Jerusalem's silent intifada', *Al-Monitor*, October 23 2014, at: http://tinyurl.com/ n3ne2xp (accessed March 14, 2015).

Challand, B., 'Looking beyond the pale: International donors and civil society promotion in Palestine', *Palestine–Israel Journal*, vol. 12, no. 1 (2005).

Chenoweth, E. and Stephan, M. J., *Why civil resistance works: The strategic logic of nonviolent conflict*. New York: Columbia University Press, 2011.

Chomsky, N., 'On Israel–Palestine and BDS', *The Nation*, July 21–28, 2014.

Clark, H., *Civil resistance in Kosovo*. London: Pluto Press, 2000.

Clark, H. (ed.), *People power: Unarmed resistance and global solidarity*. London: Pluto Press, 2009.

Cohn, M., 'Israel's war against "BDS" movement', *Consortium News*, March 24, 2014.

Cook, J., *Blood and religion: The unmasking of the Jewish and democratic state*. London: Pluto Press, 2006.

Corrigan, E. C., 'Is anti-Zionism anti-Semitic? Jewish Critics Speak', *Middle East Policy*, vol. 16, no. 4 (Winter 2009), pp. 146–59.

Crow, R. E., Grant, P. and Ibrahim, S. E. (eds), *Arab nonviolent political struggle in the Middle East*. Boulder, CO: Lynne Rienner, 1990.

Dajani, S. A., *Ruling Palestine: A history of the legally sanctioned Jewish-Israeli seizure of land and housing in Palestine*. Geneva and Bethlehem: Centre on Housing Rights and Evictions (COHRE) and BADIL Resource Center for Palestinian Residency and Refugee Rights, 2005.

Dale, T., 'The right to speak up in Gaza', *Red Pepper*, April 2012, at: www.redpepper.org. uk/the-right-to-speak-up-in-gaza/ (accessed March 14, 2015).

Darweish, M., 'Human rights and the imbalance of power: The Palestinian–Israeli conflict', in V. Dudouet and B. Schmelzle, eds, *Human rights and conflict transformation: The challenges of just peace*, Berlin: Berghof Conflict Research Centre, 2010, pp. 85–94.

Darweish, M., 'Olive trees: Livelihoods and resistance', in A. Özerdem and R. Roberts (eds), *Challenging post-conflict environments: Sustainable agriculture*. Ashgate: Farnham, 2012, pp. 175–87.

Darweish, M. and Rigby, A., *Palestinians in Israel: Nationality and citizenship*. Bradford: University of Bradford, 1995.

Della Porta, D. and Tarrow, S. (eds), *Transnational protest and global activism*. Lanham, MD: Rowman & Littlefield, 2005.

Derfner, L., 'Israel's watershed moment that wasn't', *+972*, September 12, 2014.

Dudouet, V., 'Cross-border nonviolent advocacy during the second Palestinian intifada: The *International Solidarity Movement*', in H. Clark (ed.), *People power: Unarmed resistance and global solidarity*. London: Pluto Press, 2009, pp. 125–34.

Dudouet, V. and B. Schmelzle (eds), *Human rights and conflict transformation: The challenges of just peace*. Berlin: Berghof Conflict Research Centre, 2010, pp. 85–94.

Eguren, L. E. and Mahony, L., *Unarmed bodyguards: International accompaniment for the protection of human rights*. West Hartford, CT: Kumarian Press, 1997.

El Fassad, A., 'What is it that Palestinians commemorate on Land Day?', *The electronic Intifada*, March 30, 2001, at: http://tinyurl.com/opvjhhn (accessed March 14, 2015).

Ellman, M. and Laacher, S., *Migrant workers in Israel - A contemporary form of slavery*. Euro-Mediterranean Human Rights Network and International Federation for Human Rights, 2003, at: http://tinyurl.com/pbk8ovv (accessed February 3, 2015).

Ewins, R., 'International Moves Against Apartheid', *Textuary*, 1995, at: http://tinyurl.com/pj73wyj (accessed March 14, 2015).

Fanon, F., *The wretched of the Earth*. Harmondsworth: Penguin, 1967.

Flapan, S., *Zionism and the Palestinians*. London: Croom Helm, 1979.

Foot, M. R. D., *Resistance: European resistance to Nazism 1940–45*, London: Eyre Methuen, 1976.

Galtung, J., *Nonviolence and Israel/Palestine*. Honolulu, HI: University of Hawaii Press, 1989.

Gor, H. (ed.), *The militarisation of education*. Tel Aviv: Babel Press, 2005, (Hebrew).

Gordon, U. and Grietzer, O. (eds), *Anarchists against the wall: Direct action and solidarity with the Palestinian popular resistance struggle*. Oakland, CA: AK Press and the Institute of Anarchist Studies, 2013.

Graham-Brown, S., *Education, repression and liberation: Palestinians*. London: World University Service, 1965.

Gregg, R. B., *The power of non-violence*. Nyack, NY: Fellowship Publications, 1959.

Gresh, A., *The PLO: The struggle within*. London: Zed Books, 1988.

Grossman, D., 'On hope and despair in the Middle East', *Haaretz*, July 8, 2014.

Grundy, K., *South Africa: Domestic crisis and global challenge*. Boulder, CO: Westview Press, 1991.

Guarnieri, M., 'Palestinians beaten, arrested during protest at settlement supermarket', *+972*, October 24, 2012.

Hallward, M. C., *Transnational activism and the Israeli–Palestinian boycott*. Basingstoke: Palgrave-Macmillan, 2013.

Hammer, J., 'Grandmothers on Guard', *Mother Jones*, November–December 2004, at: http://tinyurl.com/m7zjb5 (accessed March 14, 2015).

Hassan, B., 'New Palestinian campaign to support Druze conscientious objectors', *Middle East Monitor*, March 20, 2014, at: http://tinyurl.com/orv3tlj (accessed March 14, 2015).

Hermann, T., *The Israeli peace movement: A shattered dream*. Cambridge: Cambridge University Press, 2009.

Herzog, S. and Hai, A., 'What do people mean when they say "people-to-people"?', *Palestine-Israel Journal*, vols 12–13, no. 4 (2005–06), at: http://www.pij.org/details.php?id=395 (accessed July 28, 2014).

Hever, S., *The political economy of Israel's occupation: Repression beyond exploitation*. London: Pluto Press, 2010.

Hiltermann, J. R., *Behind the intifada: Labor and women's movements in the occupied territories*. Princeton, NJ: Princeton University Press, 1991.

Hirsch, A., 'The United States and South Africa since 1948', *Social Dynamics*, vol. 15, no. 2 (1989), pp. 63–78.

Hoffman, A., *My happiness bears no relation to happiness: A poet's life in the Palestinian century*. New Haven, CT: Yale University Press, 2009.

Horowitz, A., 'Gaza "March 15" protests continue amidst ongoing crackdown', *Mondoweiss*, March 18, 2011, at: http://tinyurl.com/otjye3c (accessed March 14, 2015).

Hourani, A., *A history of the Arab peoples*. London: Faber & Faber, 1991.

Kahwaji, H., *The full story of the land movement*, Jerusalem: Alarabi, 1987, (Arabic).

Kalman, M., 'Idealistic blogger "was more Palestinian than the criminals who killed him"', *The Independent*, April 16, 2011, at: http://tinyurl.com/3z2ocvo (accessed March 14, 2015).

Kaminer, R., *The politics of protest: The Israeli peace movement and the Palestinian Intifada.* Brighton: Sussex Academic Press, 1996.

Kanaaneh, H., *A doctor in Galilee: The life and struggle of a Palestinian in Israel.* London: Pluto Press, 2008.

Odeh Kassis, R., *Kairos for Palestine.* Ramallah: Badayl/Alternatives, 2011.

Kayyali, A. S., *The Palestinian Arab reactions to Zionism and the British mandate, 1917–1939.* University of London, doctoral thesis, February, 1970.

Keating, M., Le More, A. and Lowe, R. (eds), *Aid, diplomacy and facts on the ground: The case of Palestine.* London: Chatham House, 2005.

Keck, M. E. and Sikkink, K., 'Transnational advocacy networks in international and regional politics', *International Social Science Journal,* vol. 51, no. 159 (March 1999), pp. 89–101.

Keller, A., *Terrible days: Social divisions and political paradoxes in Israel.* Amstelveen: Cypres, 1987.

Kern, K., *As resident aliens: Christian peacemaker teams in the West Bank, 1995–2005.* Eugene, OR: Cascade Books, 2010.

Khalidi, R., *Palestinian identity: The construction of modern national consciousness.* New York: Columbia University Press, 1997.

Khalidi, R., *The iron cage: The story of the Palestinian struggle for statehood.* Oxford: Oneworld, 2007.

Khalidi, W. (ed.), *All that remains: The Palestinian villages occupied and depopulated by Israel in 1948.* Washington, DC: Institute for Palestine Studies, 1992.

King, M. E., *A Quiet Revolution: The first Palestinian intifada and nonviolent resistance.* New York: Nation Books, 2007.

Krämer, G., *A history of Palestine: From the Ottoman conquest to the founding of the State of Israel.* Princeton, NJ: Princeton University Press, 2008.

Lakey, G., *Strategy for a living revolution.* San Francisco, CA: W. H. Freeman, 1973.

Levinson, C. and Solomon, J., 'Israel's Isolation Deepens', *The Wall Street Journal,* June 3, 2010.

Leon, D., 'Binationalism: A bridge over the chasm', *Palestine-Israel Journal,* vol. 6, no. 2 (July 1999).

Lim, A. (ed), *The case for sanction against Israel.* London, Verso, 2012.

Lodge, T., 'The interplay of nonviolent and violent action in the movement against apartheid in South Africa, 1983–94', in A. Roberts and T. Garton Ash (eds), *Civil resistance and power politics: The experience of nonviolent action from Gandhi to the present.* Oxford: Oxford University Press, 2009, pp. 213–30.

Lustick, I., *The Arabs in the Jewish State: Israel's control of the national minority.* Austin, TX: University of Texas Press, 1980.

McAdam, D., *Political process and the development of black insurgency, 1930–1970.* Chicago, IL: University of Chicago Press, 1999.

McGreal, C., 'Abbas defies US with formal call for Palestinian recognition by UN', *The Guardian,* September 23, 2014, at http://tinyurl.com/ld9mzmh (accessed March 14, 2015).

McIntyre, J., 'Interview: Budrus "built a model of civil resistance"', *The electronic intifada,* November 4, 2010, at: http://tinyurl.com/qbbut6b (accessed March 13, 2015).

Mahony, L. and Eguren, L. E., *Unarmed bodyguards: International accompaniment for the protection of human rights.* West Hartford, CT: Kumarian Press, 1997.

Mandel, N. J., *The Arabs and Zionism before World War I.* Berkeley, CA: University of California Press, 1976.

Mar'i, S. K., *Arab education in Israel.* Syracuse, NY: Syracuse University Press, 1978.

Martin, B., *Justice ignited: The dynamics of backfire*. Lanham, MD: Rowman & Littlefield, 2007.

Matar, H., 'Palestinian women take back spring as settlers, soldiers look on', *+972*, April 22, 2012, at: http://tinyurl.com/qx6x6yl (accessed March 14, 2015).

Matar, H., 'Short-term memory loss champions of the world: Gaza? What Gaza?', *+972*, September 13, 2014.

Moore, B. (ed.), *Resistance in Western Europe*. Oxford: Berg, 2000.

Morris, B., *Israel's border wars, 1949–1956*. Oxford: Clarendon Press, 1988.

Morris, B. *The birth of the Palestinian refugee problem revisited*. Cambridge: Cambridge University Press, 2003.

Morris, B., *1948: A history of the first Arab–Israeli war*. New Haven, CT: Yale University Press, 2008.

Moser-Puangsuwan, Y. and Weber, T. (eds), *Nonviolent intervention across borders: A recurrent vision*. Honolulu, HI: Matsunaga Institute for Peace, 2000.

Nasser, I., 'In Bab Al-Shams, Palestinians create new facts on the ground', *+972 Blog*, January 25, 2013, at: http://tinyurl.com/pjbl554 (accessed March 14, 2015).

Nepstad, S. E., *Nonviolent revolutions: Civil resistance in the late 20th century*, New York: Oxford University Press, 2011.

Norman, J., *The second intifada: civil resistance*. New York: Routledge, 2010.

Omer-Man, M., 'Breaking down barriers in the South Hebron Hills', *Common Ground News Service*, 5 April, 2011, at: http://tinyurl.com/kjm35to (accessed March 14, 2015).

Oren, M. B., *Six days of war: June 1967 and the making of the modern Middle East*. New York: Oxford University Press, 2002.

Oren, Y., 'Israeli Society and Jewish–Palestinian reconciliation: "Ethnocracy" and its Territorial Contradictions', *Middle East Journal*, vol. 51, no. 4 (1997).

Overy, B., *Gandhi as political organiser: An analysis of local and national campaigns in India 1915–1922*, unpublished Ph.D. thesis, University of Bradford, 1982, at: http://tinyurl.com/omeuz24 (accessed December 5, 2014).

Pappe, I., *A history of modern Palestine*. Cambridge: Cambridge University Press, 2006.

Pappe, I., *The forgotten Palestinians: A history of the Palestinians in Israel*. New Haven, CT: Yale University Press, 2011.

Parry, W., *Against the wall: The art of resistance in Palestine*. London: Pluto Press, 2010.

Parsons, N., *The politics of the Palestinian authority: From Oslo to Al-Aqsa*. London: Routledge, 2005.

Pearlman, W., *Occupied voices: Stories of everyday life from the second intifada*. New York: Thunder's Mouth Press/ Nation Books, 2003.

Pearlman, W., *Violence, nonviolence, and the Palestinian national movement*. New York: Cambridge University Press, 2011.

Popovic, S., *et al.*, *A guide to effective nonviolent struggle*. Belgrade: Centre for Applied Nonviolent Action and Strategies, 2007.

Porath, Y., *The emergence of the Palestinian-Arab national movement, 1918–1929*. London: Frank Cass, 1974.

Porath, Y., *The Palestinian Arab national movement, 1929–1939: From riots to rebellion*. London: Frank Cass, 1977.

Quandt, W., *Camp David: Peacemaking and politics*. Washington, DC: Brookings Institution Press, 1986.

Qumsiyeh, M. B., *Popular resistance in Palestine: A history of hope and empowerment*. London: Pluto Press, 2011.

Randle, M., *Civil resistance*. London: Fontana, 1994.

Randle, M. (ed.), *Challenge to nonviolence*. Bradford, University of Bradford, 2002.

Rapoport, M., *Shady dealings in Silwan*. Jerusalem: Ir Amin, 2009, at: www.ir-amim.org.il/sites/default/files/Silwanreporteng.pdf (accessed March 14, 2015).

Reshef, T., *Peace now: From the officers' letter to the peace now*. Jerusalem: Keter Publishing House, 1996.

Rigby, A., *Living the intifada*. London: Zed Books, 1991.

Rigby, A., *The legacy of the past: The problem of collaborators and the Palestinian case*. East Jerusalem: PASSIA, 1997.

Rigby, A., *Justice and reconciliation*. Boulder, CO: Lynne Rienner, 2001.

Rigby, A., *Palestinian resistance and nonviolence*. East Jerusalem: PASSIA, 2010.

Rings, W., *Life with the enemy: Collaboration and resistance in Hitler's Europe 1939–1945*. Garden City, NY: Doubleday, 1982.

Roberts, A. (ed.), *The strategy of civilian defence: Non-violent resistance to aggression*. London: Faber & Faber, 1967.

Roberts, A. and Garton Ash, T. (eds), *Civil resistance and power politics: The experience of non-violent Action from Gandhi to the present*. Oxford: Oxford University Press, 2000.

Roy, A., 'Gandhi, but with guns: Part One', *The Guardian*, March 27, 2010, at: http://tinyurl.com/olz8g6v (accessed March 14, 2015).

Roy, S., *Failing peace: Gaza and the Palestinian–Israeli conflict*. London: Pluto Press, 2007.

Sandercock J. *et al.*, *Peace under fire: Israel/Palestine and the international solidarity movement*. London: Verso, 2004.

Sayigh, R., *Palestinians: From peasants to revolutionaries*. London: Zed Books, 1979.

Schock, K., *Unarmed insurrections: People power movements in nondemocracies*. Minneapolis, MN: University of Minnesota, 2005.

Schock, K., 'The practice and study of civil resistance', *Journal of Peace Research*, vol. 50, no. 3 (2013), pp. 277–90.

Scott, J. C., *Domination and the arts of resistance: Hidden transcripts*. New Haven, CT: Yale University Press, 1990.

Selby, J., 'NFL player Reggie Bush compares Ferguson "racial injustice" to Palestinian casualties after the Israel-Gaza conflict', *The Independent*, November 28, 2014.

Semelin, J., *Unarmed against Hitler: Civilian resistance in Europe, 1939–1943*. Westport, CT: Praeger, 1993.

Sharoni, S., *Gender and the Israeli–Palestinian conflict: The politics of women's resistance*. Syracuse, NY: Syracuse University Press, 1995.

Sharp, G., *The politics of nonviolent action*, (3 volumes). Boston, MA: Porter Sargent, 1973.

Sharp, G. *Social power and political freedom*. Boston, MA: Porter Sargent, 1980.

Sharp, G., *Waging nonviolent struggle: 20th century practice and 21st century potential*. Boston, MA: Extending Horizon Books, 2005.

Shearer, D. and Pickup, F., 'Dilemmas for aid policy in Lebanon and the occupied Palestinian territories', *Humanitarian Exchange*, no. 37 (March 2007), pp. 4–6.

Sherwood, H., 'Israeli soldier clubs Danish protester with rifle', *The Guardian*, April 16, 2012, at: http://tinyurl.com/pe9v6w5 (accessed March 14, 2015).

Shlaim, A., *The politics of partition: King Abdullah, the Zionists and Palestine 1921–1951*. Oxford: Oxford University Press, 1990.

Shulman, D., *Dark hope: Working for peace in Israel and Palestine*. Chicago, IL: University of Chicago Press, 2007.

Speakman, P., 'Netanyahu's party platform "flatly rejects" establishment of Palestinian state', *Mondoweiss*, November 3, 2011, at: http://tinyurl.com/mxxtrwc (accessed March 14, 2015).

Stahl, Z., *The road to dispossession: a case study – the outpost of Adei Ad*. Tel Aviv: Yesh Din, 2013.

Stephan, M. (ed.), *Civilian jihad: Nonviolent struggle, democratization and governance in the Middle East*. New York: Palgrave Macmillan, 2009.

Stohlman, N. and Aladin, L. (eds), *Live from Palestine: International and Palestinian direct action against the Israeli occupation*. Cambridge, MA: South End Press, 2003.

Tamari, S., 'What the uprising means', *Middle East Report*, May–June 1988, p. 26.

Tarrow, S., *The new transnational activism*. Cambridge: Cambridge University Press, 2005.

Townshend, C., 'The first intifada: Rebellion in Palestine 1936–39', *History Today*, vol. 39, no. 7 (July 1989), at: http://tinyurl.com/nfdy3kb (accessed March 14, 2015).

The Palestine question in maps, Jerusalem/ Al Quds: PASSIA (Palestinian Academic Society for the Study of International Affairs), 2002.

Touma, E., *The roots of the Palestinian question*. (Arabic), Jerusalem: n.p., 1976.

Touma, E., 'The history of Rakah in Israel: an interview with Emile Touma', *Leviathan*, (Boston) vol. 3, (Fall 1980).

Trading away peace: How Europe helps sustain illegal Israeli settlements, October 2012, at: www.fidh.org/IMG/pdf/trading.pdf (accessed March 14, 2015).

Usher, G., *Palestine in crisis: The struggle for peace and political independence after Oslo*. London: Pluto Press, 1995.

Usher, G., 'Uprising wipes off Green Line', *Al-Ahram*, no. 503, October 12–18, 2000, at: http://weekly.ahram.org.eg/2000/503/re6.htm (accessed March 14, 2015).

Wajdi, J., *In the state of the Jews: 1949–2006. Umm al-Fahim and Lajjun. A journey through time*. Jerusalem: Al Resala Press, 2007, (Arabic).

White, B., *Palestinians in Israel: Segregation, discrimination and democracy*. London: Pluto Press, 2012.

Zacharia, J., 'Palestinians turn to boycott in West Bank', *Washington Post*, May 16, 2010.

INDEX

Compiled by Sue Carlton